THREAT POLITICS

Critical Security Series

Series Editors:
Neil Renwick and Nana Poku

Editorial Board:
Richard Bedford, *University of Waikato*
Tony Evans, *University of Southampton*
Tony Mcgrew, *University of Southampton*
Mark Miller, *University of Delaware*
Robert Morrell, *University of Natal*
David Newman, *Ben Gurion University*
Peter Vale, *University of Western Cape*
Fiona Robinson, *Carleton University*

Threat Politics
New perspectives on security, risk and crisis management

Edited by
JOHAN ERIKSSON
Södertörn University College, Sweden

LONDON AND NEW YORK

First published 2001 by Ashgate Publishing

Reissued 2018 by Routledge
2 Park Square, Milton Park, Abingdon, Oxon OX14 4RN
711 Third Avenue, New York, NY 10017, USA

Routledge is an imprint of the Taylor & Francis Group, an informa business

Copyright © Johan Eriksson 2001

Johan Eriksson has asserted his moral right under the Copyright, Designs and Patents Act, 1988, to be identified as the author of this work.

All rights reserved. No part of this book may be reprinted or reproduced or utilised in any form or by any electronic, mechanical, or other means, now known or hereafter invented, including photocopying and recording, or in any information storage or retrieval system, without permission in writing from the publishers.

Notice:
Product or corporate names may be trademarks or registered trademarks, and are used only for identification and explanation without intent to infringe.

Publisher's Note
The publisher has gone to great lengths to ensure the quality of this reprint but points out that some imperfections in the original copies may be apparent.

Disclaimer
The publisher has made every effort to trace copyright holders and welcomes correspondence from those they have been unable to contact.

A Library of Congress record exists under LC control number: 2001094268

ISBN 13: 978-1-138-73649-8 (hbk)
ISBN 13: 978-1-138-73648-1 (pbk)
ISBN 13: 978-1-315-18591-0 (ebk)

Contents

List of Figures and Tables vii
About the Contributors ix
Acknowledgements xii

Introduction 1
Johan Eriksson

PART I: OPINION IN FOCUS

1 Risk Perceptions: Taking on Societal Salience 21
  Lennart Sjöberg

2 Cultural Theory, Risk Perceptions among Political Elites and Public Opinion 38
  Ulf Bjereld

PART II: ACTORS IN FOCUS

3 Mediated Threats 61
  Alexa Robertson

4 Verbal Politics of Estonian Policy-makers: Reframing Security and Identity 84
  Erik Noreen

5 Threat Politics and Baltic Sea Business 100
  Michael Karlsson

PART III: ISSUES IN FOCUS

6 Securitising Submarine Intrusions   123
   Fredrik Bynander

7 Securitising IT   145
   Johan Eriksson

8 Framing the Palme Assassination   164
   Eric K. Stern and Dan Hansén

9 Framing an American Threat: The European Commission
   and the Technology Gap   189
   Ulrika Mörth

Conclusion: Towards a Theory of Threat Politics   210
Johan Eriksson

Bibliography   226
Index   252

List of Figures and Tables

Figure 5.1	Eight threat images framed as affecting the willingness of leaders of major corporations to seize a window of opportunity	109
Figure 6.1	Number of indications cited in the Annual Submarine Commission Report, 1981-1994	126
Table 1.1	Means of attitude (good-bad), perceived risk and benefit of energy production systems (scale 1-7)	23
Table 1.2	Regression analysis of the public's attitude to energy production systems	24
Table 1.3	Regression analysis of experts' attitude to energy production systems	24
Table 1.4	Mean ratings of demand for risk mitigation, to be done by self or government (national or local). Scale 0-7	28
Table 2.1	Concern about the world political situation, 1980-1999 (the average percentage of Swedes who expressed very great to rather great concern)	39
Table 2.2	Perceived risk for a major war in Europe, 1980-1999 (average percentage who considered the risk great to very great)	40
Table 2.3	Risk perceptions among Swedish members of Parliament and voters with regard to high unemployment, environmental pollution, and an increase in the number of refugees (1994). Percentage who answered 'very concerned'	47

Table 2.4	Risk perceptions according to sex among Swedish members of Parliament and voters with regard to high unemployment, environmental pollution, and an increase in the number of refugees (1994). Percentage who answered 'very concerned'	48
Table 2.5	Risk perceptions according to age among Swedish members of Parliament and voters with regard to high unemployment, environmental pollution, and an increase in the number of refugees (1994). Percentage who answered 'very concerned'	49
Table 2.6	According to political party, risk perceptions among Swedish members of Parliament and voters with regard to high unemployment, environmental pollution, and an increase in the number of refugees (1994). Percentage who answered 'very concerned'	50
Table 3.1	Distribution of news items in *BBC World News*, *Euronews*, and Swedish Television's *Rapport*. Saturdays, January, February and November 1998	75
Table 3.2	Types of threat depicted in *BBC World News*, *Euronews*, and Swedish Television's *Rapport*. Saturdays, January, February and November 1998	75
Table 5.1	Three perspectives on international political economy and the type of threat frames that may be derived from them	102
Table 5.2	Members of the Baltic Sea Business Summit, January 1998	107
Table 6.1	Events and actions in the submarine defence, 1980-1984	125
Table 8.1	Overview of threat frames and main framing actors	173

About the Contributors

Ulf Bjereld is Professor at the Department of Political Science at Göteborg University. He has published several books in Swedish on foreign policy, and public opinion. Recent articles appear in *International Studies Quarterly, Journal of Peace Research* and *Scandinavian Political Studies*.

Fredrik Bynander is PhD candidate in Political Science and lecturer at the Universities of Uppsala and Växjö. He is the author of *Crisis Analogies*, and co-editor of *Crisis and Internationalization* (with Eric K. Stern), and *Polish Crisis Management* (with Bengt Sundelius). In addition, he has published articles in *Cooperation and Conflict*, and *Journal of Contingencies and Crisis Management*.

Johan Eriksson is Assistant Professor in Political Science at Södertörn University College, and Research Fellow at the Swedish Institute of International Affairs, Stockholm. Eriksson is the author/co-editor of five volumes on security policy, and ethnic conflicts, including *Reconstructing Survival* (with Peter Bröms and Bo Svensson); and *Partition and Redemption: A Machiavellian Analysis of Sami and Basque Patriotism*. In addition, Eriksson has contributed to four edited volumes, and has published in *Cooperation and Conflict*, and *Journal of Crisis Management and Contingencies*.

Dan Hansén is PhD candidate in Political Science at the Department of Public Administration, Leiden University, and analyst at the Centre for Crisis Management Research and Training (CRISMART) at the Swedish National Defence College. He is the author of *The Occupation of the West German Embassy in Stockholm, 1975*, and *Crisis Management in a Transitional Society* (with Eric K. Stern). A recent work co-authored with

Eric K. Stern appears in *From Crisis to Contingencies: A Global Perspective* (edited by Uriel Rosenthal, Louise Comfort and Arjen Boin).

Michael Karlsson is Assistant Professor in Political Science at Södertörn University College. His research focuses on Swedish foreign policy, Swedish interest groups and the EU, and transnational relations in the Baltic Sea region. His most recent publications appear in *Comparing Finnish and Swedish Security Policy* (edited by Teija Tiilikainen et al); *Sweden and the European Union Evaluated* (edited by Lee Miles); and *WeltTrends*.

Ulrika Mörth is Assistant Professor in Political Science at Stockholm University. Since 1996 she is a researcher at SCORE—Stockholm Centre for Organizational Research. Recent works appear in *Sweden and the EU Evaluated* (edited by Lee Miles); *State, Society and the UN System: Changing Perspectives on Multilateralism* (edited by Keith Krause and A. Knight); *Cooperation and Conflict*, and *Journal of European Public Policy*.

Erik Noreen is Assistant Professor and Director of Studies at the Department of Peace and Conflict Research, Uppsala University. His research focuses on foreign policy theory and contemporary history of the Nordic and Baltic countries. He has contributed to several edited volumes, including *European Polyphony: Perspectives Beyond East-West Confrontation* (edited by Ole Wæver et al), and *50 Years After World War II: International Politics in the Baltic Sea Region 1945-1995* (edited by H. Runblom et al).

Alexa Robertson is Assistant Professor in Political Science at Stockholm University. Robertson has done research and taught on the international role of the media, with an emphasis on European politics and a comparative approach. Her recent publications include *Depictions of the European Union*. Chapters have been contributed to several edited volumes, including *Collective Identities in an Era of Transformations* (edited by Klas-Göran Karlsson et al), and *MZES Jahrbuch* (edited by Jan van Deth and Thomas Khönig).

Lennart Sjöberg is Professor in Economic Psychology at the Stockholm School of Economics where he is also head of the Centre for Risk Analysis. He has published widely on risk issues, including several articles in *Acta Psychologica, Risk Analysis, Risk—Health, Safety and Environment*, and *Journal of Risk Research*.

Eric K. Stern has a PhD in Political Science from Stockholm University. He is Scientific Coordinator of the Centre for Crisis Management Research and Training (CRISMART) at the Swedish National Defence College. Dr. Stern is the author/co-editor of seven books, including *Crisis Decision-making: A Cognitive Institutional Approach*; *Crisis Management in Estonia: Theory and Practice* (co-edited with Daniel Nohrstedt); *Crisis and Internationalization* (co-edited with Fredrik Bynander); *Beyond Groupthink: Political Group Dynamics and Foreign Policymaking* (co-edited with Bengt Sundelius and Paul 't Hart). In addition, Stern has published articles in *International Studies Quarterly, Mershon International Studies Review, Journal of Contingencies and Crisis Management*, and *Cooperation and Conflict*.

Acknowledgements

The idea of studying threat politics—why some threat images but not others take on salience in politics and societal debate—originated in 1998 in conversations between Erik Noreen, Gunnar Sjöstedt and myself. We found that our individual research projects at the time had several common denominators. In October 1999, we jointly organised a conference on threat images and security policy, held at the Swedish Institute of International Affairs, Stockholm. Out of this the idea of producing a book on threat politics emerged.

The Swedish Agency of Civil Emergency Planning, and the Swedish Foreign Ministry provided funding for the project. I gratefully acknowledge this support.

Among the individuals that have contributed ideas and insights for this book, I particularly want to thank Christopher Jones and Olav F. Knudsen. Many other colleagues have contributed in various ways, and I would like to express my sincere thanks to all of you collectively. Finally, I thank Stephanie Buus for translating one of the chapters; Jonas Holmgren and Jan Softa for assisting in preparing the bibliography; and everyone at Ashgate for guiding me through the editing process.

Johan Eriksson
Stockholm

Introduction
JOHAN ERIKSSON

More people seem to be afraid of more things than perhaps ever before. In most western countries news reports, movies and fiction literature, but also government policy and academic research are concerned with an increasingly broad range of threats and risks. These seem to include almost every imaginable horror. In addition to the traditional fear of war, there is also genocide, terrorism, organised crime, environmental degradation, epidemics, economic crises, attacks on information systems, and so the list goes on. Examples from news reporting abound: real-time blood, fear and death have become the leading items of live broadcasting. Such images are often the first that comes to mind whenever Rwanda, Kosovo or East Timor is mentioned. In movies and fiction literature, playing with people's fears has always been a common trick. Today however there are many new themes of fear in fiction as well as in politics, of which many concern a wider agenda of threats, including the increasingly popular themes of Armageddon—global and even extraterrestrial threats to Earth herself.

Of course people have always had a broad range of fears, ranging from fear of spiders to fear of attacks from aliens of either a terrestrial or an extraterrestrial nature. Two changes however make contemporary fears qualitatively different: First, a number of new types of fears have emerged, most of which are related to modernisation—a basic theme in studies of 'risk society' (Beck, 1992; 1999; Franklin, 1998; Adam, Beck and Van Loon, 2000). Of this many examples can be given, but some of the more apparent include the vulnerability of societies depending on information technology, and fear of nuclear catastrophes, such as the Chernobyl accident in 1986. Many problems are 'manufactured' and difficult to calculate, such as the BSE disease and the Y2K computer bug. IT insecurity is one of the most recent items on the threat agenda, not least in Europe and North America. That this is directly linked to modernisation is obvious; 'cyberwar' and the Y2K bug would not exist without the development of a modern computerised society.

The linkage to modernisation is similar in the cases of nuclear accidents, acid rain and other environmental issues. And, due to globalisation of travel and migration, epidemics are no longer isolated to specific localities. Nevertheless, global problems are not automatically put on policy agendas. In the spring of 2000, almost twenty years after the discovery of the HIV/AIDS pandemic, U.S. President Bill Clinton officially addressed the issue as a threat to national and international security.

Second, this broad variety of fears is no longer only a concern for individuals, but has become increasingly politicised. Threats and risks are now officially institutionalised to a much greater extent than was previously the case, especially in comparison with the old night-watchman state. Legislation initiatives related to threats and risks have increased dramatically. In Sweden for instance parliamentarians have tripled such initiatives since the 1960s (Sjöberg, af Wåhlberg and Kvist, 1998). Also, a number of initiatives have been taken to broaden the security concept at the global level, for instance by several UN commissions (Stern, 1999a). The world summit on terrorism held in the Middle East some years ago is also worth mentioning. Moreover, in most western countries there is a growing number of special agencies and institutions responsible for an increasing number of imagined threats. Nuclear insecurity, cyberterrorism, pandemics, traffic accidents, and a great many more fears today have their own specially designated institutions. The most recently institutionalised threats are probably the imagined dangers and vulnerabilities of the information society. In private business, these issues have been addressed by a growing number of specialised corporations.

In addition, established security organisations take on responsibility for a wider range of threats and risks than they originally were designed for. This is particularly obvious in the case of the military. In addition to the traditional task of fighting wars, the military is taking increasing responsibility for peacetime operations, for instance large-scale rescue and relief operations, information warfare, as well as fighting terrorism and organised crime.

Furthermore, despite the new responsibilities of governmental security organisations, the welfare state and the military defence forces are being downsized in most western countries. This has provided an opportunity for privatisation of some aspects of security: gated communities for families, private guards and security organisations for corporations, and privatised policing of public facilities such as subways and shopping centres. Hence, while the scaling down of the welfare state and military defence opens up for private security initiatives, governmental security organisations take on new responsibilities.

Scope of Inquiry

Threats as Images

Threat images involve a sense of endangered values and a perceived inability to control events (Milburn and Watman, 1981, pp. 8-11; Johnson, 1997, p. 12). The perceived source of this danger can be specific, such as a particular event, condition or actor. In addition, social psychology tells us that the sources of threat images do not necessarily have to be specific or known. General feelings of uncertainty about the course of events and a lack of capacity to control them may produce a sense of fear. Philosopher John Dewey argues that it is not uncertainty as such that men dislike, but the possibility that it involves unknown perils of evil (Dewey, 1929, ch. 1; cf. Johnson 1997, pp. 14-15).

Importantly, this understanding of threat images is broader than is common in both security studies and crisis management studies. Both have tended to emphasise perceived threats to existential values of societies, and situations characterised by urgency and intense political activity (Buzan et al 1998; Stern 1999b). The relatively broader understanding in risk studies is closer to our conceptualisation, as it nominally incorporates everything that people are afraid of (Wildavsky and Dake, 1991; Löfstedt and Frewer, 1998).

On the other hand, risk studies have tended to focus strictly on individual risk perceptions. In this book, we are particularly concerned with how threat images of individuals, groups and institutions become the concern of politics and societal debate.

When Fear Takes on Societal Salience

The overarching aim is to understand why and how things we can be afraid of take on *societal salience*. The notion of societal salience is intended to capture things that, in a given time and place, are widely seen as the most important and topical issues. This may be observed in many different forms, for instance as current news headlines, as major items in political debate and policy making, and as major concerns among public opinion. Neonazism is a good example of something that recurrently takes on societal salience. In late 1999, this happened in Sweden when the four major newspapers published a joint investigation of, as well as a manifesto against Neonazism. They also published photographs of sixty young men accused of being leading individuals in Swedish Neonazi movements. The societal salience of things depends on *inter alia* whether the media, government, social movements, academia and other opinion makers pay serious attention to them.

The concept is necessarily and deliberately broad and open. The reason for employing the concept of societal salience rather than the related notion of political agenda—a more familiar concept in the social sciences—is that agenda setting is associated with a particular set of theories in political science and media studies (Kingdon, 1995; Hinnfors, 1995; Eriksson, 2000). In general, agenda setting is seen as preceding stage to public policy making, and this perspective is too limited for our purposes. In some but hardly all contributions to this book, societal salience is equitable with the political agenda. The processes in which issues take on societal salience in for example the media or among public opinion can be analysed in their own right, without necessarily making a connection to policy making. Societal salience is a more comprehensive concept, and agenda setting can be seen as only one way in which issues take on societal salience.

Moreover, things that take on societal salience do not necessarily have the same meaning or connotations for everyone. People may broadly agree on what are the most important issues of the day, but not necessarily what they mean, how they should be understood or indeed what can be done about them. On the contrary, what counts as meaning or what becomes a shared narrative is a fundamentally political matter.

Threat Politics

The politics of threat images is therefore the major theme in this study. There are more specifically two aspects of this. The first is the struggle about what should and should not take on societal salience. Of this an example is the debate within security studies between those who defend a traditional military and state-centric view of security, and those who wish to apply the concept of security to a wider range of perceived non-military threats (Buzan, Wæver and de Wilde, 1998). The second is the struggle about how the ensuing result should be understood, what counts as shared meaning, which is often called the framing aspect. In practice these two aspects are intertwined. Analytically, however, they can be separated. This makes it possible to study the relationship between the two, i.e. how and why different ways of framing impact on the societal salience of the subject matter.

The interplay between framing and societal salience will be elaborated in a subsequent section. For this purpose it is necessary to ask who is doing the framing, for what reasons, how they are the doing it, and under what circumstances does their framing have a political impact. Is it true, as critical theorists constantly argue, that the privilege of defining the major problems of our society always stays with a limited political elite, usually seen as the government (Wyn Jones, 1999)? Or is this a more open ended empirical question, with answers varying greatly depending on context? In any case, it seems safe to suggest that this is and will always be a question of politics and power, winners and losers. In the words of Cameron:

> Some people and institutions (those which codify and regulate public usage, including the mass media) have more influence than others in determining which meanings will have the widest circulation and credibility in a given time and place. [...] It is always worth asking why, and from whose point of view, one way of using language seems obvious, natural and neutral, while another seems ludicrous, loaded and perverse. (Cameron, 1994, pp. 23, 29)

Hence, we are concerned with something more than mere aggregations of individual beliefs and perceptions. Framing is the power struggle for a shared narrative, in our case about what counts as 'threat,' 'risk' and similar negative concerns. The political process of framing is about how policy makers as well as nonofficial agents such as the media, public opinion, or academia portray or even construct things they are afraid of, or think people should be afraid of. Above all, this process is about establishing or maintaining the power of symbols and metaphors, in this case the high political notions of threat, risk and security (Chilton, 1996). There are a number of questions relating to this: What threat images do public authorities, media, business, public opinion, academia, and other agents address? Who gains and who loses by portraying something as a threat or not? How is threat politics treated in security studies, risk studies, and crisis studies? What can be gained from learning across these fields of study? What obstructs and what facilitates change in threat images and their societal significance?

Towards a Comprehensive Approach

What, then, does this book contribute? First, this book bridges the gap between thematically related but academically disassociated fields of study, specifically security studies, risk studies, and crisis management studies. Thus a cross-disciplinary discussion is introduced, and valuable lessons from this are drawn.

Second, this study emphasises and, above all, brings together important agents and arenas previously neglected in studies of threats and risks, especially the roles played by public opinion, the media, and business.

Third, in contrast to the traditional and rather narrow focus on interstate military conflicts in existing studies of the politics of threat, this book also addresses the threat politics of other issues of contemporary saliency, for instance information technology, economic competitiveness, and assassination of political leaders.

Finally, this volume combines theory and empirical observation. In much of the literature on the subject, there is an unfortunate tendency to go either into a relatively empirical but mostly atheoretical direction (Dunn, 1997; Johnson, 1997; Fordham, 1998), or into a theoretical (Buzan, Wæver and de Wilde, 1998; Wyn Jones, 1999; Beck, 1992) and even meta-theoretical direction (Dillon, 1996). It is necessary to go beyond both the absence of theorising in much empirical studies, and the unwillingness to conduct systematic empirical inquiry in much of the theoretical work. Thus, this book includes theoretically informed and empirically rich case studies of how threat images take on societal salience.

Threat Politics: A Conceptual Framework

Frame Analysis

How, then, do threat images take on societal salience? If we are to understand the process of threat politics strings need to be pulled together. We suggest that this can be done by applying the concept of framing, 'which denotes an active process-derived phenomenon that implies agency and contention at the level of reality-construction' (Snow and Benford, 1998, p. 136). The concept of framing is neither disciplinary specific nor particularly novel. Originally developed by sociologist Erving Goffman (1974), the concept of framing has mostly been applied in media and communication studies (Entman, 1993), in social movement theory (Snow and Benford, 1998) and more recently in political science (Schön and Rein, 1994; Jachtenfuchs, 1998). To our knowledge, it has not been systematically applied in a study of the politics of threats and risks. Yet the concept of framing appears to provide the logic and coherence required for understanding the process of threat politics.

In academic discourse, the concept of framing 'refers to an interpretive schemata that simplifies and condenses the world out there by selectively punctuating and encoding objects, situations, events, experiences, and sequences of actions within one's present or past' (Snow and Benford, 1992, p. 137; cf. Goffman, 1974, p. 21). Thus the verb framing refers to the process whereby an agent is developing a particular interpretive schema. Framing is one of those heuristics people employ to make sense of the complex world they live in. In short, a framing perspective implies taking seriously those things that are always interpreted *as* something. Framing has become the focus of a literature of its own, but it refers to essentially the same things as in the literature on belief systems and schema theory. Moreover, Schön and Rein (1994, p. 29) see framing as 'symbolic contests over the social meaning of an issue domain, where meaning implies not only what is at issue, but what is to be done' (cf. Fischer and Forester, 1993, p. 146). This puts focus on framing as a matter of politics, a theme to which we soon will return.

Images and Frames

In everyday language, 'image,' 'perception,' 'frame,' 'scheme,' 'narrative' and similar terms are often used interchangeably. In this book, however, there are analytical reasons for being more specific. The basic terms to be applied throughout this volume are *image* and *frame*, and an important distinction is made between the two. On occasion, however, the term perception will be employed, since this is commonly used in risk studies (see chapter 1 and 2). In addition, the term narrative is employed in Alexa Robertson's chapter on the media.

Images are general perceptions of reality, such as identifying an actor, event or condition as malign or benign. Frames, on the other hand, contain more specific and confined meanings than images do. The frames isolates parts of the field of vision, puts images into particular contexts, and equip them with certain connotations (see Robertson in this volume, ch. 3). The reason for distinguishing between image and frame is that a single image can be framed in different ways. Of this an example is seeing unemployment as a threat (see chapter 2). This is the image—presenting unemployment as a negative condition. Yet this image can be framed differently depending on what is seen as threatened by unemployment. While liberals tend to frame unemployment as a threat to the well-being of individuals who are out of jobs, conservatives frame it as demoralising and therefore as a threat to the integrity of the social spirit, and environmentalists as a threat in that focusing on this issue runs the risk of drawing attention from environmental pollution. There are other frames of the same image floating around in the societal debate, though these three are sufficient for demonstrating the significance of framing.

Threat Framing: Securitisation and Beyond

The concept of framing emphasises the perceptual, interpretative and representative aspects of security. Threats, risks, dangers—or whatever they are called—are social constructions. More specifically, threats are images with negative connotations. This corresponds to how threats are understood in securitisation theory, developed by the 'Copenhagen school'[1] of security studies:

> In security discourse, an issue is dramatised and presented as an issue of supreme priority; thus, by labelling it as *security*, n agent claims a need for and a right to treat it by extraordinary means. For the analyst to grasp this act, the task is not to assess some objective threats that 'really' endanger some object to be defended or secured; rather, it is to understand the processes of constructing a shared understanding of what is to be considered and collectively responded to as a threat. [...] The securitisation approach serves to underline the responsibility of talking security, the responsibility of actors as well as analysts who choose to frame an issue as a security issue. They cannot hide behind the claim that anything in itself constitutes a security issue. (Buzan, Wæver and de Wilde, 1998, pp. 26, 34; cf. Wæver, 1995)

However, 'security' and 'threats' can be framed in other ways than the specific frame implied by securitisation. The Copenhagen school assumes that the connotations of security are givens (existential threats requiring emergency measures), and that only the threats and the core values of security are variables. There are indeed cases in which threat framing have exactly these consequences, especially when issues are conceived of as threats implying hostility. This is illustrated in two of the ensuing case studies that explicitly employ the securitisation concept (ch. 6 and 7). As a general theoretical approach, however, the concept of securitisation is too limited, as evidenced by the political success for alternative concepts like 'common security' and 'cooperative security' (Chilton, 1996; Snyder, 1999; Wyn Jones, 1999, p. 157-58; Stern, 1999a, p. 133-34). By adopting a framing perspective, securitisation is seen as only one type of threat framing among others, albeit one of the most important.

Framing is largely about competing problem definitions, which makes this approach particularly suitable to the study of threat politics. The 'privilege of formulating problems' is a basic element of societal and political power (Gustafsson, 1988; cf. Rochefort and Cobb, 1994; Sylvan and Ross, 1998). In framing theory a basic distinction is made between the 'diagnostic' and 'prognostic' functions of frames (Snow and Benford, 1992). The 'diagnostic' function is about the diagnosis of a perceived problem, which is about blaming or identifying the causes of a problem. The 'prognostic' function is about the search for solutions to this problem (Schön and Rein, 1994, p. 29; Jachtenfuchs, 1996). In the present study, however, we are mainly concerned with the 'diagnostic' function. Snow and Benford argue that frames:

> serve as accenting devices that either underscore and embellish the seriousness and injustice of a social condition or redefine as unjust and immoral what was previously seen as unfortunate but perhaps tolerable. In either case, activists employ collective action frames to punctuate or single out some existing social condition or aspect of life and define it as unjust, intolerable, and deserving of corrective action. (Snow and Benford, 1992, p. 137)

Likewise, in agenda setting theory, focus is strictly on 'problems.' Kingdon makes an interesting observation that corresponds to framing, though he uses the words 'problem definition' and 'categorisation.' He argues that there is a difference between conditions and problems, and that '[c]onditions come to be defined as problems, and have a better chance of rising on the agenda, when we come to believe that we should do something to change them' (Kingdon, 1995, p. 198).

Against this background, a basic contention of this book is that much of the confusion on whether threats are imagined or actual seems to stem from either a failure or unwillingness to distinguish between *frames* and *the referent objects* of these frames. The usefulness of this distinction is illustrated by a few examples. While some might frame a foreign army crossing the border as a security threat, others might see it as a welcome liberation. Violence, disease, and even death itself are sometimes framed in positive ways. Moral reasoning, political correctness, and widely shared narratives must not prevent discussion of the theoretical possibility of alternative frames.

Frames of What?

The framing literature provides theoretically elaborated discussions of frames and framing processes, but is surprisingly blunt on the referent objects of frames. Studies have been made of how different frames have become mobilising forces, such as the peace movement's 'freeze' frame (Snow and Benford, 1992), the various frames of HIV/AIDS in international agenda setting (Jönsson et al, 1995), and the EU commission's framing of the 'defence industry' (Mörth, 1999). These studies provide examples of how framing works. But little is known of whether and how the distinctive features of the phenomena have an impact on framing. If something is framed as a threat, how can this something be understood in the first place? Referring to 'conditions' (Snow and Benford, 1992, p. 137; Kingdon, 1995, pp. 109, 198) that are not theoretically elaborated is hardly satisfying. Theorising is needed not only of framing but also of the *referent objects* of framing.

As a step in this direction we suggest a distinction between three types of referent objects that may or may not be framed as threats: *events*, *structural conditions* and *actors*. This is a development of Sundelius' distinction between threats that arise from structural processes and those that are related to malignant actors (Sundelius, 1983). In the present study, the notion of events is added, and the phenomena are not seen as threats in themselves, but as referent objects of threat frames. The existence of transnational networks of organised crime is a *structural condition*, but each specific crime is an *event*, and each crime is committed by some specific *actor(s)*.

Events such as a kidnap, a murder, an air crash or the outbreak of war provide the necessary drama to make the media and decision makers pay serious attention to them. It could be argued that an event cannot be threatening in itself, but that it points to actors or structural conditions that are threatening. However, the point of addressing events as possible threats is not to discuss the underlying logic (or lack of it), but to clarify that sometimes people talk about events as threatening without making any connection to actors or structural conditions. In addition, the push provided by dramatic events is a major concern in agenda setting theory (Kingdon, 1995, pp. 94-100), and is the very subject matter of crisis studies (Stern, 1999b). The societal significance of an event framed as a threat is usually only temporary, particularly in the media. When the event is over, the news value is lost and the significance of the issue rapidly fades.

In contrast, structural conditions like pollution, vulnerability in IT systems, and budget deficits do not imply the same kind of drama and urgency as focusing events. Therefore it is often more difficult for structural conditions that are framed as threats to take on societal salience. If this has been successful, however, these structural conditions have such a strong mobilising potency that they maintain their societal salience for a much longer time than any single dramatic event. Many examples of such 'master frames' (Snow and Benford, 1992) can be given, but the 'Cold War' and its associated 'terror balance' are good illustrations of frames with remarkable staying power—referring to structural conditions rather than dramatic events. If master frames are to be toppled, something similar to Kuhn's notion of paradigm shift is required (Kuhn, 1996).

The third type of referent issue, actors, does not have the same time implications as events and structural conditions. The threat image of an actor can be short lived, as illustrated by the brief but significant salience in western media and politics of the perceived threat from Russian ultranationalist Zhirinovsky in the early to mid 1990s. Actor threat frames can also have an almost perpetual quality, as illustrated by the alienation of Roms ('Gypsies'). The specific feature of actors as potential sources of threat frames is that they are immediate sources of blame, hostility or hatred. That is, they have a strong 'diagnostic function' (Snow and Benford, 1992). In contrast, events and structural conditions are not necessarily attributed with blame and hostility. They might as well be framed as tragedies for which no particular agent is responsible. However, the threat framing of events, structural conditions and actors is often interconnected. Particular structural conditions, such as unemployment, often provoke the attribution of blame by framing some actors as culpable.

Immigrant minorities have often been the targets of this kind of threat framing.

This reasoning strengthens our criticism of the securitisation perspective's view of security as something static and rather negative. It has been argued that securitisation implies taking politics out of the normal democratic realm, and that it increases the risk for militarisation, hostility, and enemy images (Buzan, Wæver and de Wilde, 1998; Wæver et al, 1993; Huysmans, 1995). In contrast, our distinction between events, structural conditions and actors clarifies that the connotations of 'threat' and 'security' are not necessarily or always the same. Enemy images are an immediate consequence of framing actors as threats. However, enemy images may but do not necessarily follow from framing for instance radioactive fallout or unemployment as threats and risks.

In addition, a distinction can be made between *specific* and *diffuse* sources of threat images. It can be argued that one cannot fear what one does not know exists. Threat images of HIV/AIDS or the Y2K bug did not exist before these realities were discovered. Providing new threat frames are in fact largely about previously unknown phenomena, or about how previously stable conditions have become aggravated. This might include everything from discovering new viruses to monitoring arms development and earthquakes. Even fearing the unknown is about some imagined danger, though in this case it is the very diffuse or unspecific nature of this that produces the sense of threat (Johnson, 1997, pp. 13-15; Dewey, 1929). If we are not certain about the ways in which a newly discovered pandemic is transmitted, then panic is not far away.

Furthermore, some threat images are not always publicly expressed by those who feel threatened, which can for instance be the case with abused children and women (Hansen, 1999). This touches upon the problem of giving voice to issues that are off the political agenda. Hence, there is no simple or direct relationship between threat images and their referent phenomena. Some things are spelled out as threats while others are not, and threat images might be formed without any connection to known realities.

Threat Politics: How Framing Takes on Societal Salience

What makes some threat images take on societal salience while others do not? This question puts the focus on the politics of framing. It is about the symbolic contest over meaning in society, rather than the framing of problems on the individual level. It is about the struggle to maintain and challenge widely shared frames, established definitions, traditional views, and connotations (Schön and Rein, 1994, p. 29; Jachtenfuchs, 1996; Mörth, 2000). This corresponds to a broad range of similar conceptualisations. In the framing literature, we find notions such as 'master frames' and 'collective action frames' (Snow and Benford, 1992). Particular events, conditions and actors can be framed in different ways, and different frames may have different effects on policy choices and outcomes (Rochefort and Cobb, 1994, p. 26; Tversky and Kahneman, 1981).

Writing from a constructivist IR perspective, Ruggie discusses shared narratives that imply collective intentionality, such as the mutual recognition of sovereignty (Ruggie 1998, pp. 20-21). Ruggie develops this by making a distinction between 'regulative rules' and 'constitutive rules.' While regulative rules are intended to have causal effects, for instance making people to pay their bills before the end of the month, constitutive rules 'define the set of practices that make up any particular consciously organised social activity—that is to say, they specify *what counts* as that activity' (Ruggie, 1998, p. 22). Ruggie exemplifies constitutive rules with chess rules. It is the collective frame, or shared understanding, of these rules that makes playing chess possible. Thus the politics of framing is not only about competing problem conceptions, but also about determining the rules of the game.

This brings us to the first of four variable conditions that may facilitate or obstruct threat framing: *the framing actor*. Anyone can be a framing actor, but some of the more significant ones tend to be politicians, bureaucrats, experts, the media, pressure groups, and academics. If 'threats' are to take on societal salience, they have to be articulated by influential actors. This corresponds to the Copenhagen school's notion of 'securitising actors,' and to the concept of 'policy entrepreneurs' in agenda setting theory (Buzan, Wæver and de Wilde, 1998, pp. 40-42; Kingdon, 1995). It is commonly argued that governmental elites maintain a dominant position when it comes to framing threats and risks of common interest (Buzan, Wæver and de Wilde, 1998; Kingdon, 1995, pp. 68-70, 199-200; Hermann, 1990, pp. 11-12, 17-18). In particular, the realm of security is often strongly institutionalised, thus privileging the government and special security institutions such as the security policy and the military. Related to this is the notion of the military-bureaucratic-industrial-complex or, as critical theorists has reframed it, the military-industrial-academic-complex (Wyn Jones, 1999, p. 147). The existence of such exclusive elite communities has been corroborated by a few empirical studies (Horowitz, 1963; Hart, 1976). However, it also acknowledged that this dominance for state elites is neither static nor absolute (Buzan, Wæver and de Wilde, 1998, pp. 31-32). As argued in our own case studies, the media and academics are significant framing agents. If the master hypothesis is that state elites and the security institutions still dominate threat politics, there is good reason to explore this in more detail, empirically as well as theoretically.

Second, the *type of referent object* has an impact on whether threat framing takes on societal salience or not. As discussed above, dramatic events take on societal salience more easily than both structural conditions and actors framed as threats. Focusing dramatic events and crises are important as they often provide the push that makes people pay serious attention to a problem agenda (Kingdon, 1995, pp. 90-109; Jervis, 1976, ch. 6). Harrisburg, Pennsylvania and Chernobyl, Ukraine are key examples of events that pushed the problems of nuclear safety into a top position on national agendas. But the salience of events is usually only temporal. Accordingly, the media is often the most significant framing agent of events (Tuchman, 1978; McQuail, 1994, p. 335). Structural conditions seldom imply the same kind of urgency and drama. When these are articulated as threats, it is more common that the framing agents are policy makers, pressure groups, and academics rather than the media. Furthermore, frequency of activities and severity of outcomes have an impact on whether frames take on societal salience or not (Rochefort and Cobb, 1998; cf. Sjöberg in this volume, ch. 1).

Third, the *frame characteristics* are important. Frames can be *elaborated* as well as *restricted*. The former type is inclusive and allows for extension and amplification, while the latter provides a constricted range of connotations and articulations (Snow and Benford, 1992, pp. 139-40). The 'essentially contested concept of security' is an example of an elaborated frame. As the debate for and against a widened security concept illustrates, this frame may be associated with negative as well as positive connotations. This is most notably the case if security is hyphenated. For example, while 'common security' has obvious positive connotations, 'national security' is traditionally associated with fear and protection from foreign aggression. The politics of restricted frames is mostly about what issues should be framed, and much less about the meaning of the frame itself. Elaborated frames, on the other hand, not only permit political struggles about the application, but also about the very meaning and connotations of the frame. As Snow and Benford put it: 'the elaborated master frame allows for numerous aggrieved groups to tap it and elaborate their grievances in terms of its basic problem-solving schema' (Snow and Benford, 1992, p. 140).

Fourth, threat politics is largely a struggle about *frame continuity or change*. In the literature on problem definition, framing and agenda setting, it is argued that if a previously neglected issue is to take on salience and get onto political agendas, this often requires frame restructuring (Schön and Rein, 1994; Kingdon, 1995; Jönsson et al, 1995). It is difficult to challenge the staying power of institutionalised threat frames, such as the established connotations of 'national security' as having to do primarily with state sovereignty and foreign aggression. The breakthrough for the reframing of security required nothing less than the end of the Cold War—a major window of opportunity. This corresponds to Kuhn's notions of paradigm and paradigm shifts in scientific thinking (Kuhn, 1996)—that is the powerful intellectual hegemony and rigidity of established master frames. Thus, the framing process is affected by the degree of consensus or conflict. When framing actors disagree either on the meaning or the application of a frame, political debates, turf battles, and 'forum shopping' can be expected (Jönsson et al, 1995).

Finally, there is also the possibility that though political actors pay serious attention to a threat frame, the issue has a very low societal salience. The key words here are visibility and public attention. Issues can be treated as threats even if they are not officially recognised as such. Political practice is sometimes about saying one thing and doing something completely different. This philosophy was institutionalised in Finnish as well as Swedish cold war security policy toward Russia; be prepared for Russian invasion, but avoid openly depicting Russia as a security threat.

Structure of the Book

The book is divided into three parts, with different focuses and modes of analysis. In the first part—*Opinion in Focus*—the analyses focus on risk perceptions among public opinion and political elites. In the second part—*Actors in Focus*—the threat politics of particular actors are addressed, with open-ended answers as to what threat images take on societal salience. Emphasis here is on the media, governmental elites, and business actors. In the third part—*Issues in Focus*—analyses begin in the opposite end. Here the processes of how particular issues have been framed as threats are analysed, tracing the framing process across arenas and agents. In a concluding chapter the themes of the previous chapters and the mixture of approaches are brought together. The chapter makes an assessment of the conditions that facilitate and obstruct the processes in which threat images take on societal salience.

Finally, it should be noted that the book is neither descriptively nor analytically comprehensive. Geographically, there is a northern European focus; tough some case studies go beyond this. The choice of geographical focus, actors and issues covered in this book is pragmatic, based on the experience and research foci that the contributors already have. Yet the contributions to this volume are sufficient for the purpose of posing important questions on threat politics, serving as illustrations, and for combining insights from academically separated but thematically overlapping fields of study. This specifically involves risk studies, security studies and crisis management—research fields between which there have been far too little communication.

Note

1 Since the late 1980s, Barry Buzan, Ole Wæver and their colleagues have developed a creative research agenda of security studies, with emphasis on a widened security concept. The 'Copenhagen school'—a label suggested by one of their critics (McSweeney, 1996)—has attained noticeable interest within academic International Relations, as witnessed in the series of reviews, critiques, and amendments (McSweeney, 1996; Buzan and Wæver, 1997; Wæver, 1999; Neumann, 1998; Hansen, 1999; Eriksson, 1999a, 1999b, 2000, 2001; Wagnsson, 2000; Matz, 2001). For a comprehensive review of the creative development of this 'school,' see Huysmanns (1998). The most important contribution of the 'Copenhagen school' is the development of Ole Wæver's securitisation theory (Wæver, 1989, 1995, 1997; Buzan, Wæver and de Wilde, 1998; Buzan, 1998).

Part I
Opinion in Focus

1 Risk Perceptions: Taking on Societal Salience

LENNART SJÖBERG

Threats and risks have come to be an important focus in current policy debates and decision-making. A crucial issue, which has been the topic in much of Risk Studies, is how people perceive risks, and what factors affect such perceptions. Several distinctions are made in this chapter, especially between personal (risk to oneself) and general (risk to others) risks that appear to have quite different dynamics. What people demand in terms of risk mitigation is mostly related to consequences of adverse events, not risks or probabilities or even to 'riskiness' of activities. In many cases, personal responsibility is seen as drastically smaller than those of the government.

Threats or Risks? A Note on Terminology

This book mostly employs the word threat, but this chapter is about risk. The position taken here, however, is that if there is a difference between the two, it is hardly of any practical importance. One could argue that the word threat refers to a hazard close in time and very likely to strike, as suggested by some active in this field, but that is hardly a position that is easy to defend on the basis of everyday language. In technical language we are of course free to define terms as we wish, at the peril of not being understood in everyday discourse. Therefore risk and threat can be treated as synonyms.

Other misunderstandings concern the word risk. Some people seem to believe that the word is reserved for a special technical use, such as expected value or probability of an adverse event.[1] All this is very confusing and illustrates the danger of not making a clear distinction between natural and technical language. Therefore—as noted in the introduction to this book—risk is seen as equitable with threat and similar words, and thus defined with reference to how it is used in everyday contexts. What relations it may have to subjectively perceived probability is an open empirical question. In accordance with the framing perspective adopted in this volume, I am only concerned with *perceived*^{2} risk, which may or may not be related to 'real' risk.

In an international perspective, the UK Royal Society commissioned a group of researchers to do a review of risk perception, analysis and management back in 1991 (Royal Society Study Group 1992). This report gave rise to a very strong reaction and heated debate still being mentioned in UK literature. Social scientists tended to take a constructivist standpoint, while the natural scientists took a realist standpoint. However, it is obvious that both must be pertinent in risk discussions. First, risk is an *expectation* of an (adverse) event, and hence it is a social construction like all expectations. It is in our minds and nowhere else. Second, it is an expectation *about* something, i.e. about an external event, actor or structural condition of some kind (cf. Introduction). Hence, it refers to reality. Risk analysis must therefore proceed along both lines, both to understand how people perceive and construe risk, and what the issues risk perceptions are referring to. Even if there is a desire for understanding what the 'real risks' are, one must always remember that what real risks are of concern is not God given but a matter of social judgment. And how people react to the risk information that scientists provide is also a matter for the social scientist to analyse, as is, indeed, the question of how scientists and experts themselves frame risks.

The Salience of Risk: Public Opinion vs. Experts

Risk perception has been a topic of interest to researchers and policy-makers at least since the end of the 1960s, beginning with a seminal article by Starr (1969). Considerable research has been devoted to the question of how people perceive risks. The reason for this large and sustaining interest is probably that it is widely believed that risks and risk perceptions are important to policy-makers. Even if perceived risk is weak as an explanatory variable of individual behaviour, it is probably important for policy related attitudes (Sjöberg, 1999d; Sjöberg, 1999e). For example, it has been found that Swedish parliamentarians have tripled their initiatives in risk related legislation since the 1960s (Sjöberg and others, 1998).

How salient are risks? In a Swedish survey concerned with risk perception and the attitude to various technologies for energy production (Sjöberg, 1999e), a number of questions about various energy production systems, their risks and benefits were posed to members of the general public and to nuclear waste experts. The answers to these questions provide a picture of the general differences in attitude that characterised the experts and the public with regard to these issues. The means are given in Table 1.1.[3]

Table 1.1 Means of attitude (good-bad), perceived risk and benefit of energy production systems (scale 1-7)

System	Attitude		Risk		Benefit	
	Public	Expert	Public	Expert	Public	Expert
Hydro	5.66	5.91	1.44	1.47	4.89	5.45
Coal	2.56	2.50	4.21	4.16	3.09	3.80
Nuclear	3.99	5.41	4.00	2.03	4.56	5.31
Oil	3.21	2.67	3.92	3.74	3.75	4.00
Natural gas	4.31	3.88	3.23	3.38	4.14	4.15
Bio mass	4.67	4.02	2.47	2.83	4.04	3.51
Wind	5.78	4.57	0.87	1.36	4.26	2.94

There were some interesting differences between the two groups in Table 1.1. First, experts were more positive than the public to nuclear power, whereas the public was more positive to biomass, natural gas and wind. Second, the public considered nuclear power to be much more risky than the experts did. Third, experts perceived most systems as more useful than the public did, with the exception of bio mass and wind, where the public gave higher ratings.

Ratings of attitude to the seven energy production systems were regressed on judgments of risk and benefit of these systems (see Tables 1.2 and 1.3).

Table 1.2 Regression analysis of the public's attitude to energy production systems

System	β, risk	β, benefit	Adjusted R2
Hydro	-0.474	0.137	0.255
Coal	-0.544	0.071	0.294
Nuclear power	-0.692	0.192	0.608
Oil	-0.552	0.075	0.297
Natural gas	-0.681	-0.036	0.474
Biomass	-0.567	0.136	0.328
Wind	-0.492	0.217	0.283

Table 1.3 Regression analysis of experts' attitude to energy production systems

System	β, risk	β, benefit	Adjusted R2
Hydro	-0.030	0.170	0.000
Coal	-0.242	0.083	0.027
Nuclear power	-0.290	0.291	0.178
Oil	-0.271	0.174	0.089
Natural gas	-0.478	0.225	0.244
Biomass	-0.451	0.322	0.329
Wind	-0.313	0.524	0.355

The level of explained variance in these analyses was relatively high, with some exceptions. In both cases it is seen that risk was the more potent explanatory dimension. This was particularly clear for the public. There is an interesting exception for experts judging nuclear power. In this case, benefit obtained a β value at the same level as risk. Hence, it appears that experts' attitude to nuclear power is less risk dominated than the same attitude held by the public. As was shown in Table 1.1, the experts also rated nuclear power risk as much lower than the public did.[4]

Why does risk take on salience? We have just seen risk to be a dominating factor in accounting for attitude, benefits being much less important. In related studies, we found that people are more easily sensitised to risk than to safety

(Sjöberg and Drottz-Sjöberg, 1993). Mood states are more influenced by negative expectations than by positive ones (Sjöberg, 1989a). People seem to be more eager to avoid risks than to pursue chances.

The Impact of Framing: Personal vs. General Risk

Research on risk perception has usually employed an undifferentiated concept of perceived risk. In other words, respondents are not given any further specification or clarification of the concept. Yet, people do make a clear distinction between risk to themselves and risk to others, i.e. personal vs. general risk (Drottz-Sjöberg, 1993; Sjöberg and Drottz-Sjöberg, 1994). When the target is not specified it is unclear which definition of risk people choose to work with. In one study it was found that respondents seemed to choose to rate general risk under non-specific instructions. In a recent study (Sjöberg, 2000a), we have been able to replicate and extend this finding.

In many studies it has been found that personal risks are judged as smaller than general risks, especially so-called lifestyle risks, i.e. risks of smoking, drinking alcohol and the like (Sjöberg, 1999b). The difference between personal and general risk is not constant, and has been found to be smaller for risks that are imposed on the respondent and not related to his or her own behavior (Sjöberg, 2000a). The personal/general distinction is crucial to the understanding of various forms of addictive behaviour. People who smoke are aware of the risk of smoking to people in general, but see a very small risk to themselves. Failure to observe this distinction leads to misleading analysis of addictive behaviour (Viscusi, 1990).

More generally, people probably manage their own risk taking on the basis of personal rather than general risk, and personal risk is, as pointed out above, framed as very much smaller than general risk. Weinstein has described a related phenomenon called unrealistic optimism (Weinstein, 1984, 1987, 1989; Weinstein et al, 1988; Weinstein and Nicholich, 1993). Personal risks are seen as so small as to be possible to dismiss or ignore.

Furthermore, the consequences of the two risk ratings are different. Demand for risk mitigation is more strongly related to general risk, especially for lifestyle risks such as alcohol or tobacco (Sjöberg, 2000a). For risks over which we perceive no or little control, such as nuclear risks, the personal risk may be the more potent predictor of demand for risk mitigation.

The Demography of Risk Perception

Flynn and co-workers have presented some results—which according to them imply a 'white male effect' in risk perception—that there is an interaction effect of gender and 'race,' and that only white males have a distinctly different level of (low) perceived risk (Flynn et al, 1994). (No distinction was made with regard to risk target.) This phenomenon, if it exists, appears to be mostly relevant for the American society, but 'race' is often believed to be a proxy for economic and social vulnerability. We have data that may be used to throw some light on the issue in the Swedish society.

In 1996 extensive survey data were collected on risk perceptions. Mean personal and general risk ratings of 34 hazards of many different kinds were computed for each respondent. Gender, income and age all yielded statistically significant effects for both personal and general risk. However, the interactions were not significant. It was found that:

- personal risk was rated as lower than general risk;
- males gave lower risk ratings than females;
- higher income groups gave lower ratings of risk than lower income groups, thus confirming the vulnerability hypothesis.

A weak and non-significant tendency towards interaction was opposite to that expected from the 'white male effect' since women showed a stronger income effect than men. Furthermore, the effects were stronger for general than for personal risk.[5] The 'white male effect' apparently teach us little about the demographics of risk perception in Sweden.

If people perceive risk differently to themselves and others, do they also differentiate *responsibilities* for risk mitigation? That is the topic of the following section.

Is the Government Responsible?

In his famous inaugural address of 1961, U.S. President John F. Kennedy urged his audience 'not to ask what your country can do for you, but what you can do for your country.' In our risk perception research, we have in many studies asked respondents to rate how much the government should invest in terms of resources, and feel responsible, for the mitigation of various risks. Invariably, people rate such government responsibility as high. The country should do a lot for them. But what about personal responsibility for mitigating risks?

If Kennedy's admonition has been heard, people should rate their own responsibility as equally high or higher than that of the government. I present here results from a recent study where 210 young people (mean age 22 years, and 61 percent male respondents) rated demand for risk governmental and personal mitigation of 26 different hazards. The latter ratings were specifically explained to pertain both to their own risks and the risks of others. The mean ratings can be seen in Table 1.4.

It is clear that in most cases the government is seen to be much more responsible for mitigating the risk than the individual. The differences are in many cases very large. The mean difference between responsibility of the government and oneself, on the one hand, and the difference between general and personal risk, on the other were correlated -0.44. In other words, the perceived responsibility of government and oneself were most similar when there was a large difference between general and personal risk. The latter cases pertain to lifestyle risks such as Alcohol (see Table 1.4).

Again, the difference between framing risks as personal or general appear to be very relevant for understanding the salience of risk perceptions. It would be interesting to compare these results with data from other countries. One might expect that countries with a weaker tradition of welfare state politics than Sweden and with a stronger liberal individualism—for example the U.S.—might reveal a lower demand for governmental responses to perceived risks.

Table 1.4 Mean ratings of demand for risk mitigation, to be done by self or government (national or local). Scale 0-7

Hazard	Self is responsible	Government is responsible
Smoking	4.06	4.69
Alcohol	3.98	4.47
Vehicle exhausts	3.57	5.13
AIDS	4.59	4.59
Air pollution	3.78	5.57
High voltage power lines	1.55	4.22
Green house effect	3.50	5.11
Unsuitable diet	4.31	3.18
Traffic accidents	4.86	5.41
Struck by lightning	0.88	0.66
Depletion of the ozone layer	3.73	4.96
Swedish nuclear power plants	2.52	5.48
Eastern Europe nuclear power plants	2.53	4.75
Natural background radiation	1.06	1.87
Nuclear waste	2.57	5.50
Genetic manipulation	2.78	4.59
Terrorist attacks	1.66	4.27
X-ray diagnostics	1.48	3.48
Sun rays	3.35	2.65
War	3.23	5.69
Nuclear arms	3.09	5.70
Floods	1.81	3.53
Inadequate medical care when ill	3.46	6.04
Violence and aggression	4.83	5.44
Mobile telephones	2.43	2.43
BSE ('Mad cow disease')	1.58	3.84

The Media and the Societal Salience of Risk Perceptions

Mass media information may have differential effects on personal and general risk (af Wåhlberg and Sjöberg, 2000). The effects can be expected to be larger on general risk, since the media deals with general societal phenomena or well-known people, not so much with the private consumers and respondents. Campaigns that have been organised to stimulate people to more prudent behavior tend to have little or no effect (Roberts and Maccoby, 1985), and the reason can be related to the personal/general dimension. A campaign message may be seen as relevant to other people who are believed to be at risk, but not to oneself. See (Fisher and Sjöberg, 1990; Sjöberg, 1989b) for an example with regard to domestic radon.

The media is the main scapegoat in experts' debates of risk policy dilemmas, and it is frequently asserted that the media have a very large effect on risk perception (Okrent, 1998). The media is often seen as irresponsible and only interested in disseminating negative information, with a special inclination to cover low probability/high consequence risk (Cohen, 1985; Kone and Mullet, 1994). However, few references are given to support such statements.

A noteworthy exception is Combs and Slovic (1979) who reported that perceived causes of death correlated more strongly with frequency of media reporting than with actual mortality statistics. As they pointed out, this is no proof of a causal effect. Many alternative explanations are possible. Perhaps more importantly, the study pertained to illnesses and accidents rather than technologies, which are the usual topic of risk policy issues. Suppose the study would have relied on data from, e.g. genetically modified food. No deaths have been reported in the media, and none are known to have occurred. Yet, people have strong views about such hazards and perceive risks of varying intensity. Why? Perhaps it is so because the media cover them. But there are no data showing strong relations between perceived risk and amount of media coverage.

In a recent project on risk perceptions and the media in Western Europe we found no support for the media impact hypothesis. We found that perceived risk correlated only weakly (across hazards) with media coverage, whereas self-rated knowledge about the risks correlated more strongly. The former correlations were only of size 0.2, the latter about 0.6 (Sjöberg et al in preparation). Demand for risk mitigation was not correlated with media coverage.

In our study, the media gave a fairly balanced picture of risks and accidents (Nilsson et al, 1997). It was also not true that media gave priority to risks of the type small probability/large consequence. They reported, for example, many traffic accidents (large probability/moderate consequences). What was written in Swedish newspapers about Chernobyl in the spring of 1996, commemorating the Chernobyl accident in 1986, was indeed negative. However, Swedish nuclear power was given a balanced treatment. To take another example, some researchers have complained that the media did not inform sufficiently about facts in connection with the local referendum about a high level nuclear waste repository in Malå in Northern Sweden in 1997 (Findahl, 1998), but there are many other ways to get information than through the local newspaper, including the Internet.

The media often seems to be the only channel of information seriously considered when risk perception is to be accounted for. However, there are several alternatives worthy of consideration, such as movies,[6] television dramas, rumours (Kapferer, 1989), and personal contacts (Sjöberg, 1994). It is also possible that the mere connotations of terms such as 'nuclear waste' elicit risk perceptions.

The theory of social amplification of risk (Burns et al, 1993; Kasperson, 1992; Kasperson et al, 1988; Renn et al, 1992) is based, among other things, on the notion that the impact of the media is significant. We do not find that to be the case (Sjöberg, 1999f). In 1996, the media did emphasise nuclear risks and reminded the reader that it was ten years since the Chernobyl accident. Yet no change of the perceived risk of nuclear power could be noted (Sjöberg et al, 2000b). This was in spite of a clear increase of the salience of nuclear risks in at least four of the five countries studied. People had learned their lesson already in 1986, it seemed, and being reminded of it had little effect. Hence, it is debatable if a mere reminder of a hazard one already knows about is likely to have an effect on perceived risk. The very task of judging a risk is of course one such reminder by itself.

On the Limited Salience of Trust in Authorities

A further development in risk perception research has involved introducing trust as yet another determinant of risk perception, often said to be very significant (Slovic, 1993; Slovic et al, 1993). But trust correlates only about 0.3 with perceived risk (Sjöberg, 1999c). Very few of the approximately fifteen studies that have been published have indicated stronger correlations. A well-known study by Slovic et al (1991) involved asking people how their trust would be affected by various events. The conclusion was that it is easy to destroy trust, but hard to re-establish. This may be true, but the data say little since they merely reflect the beliefs that people had about how their trust would change. Such beliefs are notoriously invalid as indicators of what psychological event would in fact take place (Nisbett and Wilson, 1977).

In a recent survey, directed both to the public and to nuclear waste experts (Sjöberg et al, 2000a), the questionnaire asked for ratings of trust in the pertinent authorities for each of 22 hazards. The trust ratings were correlated with general and personal risk, for the public and for the experts. The over-all level of correlation was thus about 0.3 (somewhat higher for nuclear waste), or some ten percent of the variance explained, in good agreement with data obtained in a previous study (Sjöberg, 1999c). The experts' trust data seemed to have about the same level of correlation with risk perception as those from the public, with the exception of nuclear waste variables where the experts showed a smaller correlation. The reason is probably that their dispersions of ratings were quite small in those respects.[7]

The public sample was also given 43 items which were used in a previous study of trust and risk perception (Sjöberg, 1999c). These items measure general trust, i.e. trust without reference to any specific risk or hazard. They were factor analysed anew, since the present sample was much larger and also more representative than the original one. Five important observations could be made:[8]

- low trust in politicians;
- cynical suspiciousness;
- perceived high level of societal conflict;
- low level of trust in corporations;
- lack of trust in general honesty of people.

It was found that there was a very consistent trend for the trust dimensions to be correlated with perceived risk, but that the level of correlation was low, about 0.2. Squared multiple correlations between the five general trust factors and the indices of pooled general and personal nuclear waste risks were both

0.08. This result, about 10 percent explained variance, was in good agreement with previous research on general trust and perceived risk. However, specific risk was much higher correlated with perceived nuclear waste risks.[9] When multiple regressions were performed on the pooled indices of perceived nuclear waste risk, and trust dimensions, it was found that:

- specific risk alone accounted for 0.210 and 0.176 of the variance of perceived risk;
- this was raised, but only to 0.221 and 0.193 by the introduction of the factors of general trust;
- the only general trust factor that obtained a significant β value was lack of trust in the general honesty of people.

The present data show that trust may be a moderately important factor in risk perception, supporting the conclusion I have published elsewhere (Sjöberg, 1999c). It is important to note that trust measures need to be made specific to the hazard under investigation since general trust adds very little to the explanatory power of trust—little but still something. There may be a theoretical reason for also including the general trust dimensions.

What Explains the Demand for Risk Mitigation?

Although the perceived frequency or probability of risk might seem to be an important dimension in social policy with regard to risky technology such as nuclear power, the relationship has never been proven to be very strong. Less than 20 percent of the variance of risk tolerance, measured at the level of individual respondents, can be accounted for in typical data. In addition, perceived frequency or probability of risk has been found to be less potent a factor than the severity of consequences of an accident or otherwise unwanted event (Sjöberg, 1998b, 1999a, in press c). In contrast to the so-called Psychometric Model, which stresses the impact of frequency and probability, our research shows that it is not risk of accidents, but rather the consequences of accidents that drive demand for risk mitigation.

However, the Psychometric Model is not completely faulty, but can be can be improved, sometimes strongly so, by introducing the dimension 'Tampering with Nature.' Perhaps most important, the implications for understanding policy problems, and for risk communication, are quite different if people are no longer seen to be driven mainly by ignorance, emotions and social constraints more or less leading to opportunism.

If existing theories fail to fully explain risk perceptions, what, then, is a more successful explanation? In the case of nuclear waste hazards, we are able to suggest an answer. A more comprehensive approach can be constructed on the basis of:

- attitude to nuclear power;
- risk sensitivity (i.e. a tendency to rate all risks as large);
- specific nuclear and radiation risk factors;
- some other factors such as trust and the 'Tampering with Nature' factor mentioned above.

It is possible to construct a regression model, using these explanatory factors, which accounts for about 60 percent of the variance of risk perception (Sjöberg, 2000c). It would be interesting to investigate the generality of these findings, and also necessary since there are many indications that our reactions to nuclear hazards have some unique properties.

The Societal Salience of Risk Perceptions: Beyond 'Risk Society'

Stakeholders

In a study of how experts and the public viewed each others' risk perceptions it was found that the experts showed some bias in the way the saw the values held by the public (Sjöberg et al, 2000a). People tend to be less extreme than believed by the experts. This may be because the experts get much of their input about the public from particular 'stakeholders,' such as interest organisations, political parties, social movements, and corporations. This concept needs to be scrutinised since it is becoming quite important in studies of risk communication (North, 1998; Renn, 1998). Who is a stakeholder? How should such groups be given opportunities of influencing the process and what are the possible consequences of such a policy (Drottz-Sjöberg, 1999)? Are stakeholders to be given real power, and at whose expense? Should stakeholder committees replace the elected democratic organs of decision-making wholly or partly?

Experience of stakeholder groups is not univocal. Some years before stakeholder terminology became popular in Risk Studies, Milbraith (1981) addressed the issue. He pointed out that those who are active and take part in a process are able and willing to give of their time and energy, are quite unrepresentative of the public at large. Yet, the public may use their democratic rights when given the chance. In the two Swedish referenda about a local nuclear waste repository that have been held so far, voter turnout was very high; 76 and 87 percent, respectively.[10]

'Risk Society:' A Critique

Several critically oriented scholars have developed the so-called 'risk society' perspective (Beck, 1992; Giddens, 1991; Beck and van Loon, 2000; Lidskog, 1994). The 'risk society' thesis that risk is unique to 'modernity' simply cannot be true. Risk has always been with us; life is full of dangers, and humans always have had to try to anticipate danger.

In Sweden, there has been a major effort to understand the problems involved in finding a site for a nuclear waste repository (Sjöberg et al, in press). Studies of two municipalities have been published (Drottz-Sjöberg, 1996; Drottz-Sjöberg, 1998). Two books have been devoted to these issues (Lidskog, 1998; Nationelle samordnaren på kärnavfallsområdet, 1998). The latter studies were much influenced by the 'risk society' perspective that they seemed to accept rather uncritically (Sjöberg, 1998a).

In a case study, we investigated the first major railway disaster in Sweden, which occurred in 1864 (Sjöberg and af Wåhlberg, 1996). Although this event occurred in a technologically primitive, mainly agrarian society where people were very poor and in which the media had a limited role,[11] the perception of risk related to this event and the new technology was very strong indeed. At the same time, other hazards were more or less neglected in the media, such as fires or disasters at sea.

On the other hand, current reactions to information technology seem to illustrate a very different attitude (Sjöberg and Truedsson, in press; Truedsson and Sjöberg, 2000). There is a tremendous surge of interest in all things connected with IT and the Internet. Fortunes are made and lost over-night and, until the recent 'dotcom death,' few voices of warning were heard. The increased access to information in all respects brings with a qualitatively new stage of information access, probably comparable to the invention of printed books or modern mass media. It is a momentous change just like nuclear power was a generation ago, but we still have not seen the social and attitude backlash that is to be expected in a 'risk society.'

Can the received views of risk perception help us predict what has and will happen? If Dread and New Risk are the potent factors, railways should have been phased out in Sweden in 1864. We did not discover one such voice at the time. People were interested in the accident, what caused it and how it could be avoided. The new technology was perceived as superior to the traditional transportation alternatives of the time. Nuclear power, on the other hand, is not a unique solution to energy production, and even if fossil fuel is also disliked because of its risks, there seem to be other, clean and risk-free alternatives (hydro, wind, solar). (It can be debated if this is correct, but many people see it that way.) IT is a technology without a serious competition, just like the railways of the 1860s, and therefore serious attempts to phase it out are unlikely. How people react to a technology and its associated accidents is a function of its benefits and what alternatives are available, not only of its risks. The individual psychology of risk perception can provide only a part—although an important part—of the answer to how and why society interprets some events as threats, and what its responses are.

Why are some risks neglected by society at large and others brought forward with great power? As an example, we have found that a major risk as perceived by the public in five European countries was that of Eastern Europe nuclear power. Here we do find a certain amount of political action on behalf of Western governments, but not to the level that public fear might call for. Perhaps the reason is simply that our ability to affect the situation in countries such as Russia is very limited. In addition, a study of risk perception in Romania and Bulgaria carried out in the beginning of the 1990s (Sjöberg et al, in press) it was found that some hazards were rated as quite high, still seldom given media attention. Drinking water was one such hazard. It is possible that the reason why people were worried but the media neglected it was simply that (1) it was a hazard everybody knew about since a long time, (2) there was little hope of improvement and (3) it was easy to protect oneself from.

The route from individual risk perception to societal and political salience and action is complex. It is most likely that several factors have an impact. The actions or non-actions of elite groups is one important facet, the availability of alternative solutions another, and the existence of effective precautionary actions a third.

To sum up, this chapter has demonstrated that the societal salience of risk perceptions largely depends on whether they are framed as personal or general. In addition, the policy implications of the two are different. General risk is more important to policy attitudes for hazards perceived as being under personal control, while the opposite is true for personal risk. Societal threat images bear in an imperfect and non-obvious relationship to individual risk perception. There is need for further research to elucidate this issue.

Notes

The research presented in this chapter was supported by a grant from the Swedish Agency of Civil Emergency Planning (ÖCB). It also builds upon work conducted within the RISK-PERCOM project, supported also by the Swedish Council for Planning and Coordination of Research (FRN), the Swedish Council for Humanistic and Social Science Research (HSFR), the Swedish Nuclear Power Inspectorate (SKI), and the Swedish Radiation Protection Institute (SSI). The final stages of the work was supported by project Neglected Risks, supported by the Bank of Sweden Tercentenary Fund.

1   I have even been severely criticised for using scales of perceived risk not confined to the 0-1 interval, since probability surely must lie in that interval!
2   Perceived risk is a misnomer since risk is an expectation, not a perception. But the term seems to have stuck. At any rate, what is studied in risk perception work is beliefs, attitudes and expectations, never perceptions.
3   The use of mailed questionnaires is often seen as inefficient because it is claimed to give a low response rate. However, response rates can be boosted by a number of procedures (Dillman, 1991), chiefly reminders and incentives that were used here. A meta-analysis of response rates has shown that these tend to be very similar for in-home interviews, telephones surveys and mailed questionnaires (Hox and De Leeuw, 1994). (A previous 10

percent advantage of in-home interviews seemed to be disappearing in the 1990s). Anonymous mailed surveys furthermore appear to give more valid data than interviews (Wentland and Smith, 1993). The length of our questionnaires did not seem to deter many of the respondents, and it has indeed been found that length of questionnaire is no decisive factor in response rate (Heberlein and Baumgartner, 1978), contrary to the belief of many.

Bias in the group of respondents is usually mostly present for level of education, in risk perception surveys, as far as can be determined. Level of education is usually negatively correlated with general and personal risk at the level of -0.1 to -.2. These are low correlations. Another interesting measure is response latency, i.e. how many days elapsed before a response was delivered. The later respondents can be assumed to be more similar to the non-respondents than the earlier ones. Correlations between response latency and perceived risk of nuclear waste also tend to be very low.

Another possible source of bias is interest. It seems likely that those who are more interested in the risk topic under study will respond. However, we have found that interest in filling out the questionnaire correlated only weakly with perceived risk (both general and personal).

4   Similar results have been found in previous work in several sets of data. Risk is an important aspect of the attitudes underlying inclinations to accept or reject technologies in the energy field. Another example is associated with life values. Implied life values in various 'life saving' programs or regulations have been found to vary greatly (Ramsberg and Sjöberg, 1997), and part of the variation appears to be accounted for by variation in perceived risk (Ramsberg and Sjöberg, 1998).
5   Separate analyses that the level of single hazards showed that income effects were consistently different for personal and general risk, men and women. However, we could not locate any variable that could explain this variation.
6   One example is the movie 'The China Syndrome', which was released shortly before the Three Mile Island (TMI) accident in 1979.
7   The three trust ratings regarding nuclear waste were pooled to a common index and used as an additional explanatory variable in regression analyses (Sjöberg, 1999e). The level of explained variance increased by 0.072, 0.059, 0.010 and 0.014 for general risk, personal risk, regret of risk and dread of risk, respectively. The β values obtained for trust were in all 4 cases negative and significant: -0.296, -0.271, -0.112 and -0.135. The other β values changed but little, but it should be noted that trust emerged as the variable with the largest β weight for general and personal risk.
8   The inclusion of distrust as a separate factor was new to the present analysis.
9   As noted above, the high correlations were not true for many of the other hazards, even with specific trust rather than general trust.
10 These are impressive numbers—especially the last mentioned one that is from Malå. In the Malå referendum, no other issue was at stake in the election at the same time.
11 It was worth a comment that even few media with a limited amount of contents, such as the newspapers of the 1860s, can have play a very important role and that dissemination of news could be amazingly efficient even before there were telephones. The accident happened in the South of Sweden about 9 am on 23 December 1864, and the news made the first page on in Stockholm newspapers on the following day.

2 Cultural Theory, Risk Perceptions among Political Elites and Public Opinion

ULF BJERELD

During the days of the Cold War, the risk of a nuclear war constituted a risk perception that overshadowed everything else. The consequences of such a war were so devastating and the risk of such a war so concrete—with missiles face-to-face across Europe—that other risk perceptions (for example, environmental pollution, overpopulation, terrorism) had difficulty gaining a foothold in public debate.

Today, the situation is different. For the time being, at least, the threat of nuclear war has faded. No one believes any longer in a war between the leading powers in Europe within the foreseeable future. There is no longer any one risk perception that carries absolute primacy in relationship to the others. The lack of a predominate risk perception makes it possible for various political actors to play on different risk perceptions in their rhetoric or propaganda in ways that promote their own political position. For the Green Party and other environmental parties, it has been important to emphasise environmental pollution and threats to the environment as much as possible. For Social Democratic parties, the threat of high unemployment is most often a vote-winning issue. As a rule, populist parties or rightwing popular parties often attempt to paint a picture of immigration as a threat to the country's economy and social order.

In this book, we examine how different risk perceptions take on salience in politics and public discourse. Utilising a perspective grounded in Cultural Theory and its assumptions about how different perceptions of risk are tied to different types of cultures or lifestyles, this chapter will explore and compare risk perceptions among the general public and political elites in Sweden. This comparison will then serve as the basis for a discussion of why certain risk perceptions acquire more resonance than others in Swedish political and social debates.

The Fall of the Traditional Threat Image

Before entering into a discussion of Cultural Theory and the ways it might be used to explain and grasp the occurrence of risk perceptions in modern society, it may be useful to examine how the 'traditional' risk perception in the form of concern about the world political situation and major war in Europe developed over time. Is it, in fact, true that the end of the Cold War has meant that our concern and fears about these phenomena have drastically decreased? Table 2.1 shows the percentage of Swedes who expressed concern about the world political situation in the period 1980-1999.

Table 2.1 Concern about the world political situation, 1980-1999 (the average percentage of Swedes who expressed very great to rather great concern)

Period	Percentage expressing concern
1980-1983	74
1984-1989	53
1990-1991	52
1992-1999	48

Comments on Table 2.1: The question asked was: 'How concerned are you about the current world political situation? Are you greatly concerned, quite concerned, a bit concerned, not very concerned, or not at all concerned?' Table 2.1 shows the average percentage of those who expressed great to moderate concern during the periods in question. This study was conducted by SPF (The Swedish National Board of Psychological Defence) and discussed in Stütz (1999).

Table 2.1 suggests that the percentage of people expressing concern about the world political situation has continuously declined during the 1980s and 1990s. During the tense period at the beginning of the 1980s following such events as the Soviet Union's march into Afghanistan and unrest in Poland, 74 percent of those polled expressed concern about the political situation in the world. Following the resolution of the acute crisis in Afghanistan and the beginnings of peaceful social reform in Eastern Europe during the mid-to-late 1980s, the percentage of those expressing concern about the world political situation fell to 53 percent. In conjunction with the dissolution of the Soviet Union and the fall of the Berlin Wall, and during the period after the end of the Cold War, the percentage of those expressing concern amounted to 52 percent and 48 percent. Table 2.2 reveals the amount of perceived risk for a major war in Europe between the years 1980-1999.

Table 2.2 Perceived risk for a major war in Europe, 1980-1999 (average percentage who considered the risk great to very great)

Period	Percentage regarding the risk of war as great
1980-1983	62
1984-1989	33
1990-1991	38
1992-1999	29

Comments on Table 2.2: The question was formulated in various ways according to the situation. In all cases, however, these were variations around a general theme: 'How great do you believe the risk is that events happening in the world today will lead to a major war in Europe?' In all cases. the reply categories were 'very great,' 'fairly great,' 'fairly small,' 'very small,' and 'not at all.' Table 2.2 shows the average percentage number who answered 'very great' or 'fairly great' during the periods in question. This study was conducted by SPF (The Swedish National Board for Psychological Defence) and is discussed in Stütz (1999). See also Stütz (1999) for exact formulations of the question over time.

Table 2.2 shows that the percentage of people regarding the risk of war as great has decreased over time. During the tension-filled years of the early 1980s, 62 percent of those surveyed regarded the risk of war as great. During the mid-to-late 1980s, this number fell to 33 percent, only to rise again to 38 percent shortly before the Soviet Union's collapse and the fall of the Berlin Wall. In the period after the Cold War, the percentage of those who regard the risk of war as great has fallen to 29 percent.

Taken together, Tables 2.1 and 2.2 reveal that concern about the world political situation and the perceived risk of a major war in Europe has declined sharply since the beginning of the 1980's. The greater part of this change in risk perception occurs during the mid-to-late 1980s. In other words, the change occurs before the end of the Cold War. Nonetheless, 48 percent of those surveyed continue to express concern about the world political situation and 29 percent of those surveyed continue to regard the risk of a major war in Europe as great. The traditional risk perception has thus declined in significance, but it has not disappeared entirely.

Risk Perceptions and Cultural Theory

The traditional risk perception no longer enjoys a monopoly and has become, instead, one of many risk perceptions that might conceivably gain a foothold in Swedish politics and social debate. How, then, are we to explain and understand why certain risk perceptions gain a foothold while others do not? Two assumptions inform the view of risk perception politics that characterises this edited volume. The first assumes that there is a continuous political struggle over which risk perceptions are to dominate in Swedish politics and social debate. The other assumes that this struggle revolves around how different events within and around society are to be understood; how such events are to be 'framed' (see the introductory chapter). As an event receives a certain 'framing,' this event acquires a certain meaning, which, in turn, determines whether or not the event will be perceived as a threat. As such, the struggle over the 'framing' of an event becomes an important stage in the struggle over which risk perceptions are to achieve dominance in Swedish politics and social debate.

I believe that Cultural Theory contributes significantly to an understanding of the conditions behind the political struggle around risk perceptions and their framing. The origins and development of risk perceptions as well as the struggle over their framing do not occur in a vacuum. Human values and norms form the basis of the construction of risk perceptions, and such values and norms are created according to diverse socio-cultural bonds. American risk researchers Karl Dake and Aaron Wildavsky have attempted to explain patterns behind risk perceptions and threat perceptions on the basis of *a cultural theory of different ways of life*.[1] According to Cultural Theory, human beings can be divided up into different groups with regard to their risk perceptions. The first group is composed of those who fear economic instability and decline. The second group is composed of those who are primarily afraid of ecological instability and environmental pollution. The third group is composed of those whose greatest fear is the dissolution of the social order. According to Cultural Theory, these differing types of risk perception are systematically connected to the individual's social relations as well as their understanding of nature and society.[2]

Those who have a risk perception based upon *economic decline* represent an *individualistic culture*. Individuals within this culture possess great freedom of action and minimal collective attachments. While such individuals are part of many different social networks, their group affiliation is weak. In principal, the market forms their most important social institution. Nature is a source of wealth whose accessibility grows in proportion to mankind's ability to create conditions for its use. Economic growth is a central value.

Those who have a risk perception based on ecological decline represent an *egalitarian culture*. Within this culture, group affiliation is strong, but the rules of conduct are weak. Nature is regarded as precious and fragile, and both economic growth and a market economy are perceived as threats against this vulnerable nature. On the whole, this group tends to view economic growth to be less important as a fairer distribution of existing resources would contribute to an increase in the quality of life for the majority of people. This group also calls for greater popular participation when political decisions are made.

Those who have a risk perception based on *the dissolution of the social order* represent a *hierarchical culture* or lifestyle. Within this culture, rules of conduct and regulations are encouraged, and members organise their social relations within well-defined groups. They view nature's resources as limited, and such resources must be extracted and distributed according to set rules. The market, too, ought to be regulated in several respects. Lack of authority is viewed as a societal problem.[3]

Consequently, these groups tend to have differing views as to which events constitute a threat to themselves or to society. For the individualistic group, an issue such as unemployment (economic decline) might be viewed as a primary threat, while the egalitarian group may fear environmental pollution (ecological decline), and the hierarchical group fears, for example, an increase in immigration (dissolution of the social order).

However, the differences between groups are not only expressed in terms of different perceptions of what constitutes a threat in each group. The same event may also be framed such that it is perceived within each group as more or less threatening. If unemployment is portrayed as a threat to economic growth—either for particular individuals affected by it or for society as a whole and, by extension, also for individuals—it will be the individualistic group that views unemployment as the greatest threat. If, instead, unemployment is portrayed as demoralising; as a threat to the integrity of public spirit, then it will be the hierarchical group that views unemployment as most threatening. For the egalitarian group, unemployment becomes a principal threat in that a focus on this issue runs the risk of drawing attention and resources from more central problems around mankind's relationship to the environment.

Questions involving environmental pollution and increasing numbers of refugees may also be addressed using a similar line of reasoning. Environmental pollution becomes a threat to the individualistic group principally because it draws on money and resources that would otherwise have been used to strengthen societal welfare and living standards. For the egalitarian group, environmental pollution becomes an overriding threat because it threatens the foundation of human existence. The hierarchical group, in this case, would adopt a middle position. On a general level, environmental pollution does not threaten the social order, but it is nonetheless important that experts and the authorities set aside sufficient resources in order to maintain a balance between humans and nature.

The individualistic group will view an increase in the number of refugees entering the country as threatening depending on whether this increase is perceived as positive or negative for economic growth. During times of economic prosperity and labour shortages, an increase in the number of refugees entering the country may strengthen the economy and is consequently judged as positive by the individualistic group. However, in times of recession and unemployment, this group adopts the opposite view: an increase in the number of refugees entering the country threatens to increase unemployment and worsen the national economy. For the egalitarian group, an increase in the number of refugees entering the country is scarcely considered a threat. Instead, such an increase is viewed as a way of dismantling artificial national borders and giving more people an opportunity to live in safety and economic prosperity. It is irrelevant whether this increase is harmful or beneficial to the national economy in the short-run. The hierarchical group is the one likely to view an increase in the number of refugees entering the country as most threatening. If people with other values, ideas, traditions, and, moreover, difficult memories and experiences of the time before their escape are allowed to come the country in massive numbers, this can be perceived as a threat to the social order so valued by the hierarchical group.

Importantly, all three issues as interpreted as structural conditions, regardless of culture and framing. It might be difficult to perceive it otherwise when focusing on unemployment or environmental pollution, but refugees are at least theoretically possible to perceive as an actor. This observation confirms that risk perceptions referring to structural conditions have a stronger societal salience than those concerning actors.

The dominant risk perception of before—that of a major war or even nuclear war in Europe—did not distinguish the three groups from each other in the same way that risk perceptions around unemployment, environmental pollution, and increased immigration have. All three of the groups greatly feared a major war, albeit on partly different grounds. The individualistic group feared a major war because it threatened human life and would lead to economic collapse. The egalitarian group feared a major war because it threatened human life and would lead to ecological collapse. The hierarchical group feared a major war because it threatened human life and would destroy the social order. Thus, a community of interests existed among the three groups: the risk of a major war constituted a fundamental risk perception. From there, however, strong differences of opinion were naturally to be found within as well as between the different groups about the best ways to prevent this threat from becoming a reality.[4]

We have now identified the three groups with regard to risk perceptions which, according to Cultural Theory, tend to exist in public opinion at both the mass and elite levels. It is, of course, important to realise that the three groups constitute one version of ideal types, and that similar groupings of the public opinion are decidedly more heterogeneous. In the next section, we will examine how Swedish public opinion is distributed on the mass and elite levels with respect to risk perceptions around unemployment, environmental pollution, and an increase in the number of refugees.

Risk Perceptions in Swedish Public Opinion

How is Swedish public opinion at the elite and mass levels distributed in terms of risk perceptions around unemployment, environmental pollution, and an increased number of refugees? Furthermore, which differences can we expect between the voters and their elected representatives?

With the help of earlier studies, we already know a fair amount about conformity of opinion between voters and their elected representatives in Sweden in terms of general political issues. In a work entitled *Representation from Above. Members of Parliament and Representative Democracy in Sweden*, Peter Esaisson and Sören Holmberg demonstrate that conformity of opinion between voters and members of Parliament in Sweden has increased since the 1960s. The opinions of Parliament members and voters resemble each other more in the mid-1990s than they did in the mid-1960s. If the individual political issues are grouped according to the categories of ideology (left and right-wing ideologies), growth/ecology, and social issues, we find that conformity of opinion is greatest in matters of left and right-wing ideology and smallest in terms of social issues. During the 1960s, Parliament members in all of the parties leaned more to the left than their voters. In contrast, during the 1980s and 1990s, Parliament members of the left-wing parties continued to lean somewhat more to the left than their voters while Parliament members of the right-wing parties leaned somewhat more to the right than their voters.[5]

International research on conformity of opinion between voters and their elected representatives has not been particularly comprehensive thus far. Those studies that have been conducted reveal results in line with those of the Swedish studies. For instance, conformity of opinion between voters and their elected representatives is approximately the same in Sweden as it is in France and the U.S.[6]

However, differences in the conformity of opinion between voters and their elected representatives are not the same as differences in risk perception. If we bear in mind that conformity of opinion is greatest on ideological left and right-wing issues, lowest on social issues, and that growth/economy represents a middle position, we are then able to imagine that the differences between the risk perceptions of voters and members of Parliament are smallest on unemployment issues and largest on an increase in the number of refugees. The issue of environmental pollution, in turn, occupies a middle position.

In order to receive answers to our questions, we will draw on the 1994 Parliamentary study in which all Swedish members of Parliament were surveyed about their opinions and ideas regarding a number of political issues. We will also utilise the 1994 SOM study in which a total of 2,400 persons were questioned.[7] The results will then be compared with a study by Torben Jensen (Jensen 1999) in which he investigates the risk perceptions of members of Parliament in the Nordic countries on a number of different issues.

Table 2.3 indicates risk perceptions among Swedish members of Parliament and voters with respect to high unemployment, environmental pollution, and an increase in the number of refugees.

Table 2.3 shows that members of Swedish Parliament are more concerned about unemployment than voters are. At the same time, voters are more concerned about environmental pollution and an increase in the number of refugees than members of Parliament are. Concern about an increase in the number of refugees constitutes the greatest difference between the risk perceptions of Parliament members and those of voters. Thirty percent of voters viewed an increase in the number of refugees to be a matter of great concern while only 5 percent of Parliament members held the same view. Both groups expressed a greater degree of concern over the threat of high unemployment (members of Parliament 57 percent; voters 48 percent) and environmental pollution (members of Parliament 36 percent; voters 50 percent).

Table 2.3 Risk perceptions among Swedish members of Parliament and voters with respect to high unemployment, environmental pollution, and an increase in the number of refugees (1994). Percentage who answered 'very concerned'

	Members of Parliament	Voters	Difference
High unemployment	57	48	+11
Environmental pollution	36	50	-14
Increased immigration	5	30	-25

Comments on Table 2.3: The question asked was: 'When you think about Swedish society, what concerns you most about the future?' The reply categories included 'very concerned,' 'rather concerned,' 'not very concerned,' 'not at all concerned.' Table 2.3 is based upon the 1994 Riksdag study conducted by the Department of Political Science at the University of Göteborg as well as the 1994 SOM study, conducted by the SOM Institute at the University of Göteborg.

Thus, the risk perceptions of members of Parliament members are principally directed towards threats deriving from an individualistic culture (economy/high unemployment), followed by an egalitarian culture (ecology/environmental pollution), and, to a much lesser extent, a hierarchical culture (social order/increased immigration). The risk perceptions of voters derive principally from an egalitarian culture, followed by an individual culture, and, last, a hierarchical culture. Within the electorate, differences between the three cultures are significantly smaller than is the case among members of Parliament.

Controlling for the variables of sex, age, and political affiliation, we will now examine risk perceptions among Swedish members of Parliament and voters with regard to high unemployment, environmental pollution, and an increase in the number of refugees. Table 2.4 demonstrates risk perceptions according to sex.

Table 2.4 Risk perceptions according to sex among Swedish members of Parliament and voters with regard to high unemployment, environmental pollution, and an increase in the number of refugees (1994). Percentage who answered 'very concerned'

	Members of Parliament	Voters	Difference
High unemployment			
Men	47	41	+6
Women	72	56	+16
Environmental pollution			
Men	29	43	-14
Women	45	57	-12
Increased number of refugees			
Men	5	30	-25
Women	6	30	-24

Comments on Table 2.4: See Table 2.3.

Table 2.4 shows that differences according to sex among members of Parliament and voters are relatively small as regards perceptions of risk. It is true that female members of Parliament and female voters express greater concern about unemployment and environmental pollution than their male counterparts. However, concern about unemployment and environmental pollution carry roughly the same weight among male and female voters, followed by concern about an increase in the numbers of refugees.

Table 2.5 shows risk perceptions among Swedish members of Parliament and voters according to age. This reveals that younger voters express greater concern about environmental pollution than unemployment (55 percent versus 46 percent). In turn, older voters express greater concern about unemployment than environmental pollution (58 percent versus 45 percent). Among members of Parliament, in contrast, all age groups are more concerned about unemployment than environmental pollution. Older voters express somewhat greater concern about an increase in the number of refugees (37 percent) than do the other two age groups (28 percent).

Table 2.5 Risk perceptions according to age among Swedish members of Parliament and voters with regard to high unemployment, environmental pollution, and an increase in the number of refugees (1994). Percentage who answered 'very concerned'

	Members of Parliament	Voters	Difference
High unemployment			
15-40	68	46	+22
41-60	56	45	+11
61-	40	59	-19
Environmental pollution			
15-40	49	55	-16
41-60	33	47	-14
61-	31	45	-14
Increase in number of refugees			
15-40	2	28	-26
41-60	6	28	-22
61-	0	37	-39

Comments on Table 2.5: See Table 2.3.

Table 2.6 shows risk perceptions among Swedish members of Parliament and voters according to political party. This reveals that, in comparison with their respective voters, members of Swedish Parliament from more or less all of the parties are more concerned about unemployment and less concerned about environmental pollution and an increase in the number of refugees. There are two exceptions to this. One, Moderate party voters express more concern about unemployment than Moderate Party MP's (35 percent versus 23 percent). Two, Green Party voters are less concerned about environmental pollution than Green Party MP's (80 percent versus 94 percent).

Table 2.6 According to political party, risk perceptions among Swedish members of Parliament and voters with regard to high unemployment, environmental pollution, and an increase in the number of refugees (1994). Percentage who answered 'very concerned'

	Members of Parliament	Voters	Difference
High unemployment			
The Left Party	76	54	+22
The Social Democrats	71	59	+12
The Center Party	54	41	+13
The Liberal Party	54	39	+15
The Moderate Party	23	35	-13
The Christian Democrats	53	30	+23
The Green Party	61	43	+18
Environmental pollution			
The Left Party	52	63	-11
The Social Democrats	34	49	-15
The Center Party	38	56	-18
The Liberal Party	46	50	-4
The Moderate Party	11	40	-29
The Christian Democrats	47	48	-1
The Green Party	94	80	+14
Increased number of refugees			
The Left Party	5	20	-15
The Social Democrats	4	29	-25
The Center Party	0	37	-37
The Liberal Party	0	21	-21
The Moderate Party	12	34	-22
The Christian Democrats	7	13	-6
The Green Party	6	26	-20

Comments on Table 2.6: See Table 2.3.

Among Swedish members of Parliament, concern about unemployment is greatest among the Left Party, the Social Democrats, and the Green

Party, while there is least concern among the Moderates. Concern about environmental pollution is greatest among Green Party MP's and least among Moderate MP's. Concern about an increase in the number of refugees is greatest among Moderate MP's and least among Centre Party and Liberal Party MP's. Among voters, concern about unemployment is greatest among Social Democratic and Left Party voters and least among Christian Democratic voters. Concern about environmental pollution is greatest among Green Party voters and least among Moderate party voters. Concern about an increase in the number of refugees is greatest among Centre Party and Moderate Party voters and least among those voting for the Christian Democrats, the Left Party, and the Liberal Party.

Given this information, how can we ascertain that concerns about high unemployment, environmental pollution, and an increase in the number of refugees are expressions of the individualistic, egalitarian, and hierarchical cultures, respectively? As we discussed earlier, an issue such as unemployment, for example, may be perceived as a threat to the social order depending on how the issue is framed. Likewise, an increase in the number of refugees may also be perceived as a threat to the national economy depending on the framing it receives. The three issues we have focused on in this chapter were part of a larger battery of issues in the 1994 Parliament study regarding risk perceptions held by members of Parliament. These issues were, in turn, coordinated with issues in corresponding Parliamentary studies carried out in all of the other Nordic countries. In a study based on this material, Torben Jensen has shown that the risk perceptions of Parliament members display a powerful pattern along the lines assumed by Cultural Theory. Using a factor analysis, Jensen demonstrates that concern about high unemployment varies in correlation with concern about inflation and the national debt—that is, economic factors (the individualistic culture). Concern about environmental pollution correlates with concern about nuclear power, technological growth, and a weakened social conscience (egalitarian culture). Concern about an increase in the number of refugees correlates with concerns about a lack of strong national leadership, the disintegration of established societal norms, and corruption—that is, factors we associate with the fear of a dissolution of the social order (hierarchical culture).[8] We can thereby conclude that our three issues—concern about high unemployment, environmental pollution, and an increase in the number of refugees—are correlated with the individualistic, egalitarian, and hierarchical cultures.

Jensen further demonstrates that approximately half of the MPs in the Nordic countries were most concerned about economic threats. Approximately one-third was most concerned about ecological threats while 10 percent were most concerned about tendencies toward the dissolution of the social order. This was a common tendency in Sweden, Finland, and Iceland while concern about ecological threats was greatest in Norway and Denmark. In Norway, 24 percent of its MPs were most concerned about the dissolution of the social order.

Sadly, the larger battery of issues we have discussed here was only posed in the Parliament study and not in the SOM study. Unfortunately, then, it is impossible to make any comparisons between voters and their elected representatives using this material.

Cultural Theory and Risk Perceptions in the Swedish Political Debate

Given the risk perceptions evident in Swedish public opinion and among Swedish MPs, what can we ascertain about the conditions necessary for different types of risk perceptions to gain a foothold in Swedish politics and public debate? One important point of departure for the following discussion is the premise in Cultural Theory that it is not the objective strength of a threat that forms the basis for the type of risk perceptions existing in a society. It is not the case that societies with serious environmental problems are dominated by risk perceptions focused on the environment, or that societies with high unemployment tend to be dominated by risk perceptions around unemployment or other economic problems. It is, instead, whether the society is dominated by an individualistic, egalitarian, or hierarchical culture that determines which type of risk perceptions will be given a voice in public debate and politics. As these categories represent a form of ideal types, it is only reasonable to assume that any given society consists of a combination of the three cultures, and that the content of this combination will influence perceptions of risk.

Sweden may be characterised as a mixture of egalitarian and individualistic cultures. The hierarchical culture, in contrast, holds little sway in Sweden. This picture is supported by the fact that economic threats and environmental threats dominate the risk perceptions of both MPs and voters (despite the fact that concern about an increase in the number of refugees was significantly greater among voters than MPs). We are not simply referring to the three specific issues (unemployment, environmental pollution, an increase in the number of refugees), but also to the larger battery of issues utilised by Torben Jensen in the study cited above (economy = unemployment, inflation, and national debt; ecology = environmental pollution, nuclear power, technological growth, and social awareness; social order = an increase in the number of refugees, powerful national leadership, dissolution of established societal norms, and corruption). It is, in particular, the issue of the place of environmental threats on the political agenda that distinguishes Sweden from other more hierarchical cultures in southern and eastern Europe.

As the hierarchical culture is so weak in Sweden, political parties have little to gain from framing their issues or their descriptions of reality in terms of a threat against the social order. Those groups which are against immigration to Sweden have thus had a difficult time launching the refugee question as a social order issue (for example, by claiming that immigrants have a more criminal nature than Swedes and that immigrants' values represent a threat to Swedish society). They have had more success, however, arguing that immigration hurts the national economy (increased immigration leads to increased unemployment; immigrants receive social welfare at the expense of retirees' pensions). Unemployment, in turn, is discussed either in economic terms (negative effects on society and on the individual) or in terms of the anxiety and alienation it causes the unemployed. Unemployment is rarely discussed as a threat to the social order or to social authority. In debates around the broadcast of pornographic films on television, supporters argued in terms of individual freedom, while opponents emphasised pornography's negative effects on individuals (those acting in the films or the viewers who receive a distorted view of sexuality) or a collective group (women). When it comes to the issue of sexuality, Swedish society is so non-hierarchical and anti-authoritarian that it is difficult to formulate convincing arguments about the offensiveness of pornography and its ability to damage the moral fabric of society.

Certain issues, however, are subject to arguments deriving from the hierarchical sphere. In the debate about law and order (for example, the lack of police and too many unsolved crimes), the arguments are seldom about what crime or an increase in the number of policemen will cost society in economic terms. Instead, supporters of a larger police force paint a picture of a lawless society in which everyone runs the risk of becoming the victim of a serious crime. Still, such issues pose an exception, and, when they arise, they tend to involve matters with a direct bearing on the life and health of the population (e.g. the healthcare crisis and defence cuts).

Rivalry between the cultures of individualism and egalitarianism is partly the result of the rivalry between two founding conflict dimensions in Swedish politics: Left/Right versus ecology/growth. Egalitarians tend to lean towards the Left politically, while individualists tend to lead toward the Right. At the same time, there is a distribution of persons who lean towards the Left relatively often when it concerns the ecology/growth dimension. In this respect, the Left is torn between an optimistic view of economic growth on the one hand and a desire to protect the environment—not least from capitalist interests—on the other. In Swedish politics, however, rivalry between the dimensions of Left/Right and ecology/growth tend to lean towards the benefit of the former. Despite all of the talk about post-industrialism and the information society, the Left/Right dimension remains powerful. The Swedish parties remain to a large extent class parties, and their basis can be found in the political dividing lines that emerged from the industrial revolution—primarily between labour and capital, but also between city and countryside. Voting by class (i.e. the working class votes for socialist parties, the farmers for agrarian parties, and the middle class for bourgeois parties) has certainly decreased since the 1950s. However, Sweden is one of the countries in the western world in which the practice of voting by class remains the strongest. During the 1994 general elections, for example, 70 percent of the Swedish working class voted for the Social Democrats or the Left Party. Among the middle class, the corresponding share was 41 percent.[9] In recent times, purely environmental issues have also begun to lose public interest. During the 1988 election campaign, the environment was the single issue most often named by voters as an important factor in their choice of party. Of those persons asked in the 1998 election survey, 46 percent stated that the environment was an important factor in their choice of party. During the 1991 general elections, the corresponding share was 25 percent. During the 1994 general elections, this share amounted to 20 percent. During 1998, this share had decreased to 15 percent. Instead, it is issues such as employment and welfare that dominate the agenda.[10] The diminishing importance of the ecology/growth dimension is not only reflected in a decreasing interest in environmental issues in general. The Green Party itself frames its arguments about the environment in economic terms, for example by formulating the issues in terms of 'green growth,' 'tax rotation,' and 'shortened work hours.'[11]

Accordingly, the various cultures in a society—or the dominant culture in a society—are influence the ways in which each issue is framed. This influence on the framing of an issue occurs in two ways, depending on which actor perspective we assume. Among *the electorate*, those within the respective cultures tend to frame issues in different ways. For example, individualists view unemployment as an economic threat, egalitarians view it as an ecological threat, and those from the hierarchical cultural sphere view unemployment as a threat to the social order. Framing in such cases becomes a passive, subconscious process whereby the culture and values of the individual determine how an issue is understood. For *political actors*, there is much to be gained by adjusting the argument according to the issue—to frame the issue—in such a way that it reverberates in the dominant culture groups. Sweden is characterised by a mixture of an individualistic and an egalitarian culture. Therefore, issues are framed in such a way that they suit the individualistic or the egalitarian culture—and more seldom the hierarchical culture. In this case, such framing appears to be a conscious act on the part of politicians and political parties in an attempt to set the agenda and to gain an audience for their politics. The degree to which this framing is, in fact, a conscious politics on the part of the various political actors as opposed to the subconscious result of that mixture of egalitarian and individualistic cultures in which parties and politicians act is another matter.

Notes

1. Wildavsky and Dake (1991).
2. Cultural Theory was developed during the 1970's by the British social anthropologist, Mary Douglas (see, for example, Douglas 1970, 1992). It was first and foremost Aaron Wildavsky who incorporated Cultural Theory into the field of political science during the 1980's (see, for example, Wildavsky, 1987). Cultural Theory begins with the distinction between *grid* (relationships of authority within social relations) and *group* (the social boundaries that humans establish between themselves and others). We are then presented with four different types of social relations: hierarchy (strong grid and strong group), fatalism (strong grid and weak group), egalitarianism (weak grid and strong group), and individualism (weak grid and weak group). This study omits the fatalistic group as the available material does not make it possible to conduct a study of this group. This summary of the basic assumptions of Cultural Theory builds on Grenstad and Selle (1996) as well as Jensen (1999).
3. Grenstad and Selle (1996), pp. 13 ff and 317 f. See also Jensen (1999), p. 386 f.
4. Cultural Theory has received outside criticism on two principal fronts. First, it has been accused of taking insufficient notice of the fact that individuals are often part of different cultures at the same time. Second, certain critics have suggested that the explanatory power of the theory has not been particularly great in empirical studies (see, for example, Rorty 1991 and Rothstein 1994). What remains entirely clear is that the three cultures are meant to be viewed as ideal types. It then becomes an empirical question as to the degree to which individuals can be placed within the respective categories without doing too much harm to reality. In terms of the explanatory power of Cultural Theory, it is neither better nor worse than a number of other similar theories, for example Inglehart's theory of post-material values or Rokeach value theory. In the final section of this paper, we will return to a discussion of Cultural Theory's relationship to other theories on dividing lines and societal values.
5. Esaiasson and Holmberg (1996), pp. 109 ff.
6. Esiasson and Holmberg (1996), p. 110 f.
7. The 1994 Riksdag study was conducted within the framework of a research project entitled *Riksdagen och den representativa demokratin inför 2000-talet* [The Swedish Parliament and representative democracy on the eve of the 21st Century]. This project was funded by Riksbankens Jubileumsfond and headed by Peter Esaiasson. The Riksdag study was conducted by Peter Esaiasson, Sören Holmberg, and Martin Brothén. The reply rate during the entire study totalled 97 percent. SOM stands for Society, Opinion,

and Mass media and is an annual survey conducted by the SOM Institute at University of Göteborg.The SOM Institute is headed by Sören Holmberg and Lennart Weibull. In the 1994 study, 2,400 people were questioned.
8   Jensen (1999), pp. 398 ff.
9   Gilljam and Holmberg (1995), p. 100. For a study of class voting in Sweden over time, see Oskarson (1994).
10 Gilljam and Holmberg (1995), p. 23 as well as the 1998 Election study.
11 In a study entitled 'Fem tyver på same marked' [Five twenties on the same market], Gunnar Grendstad and Hilmar Rommetvedt examine the empirical connections between the dimensions which are part of the Cultural Theory approach, and the dimensions included in four other approaches or perspectives on political dividing lines in western societies today (the Left-Right dimension, Inglehart's theory of post-material values, the Norwegian Market and Media Institute's categories of stability/change-materialism/idealism, as well as Todal Jensen's theory of relational values in the form of individualism/collectivism-authority/egalitarianism). Utilising a factor analysis, Grendstad and Rommertvedt find that the different dimensions can be classified according to three factors: equality vs. achievement incentives (which loads on hierarchy, and, in part, individualism) as well as spiritual vs. material (which loads on none of the Cultural Theory categories) (Grenstad and Rommertvedt. 1996, pp. 314 ff).

Part II
Actors in Focus

3 Mediated Threats
ALEXA ROBERTSON

On the last day of November 1999, a new chapter in Swedish media history was written. Four major newspapers momentarily abandoned their rivalry and published joint editions warning their readers of the threat posed by neo-nazism and organised crime. The four editors-in-chief explained their action on the first page of each newspaper:

> Fear is spreading and putting down roots in the judicial system and among witnesses, in politics and newsrooms. It threatens to poison democracy. There is a risk that debate will be silenced and that scrutinizing of anti-democratic forces will cease. These four national newspapers, which normally compete with each other, have chosen to pool our resources to scrutinise the threat to the community founded on the rule of law. (*Dagens Nyheter, Svenska Dagbladet, Aftonbladet, Expressen*, 30 November 1999, p. 1.)

This is just one, albeit unusually striking, example of threat politics. An understanding of why some threats rather than others take on societal salience cannot be complete without attending to the practices involved in the engagement of a variety of political actors engage in what Thompson has referred to as the creative, uncontrollable, open-ended space of the media (Thompson, 1995, p. 246). The aim of this chapter is to illustrate how the media form a site of threat politics, applying some theoretical insights to a comparative empirical analysis of news texts.

As Eriksson notes in the introduction to this volume, we have grown accustomed to 'real-time blood, fear and death' greeting us on the first pages of our morning papers and at the top of our evening news broadcasts. An oft-voiced lament is that, in a picture-driven medium like television news, the availability of dramatic and violent film footage has an unfair advantage over other news material (Gurevitch, 1996; Van Ginnekin, 1998; Robertson, 1999b). Images of conflict are widely thought to be more salient than images of the cooperation that is more characteristic of international life; violent threats to the sovereignty of Kuwaitis and Kosovars, it is argued, will pre-empt reporting of 'invisible' threats posed to the state in a globalised world by the unrestricted flow of capital, by European monetary union, and by environmental destruction that recognises no borders.

Empirical analysis, however, indicates that the threats depicted in the news media have to do with more than 'traditional' spectres of war and bloodshed. The same year in which the four newspapers raised the anti-nazi alarm, Sweden's largest broadsheet, *Dagens Nyheter*, printed 1669 articles and telegrams containing the word 'threat.' While they included stories about right-wing violence, car bombs and the Kosovo conflict, these threat stories were also about issues ranging from the millennium bug, family disputes and pensions to traffic and hormones in meat. In the same year, the leading tabloid *Aftonbladet* contained 800 such 'threat reports,' on all sorts of issues concerning armed conflict and crime, but also on the risk of inducing strokes by post-Viagra over-exertion, of infants suffering fractured skulls after being carried about in a Swedish-made harness, and the spectre of a new global disease. Banal as these problems may seem, they too are susceptible to threat framing, as the following quotation from the tabloid illustrates:

> A new influensa with global reach, a new Spanish flu or something even worse is what we should be prepared to face. There is tremendous respect for nuclear weapons because we have experienced the effects of atomic bombs. The consequences of bioterrorism are just as horrific... (*Aftonbladet*, 14 February 1999).

There is a case to be made for resting the analytical gaze on the degree of correspondence in the issues selected for publication or broadcast if media impact is to be gauged. Eilders argues, for example, that different media outlets can only constitute a unified actor capable of putting sufficient pressure on the political system if they share a focus on a particular problem and do not paralyse each other through divergent contributions (Eilders, 2000, p. 2). Certainly, the joint action of the aforementioned four newspapers sent shockwaves throughout the country that reverberated in the corridors of the powerful as well as the streets and sofas of the ordinary. Nevertheless, this chapter is not concerned with establishing similarities between media when it comes to making a given threat image salient. Instead, the focus here is on what can be learned about the ways in which they differ.

Even in the November 30th Nazi threat reporting, the same news appeared under different headings in the four Swedish newspapers. In the conservative broadsheet the threat was to the 'state governed by the rule of law;' in the liberal tabloid it was to 'justice;' in the liberal broadsheet and the social democratic tabloid it was 'democracy' that was threatened. As gatekeepers the four papers siphoned off the same news. As agenda-setters they identified the same threats. But as storytellers making sense of that threatening news, they employed different frames.

In what follows, the news media's contribution to threat politics will be considered in terms of the images portrayed and the frames in which such portrayals of threat are set out to catch the public eye. While the analytical concept of 'framing' is common to that of the other contributors to this volume, the theoretical literature underpinning this chapter emanates from the field of mass communication research rather than security and risk studies. And while the last couple of pages have concerned the Swedish press, the empirical material to which these theoretical notions are applied in what follows is comprised of television news reports, some of them Swedish, some of them not. It will be argued that while we are daily subjected to a flurry of new information about previously unenvisaged sorts of dangers, threat stories tend to be relayed within narrative structures which lend a sense of continuity to and help us find meaning in a turbulent world. In this respect I would like to qualify the claim made by Eriksson in the introductory chapter that the societal salience of an event framed as a threat is usually only temporary in the media. While a particular news event may seem to be submerged in the rapid succession of news reports that flow across our television and computer screens, its salience need not be, insofar as it fits into one of the several narratives that endure over time—narratives that become a primary source of meaning in a world of uncontrolled, confusing change (Castells, 2000, p. 3).

Understanding the Power of Images in a Mediated Environment

It may be called the Information Society (Castells again), but it can be argued that the defining feature of the political environment at the beginning of the millennium is that it is still dominated by images. Once the sun set over the Cold War era and rose on a global media age, it became routine for major international conflicts to be waged on two sites: in the disputed territories (whether in the Middle East, north Africa or in what was once the communist bloc) and on television screens throughout the world. Media market liberalisation, the concentration of ownership in multinational firms, and the increased speed, scope and efficiency of news reporting as a result of technological advancement have affected the preconditions for threats filling different news holes. Compelling pictures of dramatic conflicts are hard to resist in the competitive globalised news business, and many have commented on the resulting tendency for viewers around the world to be proffered the same views of violence. Reading secondary accounts, it is easy to form an impression that television is giving publics in Europe, at least, a shared window onto a world bristling with menace.

Care must be taken, however, not to equate globalisation with cultural homogenisation. On the contrary, the global era has been characterised by cultural diversity (at best) and (at worst) by a backlash, a resurge of ethnic conflict, religious fundamentalism and nationalism in a world popularly characterised as 'beyond nationalism' (Holsti (1982, p. x; Castells, 2000). Featherstone has noted that, rather than resulting in greater tolerance and cosmopolitanism, the increasing familiarity with 'the other' ushered in by globalisation is just as liable to result in a disturbing sense of engulfment and 'the active assertion of the integrity of national culture' (Featherstone, 1995, p. 91).

The deployment of images is an important political activity in this context. Aumont contends that, in all its relations to the real and all its functions, the image pertains ultimately to the sphere of the symbolic. Building on Gombrich, he suggests that the primary function of the image is to reassure and to consolidate and refine our relation to the world

(Aumont, 1997, p. 55-6). Two of the activities at work in this capacity are recognition and recall. The image conveys knowledge about the real in coded form (in both a semiological and linguistic sense). There are mechanisms of recall through imagery at work, and schemata are constantly corrected with the production of new knowledge and evolve over time. The 'frame' isolates part of the field of vision, singles out and enhances the perception of the images, acting as an intermediary between the spectator and the image, or as a kind of index which tells the spectator he is looking at an image which, because it is framed in a certain way, should be viewed in relation to certain conventions. Given these conventions, the viewer, 'by virtue of his or her prior knowledge, makes up for what is lacking, that is to say, he or she supplies what is not represented in the image,' drawing on the shared meanings on which national cultures are based (Aumont, 1997, p. 60).

Aumont's postulations about the role of the frame highlights the possibility that attention should not just be paid to the denotative, epistemological functions of news images, but also the settings in which such images are placed, both in terms of the broadcast or newspaper in which they appear, and in the related narratives that recur over time. Attention to these provides information about the ways the images circulating in the political environment are likely to be decoded in different contexts of meaning. What is of interest to the social scientist is the possibility that the triggering of recall and memory in the viewer or reader, and more broadly the meanings he might give to images of the outside world, is influenced or even governed by political or economic forces. Price suggests that political influence over imagery is historical fact; what he and others suggest is new(er) is the way in which the fates of governments are 'inextricably intertwined' with the structure and capacity of communications. In spite of the impossibility of the task, however, states continue to try to maintain a monopoly over imagery because democratic values need concrete loyalties:

> The millions of images that float through the public mind help determine the very nature of national allegiances, attitudes towards place, family, government and state [...] Communal symbols reinforce cohesion, affect the duration and

nature of any particular hegemony and thus have a central place in the idea of the state... (Price, 1995, p. 3).

Four decades ago, Boulding argued that, in attempting to understand international relations, it was essential to recognise that people do not respond to the 'objective' facts of the situation, whatever that may mean, but to their 'image' of the situation. 'It is what we think the world is like, not what it is really like, that determines our behaviour' (Boulding, 1959, p. 120). A variety of authors proceeded on this assumption and demonstrated the importance of perceptions of international actors and situations when it came to explaining political responses (Jervis, 1976; Sande et al, 1989; Silverstein and Holt, 1989; Peffley and Hurwitz, 1992). An early study concluded that people live in two worlds—that of first-hand experience and that of mediated experience. A factor conditioning how nations 'saw' each other was this indirect or 'extensional' world, interestingly referred to as the 'verbal world,' acquired from school and media through words (Buchanan and Cantril, 1953, p. 1).

Media Framing

The importance to political behaviour of the 'extensional' or mediated realm, filled with information about threatening 'others,' can be assumed to endure when the salience of images has displaced that of words 'in the cultural production and construction of difference' (Loshitsky, 1996, p. 335). But there is a difference between the two epochs. It is often said that things were much clearer in the 'verbal' Cold War world of Buchanan, Cantril and Jervis; a number of commentators have maintained that the Cold War provided a framework that organised, shaped and contextualised understandings about the international environment, or what Walter Lippman famously referred to as the 'maps of the world' drawn by the media in people's heads (Lippman, 1941). Schlesinger, for example, has called the Cold War 'an organising grand narrative about democracy and totalitarianism, capitalism and socialism, freedom and repression' (Schlesinger, 1997, p. 369). The old certainties dissolved together with the polar division between East and West in a process initiated by Gorbachev, hastened by the silent revolutions of 1989 and made irrevocable by the incorporation of former Warsaw Pact states in the EU and NATO in the decade that followed. The result has been a sense of dislocation; an 'inability to find the way home, to return to the lost point of coherence and order' (Featherstone, 1995, pp. 1, 95).

The changes that accompanied the dismantling of familiar power blocs, the radical restructuring of the architecture of Europe and the emergence of a host of new actors, posed substantial problems to journalists as well as policymakers. Many foreign correspondents and news editors whose careers began in the 1960s and 1970s experienced a sense of disorientation after the end of the Cold War. The black-and-white clarity of the pre-1989 period that had conditioned their news values was gone, and it was not immediately apparent what would replace it. The problem was not a lack of relevant news; the problem was how it was to be framed in the new situation that prevailed.

Framing has long been a focus of empirical attention in quantitative American media research (Iyengar, 1996; Neumann et al, 1992; Capella and Jamieson, 1996) but has also gained currency among media researchers working within a more interpretative, European tradition (Neveu, 1999; Renard, 2000; Eilders, 2000; Fairclough, 1995; Couldry, 1999). Most of these approaches take Goffman's idea of framing as their point of departure, and are agreed that what the concept addresses is the construction of political issues and that framing analysis involves the examination of how concepts are associated within discourse (Simon and Xenos, 2000). Entman still has good reason, though, for complaining that here is no general statement of framing theory (despite its omnipresence across the social sciences and humanities) that shows exactly 'how frames become embedded within and make themselves manifest in a text, or how framing influences thinking' (Entman, 1993, p. 51).

Regardless of the tradition within they work, media scholars are generally agreed that the concept of framing offers a way of getting at the power in a news text, and at the activity that takes place when meaning is created in the meeting between journalist and news consumer. 'In seeking to make sense of the political world,' write Neuman et al, 'both the media and the public employ simplifying cognitive frames as hooks to capture a piece of the abundant flow of confusing and conflicting information from Lippmann's "world outside" ' (Neuman et al, 1992, p. 60).

Researchers such as these, who work from the audience up rather than just the newsmaker down, emphasise that framing is a dynamic activity in which both the media and the public engage. They challenge classic theories of cognitive dissonance in which individuals are defined as having a set of clear-cut opinions on an issue that determine which new information will be allowed across their cognitive threshold. Such theories, it is pointed, do not stand up well in empirical tests with broadcast news. Neuman et al argue that the process is more sophisticated, with audiences interacting with journalists in producing meaning from news texts. As they envisage, it, the frame does not predetermine the information that individuals will seek, but it is likely to *shape* experiences of the world and is thus central to the process of constructing meaning. Their research shows that individuals—both those in the newsroom and those on the sofa—draw heavily on a few central frames in interpreting public issues, including the division of protagonists into 'us' and 'them' and perceptions of control by powerful others (Neuman et al, 1992, pp. 60-77).

But framing has to do with more than sense-making. It is also about making diagnoses, such as pointing out a problem and identifying who is responsible for it and prognoses, which propose solutions to problems placed on the agenda (Entman, 1993; Iyengar, 1996; Eilders and Lüter, 2000). This is what makes framing a political activity. In their analyses of editorials in the German press about the Kosovo war, Eilders and Lüter also found evidence of what they call 'motivational framing.' Originally a concept used by scholars of social movements to deal with why individuals were motivated to join protest movements, Eilders and Lüter apply it at the level of the nation, when editorialists use the public space provided by their newspapers to discuss whether and why the nation should become involved in a war. In the context of their study, they replaced the term 'motivational framing' with 'identity framing,' as media justifications for intervention in the Kosovo war were framed as nation-specific obligations resulting from historical experiences, contributions to European identity formation, and the like.

Iyengar reminds us that it is through television coverage that most people encounter the world of public affairs. This coverage, he argues, embodies two distinct frames. The episodic frame treats issues as specific events (a terrorist bombing, for example), while the thematic frame places issues in context (relating them to a structural condition or a particular set of actors), therefore portraying them more broadly and abstractly. 'The nature of television news and the increasingly competitive nature of the news business,' he writes, 'have combined to create a premium for episodic coverage of political issues.' The problem with this is that empirical studies indicate episodic framing tends to encourage viewers to hold individuals, rather than society, responsible for problems ranging from poverty and drug abuse to international conflict (Iyengar, 1996, p. 62).

Do developments in 'the news business' inevitably result in episodic framing? And, if they do in US news coverage (analyses of which Iyengar bases his conclusions on) is it also true of European television news? There are reasons for being wary of such claims, as will be explained in the next section.

Television News as a Source of Narratives

As Neumann et al demonstrate, people—journalists and their audiences alike—use heuristics like frames to make sense of a complex international domain. According to Peffley and Hurwitz (1992), general beliefs (such as images of international actors) constrain specific policy preferences (like support for arms reductions). Their research shows that the images Americans held of a former enemy like the Soviet Union (theory) both affected, and were affected by, dramatic new information from the international environment (data), supporting their hypothesis that decision-makers (a category in which I would include the journalists responsible for deciding which news gets into our daily newspapers and broadcasts) and publics alike are both 'theory-driven' and 'data-driven.' Assuming that images of actors and the options open to them are significantly affected—if not largely formed—by media portrayals of enemies and others in the changing environment, this finding suggests that attention must be paid not only to the informational aspects of news reporting (i.e. data) but, even more importantly, its sense-making or narrative function (i.e. theory).

For decades, however, political scientists have attempted to study the power of the media with the aid of concepts such as 'agenda-setting' and 'gatekeeping,' which presuppose a factual world from which news events flow. The approach has been to measure the space and prominence allotted to different views and factions on specific political issues; the emphasis in studies of news about international conflicts and crises has tended to be on the content of newspapers and news broadcasts, i.e. on *what* has been told. As a result, classic studies of gatekeeping have regretted the lack of continuity and context in foreign news reporting; the complaint that the fascination of continually breaking news tends to prevent people from reflecting on the meaning of events has been ritually made since Lazersfeld lamented in the early 1940s that 'continually new news programmes keep us from ever finding out the details of the previous news' (cited in Van Ginnekin, 1998, p. 109; Cohen, 1963, p. 99).

The problem with this view is that it assumes that news is all data and no theory, and that it is unable to deal with how media images influence viewers' perceptions (Eilders, 2000). But there are other ways of understanding how news works. Researchers from disciplines beyond the pale of political science have suggested that its informative function is secondary to its social, ritual function. Scholars interested in this socio-political or, as it is sometimes called, ideological role have been less concerned with the data—the *what*—of news, and more concerned with the theory, its technical and symbolic forms and structure—or with *how* it works. Rather than seeing the news as a source of information, these scholars consider the news as narrative, with the stories being told providing the context and continuity that foreign news studies have overlooked (Allan, 1998; Barkin, 1984; Bell, 1994; Bennett and Edelman, 1985; Elliott et al, 1986; Fairclough, 1995; Hartley, 1995; Kellner, 1995; Knight and Dean, 1982; Smith, 1979; Tuchman, 1976).

According to Gray (1992), creating a narrative means selecting incidents so as to suggest some relationship between them. In many media analyses, the terms 'narrative,' 'theme' and 'frame' are used interchangeably. Gitlin, for example, could well be describing the essential features of the narrative as defined by Gray, Martin or by Fowler (who says that narrative is the establishing of some connection between the events being recounted) when he defines 'media frames' as 'principles of selection, emphasis, and presentation composed of little tacit theories about what exists, what happens, and what matters' (Gitlin, 1980, p. 7).

What I have in mind when I refer to narratives is storytelling involving the use of frames. But while the frame is the noun, so to speak (the concept of frame implying something static, hung around a snapshot or a photograph), the narrative is more of a verb, unfolding in stages and by definition requiring a narrator. In conceiving of what it is that takes place in this process, I have found Jenck's metaphor of the 'imaginary museum' to be particularly helpful. This refers to a museum that is becoming increasingly crowded with stockpiles of media products of which people are trying to make sense. In this museum, the journalist is a curator, who arranges the items in different ways so that visitors will be able to see and make sense of them (Bondebjerg, 1992).

Seeing news as narratives rather than simply as information has two political implications. The first has to do with how a familiar 'us' is juxtaposed with threatening 'others.'

If the informational function of news is considered subordinate to its sense-making one, and the concern is to understand how the news media can unify *and* fragment, contributing to the assimilation of new information without old cognitive frameworks, schema, or theories being relinquished, then the public must be seen as comprised, not of opinion-holders who gather and process facts about international events, but as actors who create meaning together with journalists, in an interactive sense (Neumann, Just and Crigler, 1992; Stevenson, 1995; Hall, 1994; Hartley, 1995; Kellner 1995; Schudson, 1995).

The primary political role of television news is thus not to ensure that the 'well-informed citizens' conceived of in democratic theory get their daily diet of facts on which to base their political views and behaviour, but to ensure that they can identify with the dominant political community to which they belong. The analytical focus has consequently shifted to a concern with how people try to make sense of a complicated political environment in terms of media stories about 'us' and 'them;' to a search to understand how, as Price (1995, p. 3) put it, 'imagery affects loyalties.'

The second political implication has to do with how issues are structured into threats by news frames. If issues are framed differently by journalists trained in different news cultures and in news aimed at audiences in different countries, then threats will be constructed into politically salient problems (or not) in different media at different times. Despite the communications revolution, news stories vary from culture to culture, because images of international events are more than responses to external stimuli such as changes in the international environment, however dramatic those may be. Explanations of the shapes such images take, and their impact on political behaviour, must thus take account of 'subjective' factors such as the cultural meanings given to events and political relationships. Critical theorists argue that the 'institutionalised' or established meanings attached to social circumstances and situations, such as the threats posed by poverty and the explanations proffered for these states of affairs, are 'subject to the manipulation and control of power-holders in society, particularly those who are able to command access to the mass media' (Layder, 1994, p. 73, Preston, 1997). It is this consideration that makes the analysis of media images of threat—and the frames around those images, the narratives used to explain processes, conditions and events—so compelling.

Journalists are socialised in a given country, or national culture, and in a given workplace, or professional culture. They can be thought to frame the news in a way that makes sense to their compatriots, both consciously, as purveyors of 'mediated culture,' and unconsciously, as inhabitants of the same 'situated culture.' The stories told in evening broadcasts are of interest because television news does not simply 'reflect' its linguistic, social or historical determinants, but may also work on them in an active and creative way (Fairclough, 1995, p. 55; Hartley, 1995). This view of media agency does not only exist in the mind of scholars. Journalists have also expressed the possibility that the news 'construct' rather than reflect reality. As two BBC cameramen, talking about their experiences in covering the Gulf War, put it:

Every time we film something, we film what we know. How we want to film something, what we're prepared to see, what we think will get on air...

I filmed it as I would any news event really [...] I produced material that was suitable for transmission rather than perhaps reflected what was actually there.[1]

In the empirical work reported below, that possibility has been continually in mind.

Televised Threats

A key feature of political life at the end of the millennium is the internationalisation of what were considered local or domestic issues in earlier decades (Goldmann, 1999), and the increasing difficulty of applying the distinction between 'high' and 'low' politics. While the international arms trade that was a matter of elite concern in the 1970s and 1980s could rarely have anything other than abstract consequences for the average voter, the international drug trade that has caused major concern in the 1990s has an impact that is as direct on the average youth-in-the-street as on the agendas of international meetings. The same can be said of issues related to the environment and refugee flows. It is also worth pausing to reflect upon the results of study, which found that in 1997, a majority of Russian politicians identified the greatest threat to the state as emanating from *within* the country (Petersson, 1998; cf. Wagnsson, 2000). While Russia is, admittedly, something of a special case, it can no longer be assumed that 'threat' implies something foreign. The implications of insights such as these are that, when studying images of threat in television news, it is not sufficient to analyse reports of current and former enemies, or even 'foreign news' (insofar as such a genre still exists).

For this reason, and in acknowledgement of television's special nature as a medium of 'flow' the entire contents of three television news programmes were analysed to investigate the sort of threats they depicted, and the way in which such news was framed.[2] Given the argument that globalisation has entailed a qualitative change in the conditions pertaining to news reporting, the sample included programmes aimed at three different sorts of publics. One was a commercial programme produced by the world's oldest and most respected public broadcast corporation, geared towards a global audience of news consumers (*BBC World*). One was a programme with a public service mandate to help a national citizenry understand the most important events of the day (Swedish Television's *Rapport*).³ One was a hybrid that began life as a political initiative aimed at integrating viewers from different nations into a new cultural coalition, but which had reverted to private ownership by the period in question (*Euronews*).

The chosen sample was designed, on the one hand, to include reporting over a longer period of time than is the norm (three months of one year) but, on the other, to be manageable (one day each week). The study is thus based on analyses of Saturday primetime broadcasts for the months of January, February and November 1998 on *BBC World News*, *Euronews* and *Rapport*.

The items contained in the 38 broadcasts were first coded according to subject matter, location and type of threat in a quantitative content analysis. They were then subjected to a narrative analysis which involved a 'close reading' of frames. This means that the texts (i.e. the different news items) were read in such a way as to see how their structure could be thought to communicate particular messages and not others, with particular attention paid to the juxtapositions in the texts. The purpose of such analysis was to determine whether, and if so why, certain images, explanations and outcomes could be thought to seem more 'natural' than others.

It was possible to discern threats in a substantial proportion of the material, from just over a third in *Rapport* to roughly a half in *BBC World* items. This can be seen from Table 3.1. Put differently, there was considerably more reassurance than threat in the nationally-geared programme and an even balance in the global one, with *Euronews* falling in between the two extremes.

The world seen through these camera lenses is chaotic and often threatening, and it is difficult to discern any clear patterns. There is little news about former enemies likes Russia; only Iraq and the Middle East conflict serve to provide threatening continuity.

Table 3.1 Distribution of news items contained in *BBC World News*, *Euronews* and Swedish Television's *Rapport*. Saturdays, January, February and November 1998

	Threat items Jan	Total items Jan	Threat items Feb	Total items Feb	Threat items Nov	Total items Nov	Threat items Sum	Total items Sum
BBC World	33	64	23	46	17	44	73	154
Euronews	27	53	10	26	9	32	46	111
Rapport	23	60	19	56	22	50	64	166

Table 3.2 Types of threat depicted in *BBC World News*, *Euronews* and Swedish Television's *Rapport*. Saturdays, January, February and November 1998

	BBC World	Euronews	Rapport
Natural threat (severe weather, earthquake, etc.)	12	4	6
Terrorism (incl. Algeria, N. Ireland, Corsica)	12	14	10
Aggressive, oppressive regime	10	6	7
Domestic conflict (potential/actually violent)	7	5	5
Environmental destruction, threat to health	6	0	2
Ethnic conflict	6	3	4
Destabilising refugee situation	4	2	0
Other armed conflict (e.g. Middle East)	3	4	0
Economic instability	3	1	1
Accident/unsafe work or traffic conditions	2	3	4
Drug trade	2	1	1
Criminals, hooligans, youth violence	1	0	8
Neo-Nazis	1	2	3
Technology	1	0	0
Old enemy	1	0	1
Violence vs. women and children, sexual abuse	0	1	2
Human incompetence, greed (profit-seekers)	0	0	9
Don't know how to classify	0	0	1

Even if there is a certain amount of overlap in the items reported by the three broadcasters, it is not the case that these events, actors and structural conditions are always reported as entailing a threat, and the type of threat depicted was also found to vary from programme to programme, as evident from Table 3.2.

In spite of some similarity in terms of subject matter, the three different programmes create three different impressions. The *Euronews* style is impersonal and there is a feeling that the news comes 'second hand,' which is hardly surprising given that the programme relies entirely on material from agencies and has no reporters of its own in the field. The items are represented as *events*, not as threatening actors or structural conditions. In spite of containing the fewest items in the sample, it had the most reports of terrorism of the three broadcasters. 'Old enemies,' however, scarcely exist, nor 'new' threats from the environment or international crime.

In *BBC World*, however, with an impressive staff deployed throughout the globe, the old Cold War framework persists and is adapted to new sorts of issues. A recurrent feature is the inevitability of certain threatening structural conditions, and a tendency to report them so neutrally that it can be difficult to discern human agents behind them. The *BBC World* sample distinguishes itself by containing by far the most 'natural' threats and more items in which it is impossible to discern from whence a given threat emanates.

This is quite different from the world depicted in *Rapport*, in which even threats posed by nature or the unforeseen have consequences for which human agents can be held responsible. In keeping with its characteristic as a national broadcaster, *Rapport* contains more domestic threats than the others—threats emanating from Sweden comprise by far the largest category in the table given in the appendix, and there are more 'non-political' agents like criminals and hooligans. Interestingly, these two categories do not completely overlap: many of the criminals in *Rapport* news accounts are to be found in the former East Bloc. While the stereotypical Russian in *BBC World* is still a soldier, he is a drug-dealer or extortionist in *Rapport*, as will be seen below.

It has been suggested that news discourse plays an important role in affirming 'uni-accentual' values for such concepts as 'democracy' and 'the

West.' As signs or concepts take on meaning not just through being contrasted with other concepts, but also, as Bignell puts it, by virtue of the other signs that have been excluded and are not present in the text (Bignell, 1997, p. 14) a comprehensive analysis should take absences into account. Comparative studies of coverage of the same events in different national media are perhaps the only reliable way of identifying such absences. What follows is a probe of the material read closely to this end: three examples of themes pertaining to threatening situations. One has to do with the adaptation of former Warsaw Pact states to the new situation prevailing at the end of the century; the second with the potentially explosive consequences of refugee flows from Kurdistan to Western Europe; and the third with conflict between the state and the Islamic fundamentalist opposition in Algeria. As the analysis is limited to items filed by the programmes' own reporters, only texts from *BBC World* and *Rapport* bulletins are included here.

Continuity and Change in a Threatening International Environment

Former Warsaw Pact States in a New World

In a number of reports broadcast on *BBC World News* in the sample period, the enduring legacy of the communist past is a prominent frame. On 3 January 1998, for example, there is an item about Russia's development of a new ballistic missile. In spite of serious funding shortages, we are told, Russia is determined to remain a major nuclear power, and its rockets are still a claim to 'real big-power status.' The images accompanying the report are familiar ones of nuclear-tipped rockets and wintry military parades, with the brass bands and great-coated officers reminiscent of the Cold War past. In such reports, the image and aspirations of the Russian military are unchanged, even if the preconditions have altered.

A different sort of report, broadcast on *BBC World News* a week later, also implies continuity with the past. It tells of a problem shared by EU membership applicants from the former communist East Bloc—'serious pollution from decaying factories that were built up without concern for the environment in communist times.' The reporter visits an area in the Czech republic in which the forests have been almost destroyed by acid rain. Before being allowed to join the EU, it must 'clean up the legacy of the communist era' which gave the region a giant complex of power stations, refineries and petro-chemical plants. 'The result,' we are told 'is an awful spectacle. The trees that once gave rich cover to these hills are poisoned by the foul air, three quarters of them dead, or doomed to die.'

The narrative here is built around a juxtaposition that recurs in *BBC World* reports—an obsolete state-controlled industrialism against the vulnerable human beings it threatens. The legacy lives on, as land continues to be 'devoured' as industries start up the pollution chain again 'with deadly certainty.' The message is clear: 'the devastation is so extreme' that there is 'little hope' for the local people. In both the ballistic missile report and the one from the former Czechoslovakia, continuity with the familiar Cold War past is emphasised in BBC World reporting.

Items pertaining to Russia and the defence forces in *Rapport* in the same period, however, emphasise the novelty of the situation rather than continuity with the past. In one of a series of reportages on the restructuring of the Swedish armed forces, broadcast on 31 January 1998, viewers are informed that the defence establishment is undergoing the most comprehensive transformation since conscription was introduced in 1902. Referring to European integration, spending cuts and the changed situation in the former East Bloc, the Commander-in-Chief explains that 'the climate is such that everyone understands that the world situation demands a change.'

Archive footage of stalwart Warsaw Pact soldiers and impressively armed military exercises is juxtaposed with pictures of combat aircraft embalmed under tarpaulins and rusting warships lying half submerged or belly-up in foul waters, as the reporter comments: 'Today the threat is gone for the foreseeable future and the defence forces are entering a new reality that requires a new organisation.'

If the Russian military presence is no longer a threat, other *Rapport* items, again emphasising the novelty of the post-Cold-War situation, nevertheless provide images of menace. On 7 November 1998, for example, an item tells the story of the KGB's futile hunt for felons. While the methods used by the hunters are reminiscent of the Cold War, the quarry is different. They are corrupt politicians and economic criminals.

While the KGB were once known for their power and efficiency, they are portrayed in the report as devious—using prostitutes and hidden cameras to entrap government ministers—but ineffectual, capable perhaps of getting the 'small fish' who hide their stacks of dollars behind the wallpaper in their offices, but not of securing the prosecution of the 'big guys' who hide their millions in foreign banks. The reason, we are told, is that the system is rotten: it is one in which 'everyone covers for everyone else.'

Refugees and Exiles from the Outside World

A recurrent theme in reports throughout the year was the threat posed by refugee flows within Europe. *BBC World* topped its 3 January 1998 broadcast with a report of tightened border controls in Austria and France in response to waves of Kurdish migrants flooding into Italy. Even though the camera tells a silent and sympathetic story from the vantage point of the 'would-be-emigrants'—women and children adrift on boats, passive and dejected rather than aggressive—the voiceover gives official European government views on the need to police their borders and the problems in doing so under the Schengen agreement. The EU, we are told, is making it clear that it's up to Turkey to find a political solution to 'its' Kurdish problem.

Following a telegram about the shooting down of a Turkish military helicopter by the Kurdish PKK on 28 November 1998 (also covered by *BBC World*), *Rapport* took a look at 'ordinary' Kurds, not adrift but at home in a village in southeastern Turkey. First, we join in a conversation with lawyers representing the Kurdish Hadep party that has suffered the arrests of 9 of its leaders and 107 of its members. The reporter notes that while progress has been made in resolving other long-term conflicts such as those in Israel and Northern Ireland, greater efforts are needed to solve the conflict in Turkey. The Turkish side in this conflict is depicted by an empty parliament building, in which the only visible activity is a man going down a spiral staircase. However, the implied threat is defused when we go on to accompany the reporter into the village, into the busy cafe where Kurds and Turks meet over a glass of tea and a game of dominoes. The village is called 'little Sweden' because it has an Olof Palme park, an Olof Palme street, a Swedish restaurant and a Swedish travel agency. In contrast to the Turkish government building in which nothing is happening, this village, we are told, is famous for its hard-working inhabitants, many of whom have migrated to Sweden. In this news story, the Kurds are not just the concern of the Turks as in the *BBC World* item; they have to do with Sweden too. The narrative framing the report is, I would suggest, a familiar one to Swedish publics. Conflict is the result of the aggressivity or passivity of undemocratic governments: if only they are allowed to get on with their industrious lives, ordinary people tend to live harmoniously.

The Kurds are one on-going serial throughout 1998; the bloody conflict in Algeria is another. Fieldwork has indicated that television journalists have been frustrated by the conflict in Algeria, which provides an example of how the globalisation of news is effecting a qualitative change in the factors conditioning reporting. Heavy censorship by the Algerian authorities has meant that there is a dearth of pictures emanating from the conflict, and as television is a picture-driven medium, it has not been covered to the degree journalists feel it deserves (Hellman and Robertson, 1997).

This dilemma is clearly reflected in *BBC World* treatment of the killings in Algeria. News of these is inevitably presented in telegram form. An item broadcast on 10 January 1998, for example, depicts abandoned rooms and blood-splattered walls, but contains few people and certainly no acting or speaking subjects.

The absences in these cursory reports become noticeable when contrasted with *Rapport*'s coverage of the developments in Algeria. The Swedish journalist whose report was broadcast on January 10th gets into the Algerian conflict through the back door, so to speak, through the southern European port of Marseilles from which, we are told, it is only a short distance to that ostensibly remote North African world. In Marseilles she finds Algerians who are not silent, but who can and want to talk and who are angry rather than afraid.

Their community of exiles—a colourful, cosmopolitan marketplace full of life and nourishment—is sharply contrasted (in a scenography reminiscent of Camus' *The Plague*) with the dry and dusty landscape surrounding the cemeteries in their native country, filled with the corpses of the innocent by the fundamentalists.

The Algerians who tell us their story are working for a return to democracy; they are political actors rather than victims, actors with whom we can identify because they are dressed in Western clothes and speak to us in recognisable settings in a European language. They work as journalists and party activist; the local religious leader Soheib runs study circles to encourage French and Algerians to achieve mutual understanding, using dialogue rather than violence. That the Algerians can be thought to represent the forces of light in a battle against the forces of darkness is underlined by the dramaturgy of the report, which begins in the rosy dawn and ends at nightfall, with the words:

> There is no sign of a political solution in Algeria today, even if the EU is going to send its envoy. Meanwhile, the old man in Marseille will continue to pray and his leader Soheib will continue to hold his meetings. But last night he received a death threat and was offered police protection. He refused. Whether that was the right decision, no one yet knows.

Conclusion: Different Stories, Different Depictions of Threat

Comparative analysis of reports depicting different realms of threat—the dangers emanating from familiar enemy territory as well as new features of the international environment, be they destabilising refugee flows or the antidemocratic enemy within—highlights a number of differences that can be thought to have a bearing on whether, and how, the different 'imagined audiences' are cued to respond to those threats. In the world depicted by BBC journalists, the situation of the Kurdish refugees may represent a tinderbox, but it is a problem for Turkey, not 'us.' While the refugees are portrayed sympathetically, they remain at a distance from the viewer, adrift in a sea of bureaucracy. There is something resigned in the BBC treatment of them; the message (particularly when seen in the context of similar reports that recur, like a feuilleton, over time) is that refugee flows are an inevitable feature of world politics. The same can be said of the unfathomable violence in Algeria and the pessimistic tone of the Czech story. The legacy of the past means that conflicts—be they between men or between man and nature—are an abiding trait of the political environment. Viewers are not invited to respond to these images other than by becoming aware of the situations they recount.

In *Rapport*, on the other hand, the underlying narrative is one of change, as opposed to continuity, to which viewers *are* invited to respond. Ethnic and religious conflict is not inevitable in this reading. Kurds and Turks can peacefully coexist if left to get on with it, unless they are misrepresented by oppressive regimes; bloodshed such as the slaughter in Algeria is fought more effectively by the pen than the sword, by enlightenment (the study circle in Marseilles), by opinion-formation (the political activist and the journalist) and by dialogue (like in the cafe where Kurds and Turks meet). The bad news is that this can be difficult in a new anarchical post-Cold-War world, in which the nuclear threat has been replaced by one of lawlessness, with gangsters taking over from greatcoated Russian soldiers in the role of 'baddies.' In reporting police murders, the actions of neo-Nazi vandals and militant squatters in quiet Swedish communities, it emerges that this anarchy has seeped within the walls of the nation. The dilemma of globalisation is evident here, with the border between the domestic and the international erased. In this context, Swedish news consumers are not simply invited to be aware of events and threats. The summons to respond is even clearer here than in the case of the refugees, as November 30th reporting demonstrates.

Images of threat, I contend, are formed in a contradictory process, as they are affected both by the revolutionary nature of media globalisation and the conservative framing of culturally determined news media. This framing activity is where the political power of the media in general and television in particular most clearly resides. Price draws attention to the perception of interest groups that 'the mass of images off and on television' harbours the capacity of reorganising public attitudes to crime, politics and the like. 'In each of these areas,' he writes, 'an old and haunting question became newly grave in the light of disarray and undercurrents of conflict' in the nation. The question is what the range of appropriate societal response should be to the brutal and sometimes inexplicable power of the image (Price, 1995, p. 174-75). The appropriate response, it seems to me, is to do nothing, when threats are depicted as inevitable, as distant, evens as 'acts of God' as in many *BBC World* reports. A more active response may be cued by the sort of items I have found of interest in the Swedish *Rapport*, in which the international, if not the national, environment may be depicted as less threatening than in *BBC World*, but in which the threats that *can* be discerned are portrayed as the business of people 'like you and me' as well as governments.

The concern of this chapter has been with 'banal' news reporting which, I have argued, gives us access to the realm in which enduring *Weltanschauung* are conditioned—the stable narrative structures or 'theories' that can be adapted to new information about the changing environment (and vice versa). In a political landscape characterised by the rapid succession of media events it is important to attend, not just to the short-lived news item that is offered to the viewer in an episodic frame and then dextrously whipped away as soon as they are presented and replaced with others, but also to the long-running serials, the narratives which frame thematically our understandings of the outside world and condition the images of threat we may perceive as emanating from there.

Notes

1 Susan Stein and Ian Pritchard, interviewed in the BBC documentary 'The Eye of the Storm.'
2 Actually, a fourth, German television's *Heute*, has now been coded for the same period, (in fact, for all Saturdays in 1998), but I haven't had a chance to incorporate the results in this chapter.
3 *Heute* is a companion to *Rapport* in this category.

4 Verbal Politics of Estonian Policy-makers: Reframing Security and Identity

ERIK NOREEN

The memory of some half-century of Soviet occupation of Estonia is deeply engraved in the minds of the Estonian people. According to various opinion polls, 60-80 percent of the Estonian people perceived the Russian state as a threat to Estonia in the winter of 2000.[1] The point could thus be made that the Estonian government considers it logical to seek membership in a Western security structure such as NATO. History plays a major role in arguments justifying Estonia's desire to join this collective security organisation, for the major concern of policy-makers is how to avoid repeating the past mistake of being a neutral, defenceless, weak state that falls easy prey to an aggressive neighbour.

However, the fact that Russia has historically been 'bad' for Estonia and the Estonian people is not the only possible argument in support of this policy of 'Westernisation.' The instability in Russia's economic and political situation and the unpredictability of its foreign policy during the 1990s lends credence to claims that formalised security cooperation with the 'good' democracies of the Western world represents the only feasible security policy for the Estonian state.

It can also be argued that the emancipation process of leaving the 'bad' Soviet Union for the 'good' European one needs to be interpreted within the context of finding a new identity within post-Cold War Europe, as well as regaining the identity of the independent state of Estonia during the inter-war era. This argument gives rise to the question of how Russia, 'the other', is assessed within the process of forming a collective Estonian 'self'? The opinion polls mentioned above speak for themselves, but does the Estonian elite, such as the policy-makers in the Ministry of Foreign Affairs, share this threatening view of Russia?

This chapter sets out to analyse trends in the *verbal politics*[2] concerning threat framing from the second year of independence up to the year 2000, focusing on policy-makers in the Estonian Ministry of Foreign Affairs (EMFA). By analysing speeches and statements made by the Estonian security policy elite over a period of time, the framing and reframing of threats will be explained. This will be achieved by focusing on the rhetorical elaborations of historical experience, as well as current conditions. In particular, the reconstruction of national identity is addressed.

Desecuritising Russia—Widening the Threat Agenda

The post-Cold War history of Estonia can be divided into three phases (Haab, 1998): the *proto-independence* mobilisation under the last years of Russian occupation, the first years of formal independence, and the *nation-building phase*.

The first phase of proto-independence started already at the end of 1988, when popular movements openly began to manifest demands for a politically independent Estonia. The period ended in August 1991 when the provisional Estonian government—as was the case in Latvia and Lithuania—declared its country's *de jure* independence.

The second phase of independence was initiated thereafter and was completed in August 1994, when the Russian government, after drawn-out negotiations, withdrew all its troops from Estonian territory. Like the other Baltic countries, Estonia was now *de facto* independent. During this period Estonia had become a member several international organisations, including the UN, the CSCE, the Council of the Baltic Sea States, the NACC and the Council of Europe. It was also associated with the WEU. Furthermore, the Estonian government made it clear that it also wanted to join NATO and the EU.

During the present *nation-building* phase we can identify a number of contradictory landmarks with respect to Estonian-Russian relations. On the one hand the Estonian Citizenship Law and Language Law of 1995, on the other hand the outcome of the negotiations on a border agreement in 1997. On the one hand a fairly nationalistic, anti-Russian gesture, as judged by opinions among the Estonian Russian-speaking minority as well as the Russian government, on the other hand a complaisant and flexible attitude vis-à-vis Russia, as the Estonian government gave up its demands on some 2,000 square kilometres of its territory. Estonia's relations with Russia in the middle of 1990s were, according to a domestic observer, 'approached from the side of Estonia by a policy of positive engagement.' However, she continues, 'driven by historical prejudices and uncertainty as to the nature of the post-Soviet Russia, Estonia's policy towards Russia remained reserved and occasionally provocative' (Haab, 1998, p. 119).

A computer search of speeches and press releases, stored in the websites of the EMFA, using the word 'threat' (and 'threats'), resulted in 21 hits for the two-year period from July 1, 1992 to June 30, 1994. Nineteen of these were directly related to Russia, referring to Soviet-Russian military occupation forces. The documents were, thus, concerned with an assessed military threat directly against Estonia (Velliste, 1993a; Luik, 1994a; *Estonia Review* 15-21 June 1992; 27 July-2 August 1992; 15-21 March 1993; 25-27 October 1993). It is hardly an exaggeration to point out that the Estonian policy-makers were almost fixated on images of a Russian military threat during the first years of independence. How does the trend look when moving on to the next phase?

During the first years of the nation-building phase, after the Russian troop withdrawals (i.e. from 1 September 1994 to 31 August 31 1996) a corresponding computer search resulted in 19 hits, but now fewer (11 of them) were referring to Russia. In addition, four of these were emphasising that Russia did not constitute any immediate military threat against Estonia. We may thus discern a tendency among the policy-makers of the EMFA to tone down the image of a Russian threat. And this trend continued. During the very last years of the millennium, the two-year period of 1998 and 1999, there were 31 hits on threat/threats of which only 11 were related to Russia. None of these were references to Estonian policy-makers' fear of any immediate military threat. Most of them were rather indirect, for instance, references to domestic political instability in Russia (Kallas, 1996a, 1996b; Ilves, 1998c, 1999a, 1999c).

There was a significant increase in the number of references to a threat, but the threat referred to anything else other than Russia. In other words, Russia was being *desecuritised* (see Buzan, Wæver and de Wilde, 1998; cf. the introductory chapter to this volume). If these figures are expressed as a percentage of the total range of threat references during the periods investigated, in the period from 1992 to 1994 they constituted 10 percent of the total; from 1994 to 1996, 42 percent; and from 1998 to 1999, 65 percent.

What were the sources of these other, non-military, threats that seemed to play an increasing role in the statements of the EMFA? By September 1994 Foreign Minister Jüri Luik had already set the tune in his speech in the UN General Assembly. He argued that as a consequence of the fact that the Russian troops had now withdrawn from Estonian territory, his government could 'devote more energy to wider issues.' New items were being put on the agenda, such as:

> terrorism, organised crime, drug trafficking, smuggling of radioactive materials, illegal arms trading, as well as health and social issues and environmental problems. These are issues that know no borders, and combating them requires a collective effort on our part (Luik, 1994b).

It is noteworthy that this framing was continued by Luik's successor Toomas Hendrik Ilves:

> [Th]e decline of a clear adversary would bring changes to the nature of security threats faced by Europe. The appearance of new countries, ethnic strife, mass migration, environmental degradation, and economic collapse [...] (Ilves, 1997b, cf. 1997c, 1997e, 1997f).

The reasoning concerning threats was often put in a context that stressed the relationship with Europe. In a speech entitled 'Estonia's Return to Europe,' Ilves referred to threats affecting Baltic Sea states. The intention was not only to cooperate with Nordic and Baltic states to combat these types of threats, but also with Russia (Ilves, 1998a).

In sum, the assessed threats could be characterised as structural rather than actor-specific (Sundelius, 1983; cf. Introduction to this volume). It is also obvious that the statements increasingly stress non-military rather than military threats. As showns, the withdrawal of Russian troops was an event that had a desecuritising effect on the EMFA's assessment of Russia as a military actor, but a securitising effect on a wide range of other potentially threatening issues, particularly of a structural nature. Foreign Minister Ilves (1999c) made this clear when he stressed that threats were 'no longer state-driven, but rather derive from mal- or dysfunction of states.'

Reframing Security and Identity

The First Years of Independence: The Mirror of the Past

Many of the incidents that occurred between Russian occupation forces and Estonians between 1991 and 1994 are briefly described in the documentation of the EMFA. Needless to say, these events could easily be related to assessments of Russia as an immediate threat against Estonia in military terms (*Estonian Review*, 15-21 June 1992; 13-19 July 1992; 10-16 August 1992; 31 August-6 September 1992). This threat image was accentuated in that Estonia did not have much in terms of military resources to counter should Russia have intended to reinforce annexation, or simply refuse to withdraw its occupation forces from Estonian soil. Consequently, Estonian policy-makers were greatly affected by Russian statements in line with the so-called *Near Abroad* doctrine, meaning that Estonia belonged to the Near Abroad, referring to the Russian security sphere of interest. In September 1993, Foreign Minster Trimivi Velliste gave expression to this anxiety as he stressed 'the fact that a long row of high Russian officials have joined the chorus strongly suggests that in Moscow, the 'Near Abroad' is an officially-sanctioned idea whose time has come' (Velliste, 1993a, cf. 1993b-d).

During the first years of independence, however, the Estonian decision-makers' statements were not often connected to a traditional Realist framing of threats.[3] Although there were an increasing number of statements in favour of NATO, as well as a sense of the desirability of Estonian membership in the Alliance, the policy-makers did not talk about any balance-of-power in terms of military resources. For example, in a statement by Foreign Minister Luik in March 1994 there was indeed a reference to the term 'balance.' But the intention here was not, for instance, that NATO should 'counterbalance' any military power of Russia. The intention was rather that Estonia wished to integrate 'into those Western structures that may help to counterbalance the crisis in the East' (Luik, 1994a).

In Luik's list of strongly advocated organisations, only NATO did not include Russia as a member. Moreover, membership of NATO was interpreted as a final step in the process of integration ('the step-by-step approach') with European and North Atlantic states, rather than joining a defence alliance *against* any power.[4]

It would be naïve, however, to think that in the hidden agenda of the decision-makers of the EMFA there were no considerations whatsoever indicating an awareness of such realities as: a great power (particularly Russia) is not a great power if it does not seek to increase or preserve its position of power; a small state (like Estonia) has reason to fear a great power in its vicinity due to the asymmetry in resources and capabilities. After neutrality or more limited regional security arrangements had been removed from the agenda, the only feasible security policy option in this respect therefore was NATO. The point is, however, that this was not very explicit in the documents of the EMFA. We have to go to other forums to find out how the EMFA might have reasoned behind closed doors. These discussions implied hat Estonia has to join NATO and the EU because these are the only credible balancing powers vis-à-vis Russia.[5]

If this kind of Realism—focusing on current international conditions—was not clearly expressed in the documents of the EMFA, what could be said about historic frames of reference?[6] Put simply, was Estonian foreign policy 'driven by historical prejudices?' (Haab, 1998, p. 119). If so, why was history interpreted in one way rather than another?

There were, perhaps not surprisingly, expressions of the Estonians' sad history, such as the Soviet-Russian annexation, in the documents of the EMFA, as well as in the media (Tarand, 1994; Reinart, 1994). If we concentrate on the last years of occupation (1991-1994) it is however difficult to separate the current from an historic perspective. The Russian troops on Estonian territory were interpreted as a remnant of the past, as they reminded people of all the injuries inflicted by the Russians during the war years as well as during the Cold War.

One issue, which came to be securitised, was the Russian minority. This issue was framed within a historical context in a way that could make people think of a possible re-annexation, which might be exemplified as a good example of securitisation. A Russian proposal concerning political, economic and social support for the Russian-speaking minority in Estonia was thus compared with 'Hitler's programme of protecting the so-called *Volksdeutsche* living outside the boundaries that then constituted Germany. As we all know, Hitler's programme was a justification for the invasion and annexation of the Sudetenland' (Luik, 1994a). Even if a speculative analogy like this did not occur very often in the EMFA material, it occurred repeatedly in the media (*Postimees*, 21 August 1993; 25 September 1993). It could thus be seen as an indication of the tense relations between Russia and Estonia during the years just before the troop withdrawals.

The Nation-Building Phase: Joining the 'Western Family'

How can we explain the defusing of the image of the Russian threat, while the policy-makers almost simultaneously tended to stress more and more the importance of Estonian integration in 'Western structures,' and above all in NATO? Why was there a lack of analyses about the Russian military capability in the EMFA documents? Why did Russia as a security threat disappear from important policy documents in 1999 where it previously had a prominent role? (Ilves, 1999b, 1999d, 1996; Mälk, 1998).

It would appear that, to an increasing extent, the Estonian policy-makers, after the withdrawals of Russian troops, connected their language to a framework that was closer to Constructivism than Realism. The Constructivist model I am referring to here consists of more malleable and flexible elements than the stable and predictable elements of the Realist model. According to the latter, states are constantly striving for independence and power. The Constructivist point of departure is different. According to Constructivists, identities are always under construction, and consequently so are images of threat. Thomas Risse-Kappen suggests that identity formation, the definition of 'how "we" [...] also delineates the boundaries against "them," the "other" ' (Risse-Kappen, 1996, p. 367). This 'self–other' polarisation is fundamental to how threats are framed and reframed. It has also been claimed that norms and values shape identities. A case in point is the liberal values held by Estonian policy-makers that determine whether Western Europeans are perceived as 'the "in-group" of friends' or 'the "out-group" of potential foes.'[7]

However, Constructivists have paid less attention to the issue of how historical experience shapes identities. As was suggested earlier, it could be argued that the Estonians' experiences, their collective memory of the years of Soviet occupation, have shaped the process of constructing a collective identity in the post-Cold War era of independence. This would lead one to understand identity formation as a recurring process of interpretation and re-evaluation of historical experiences, which would in turn influence people's assessments of threat.

Focusing on the concept of identity it is obvious that the EMFA, to an increasing extent, referred to this term during the 1990s. The number of references to identity were thus constantly increasing; from five in 1993 to seventeen in 1999.[8] Moreover, of the total of 70 references to identity during the period of investigation, most were related to Europe. It was, for example, emphasised that national identity could be strengthened if, or rather when, Estonia became a member of the European 'family'—a metaphor that was frequently used by the EMFA (Sinijärv, 1995; Kallas, 1995, 1996a; Tarand, 1996; Ilves, 1997a, 1998b, 1999a).

Other identities were also accentuated, for example, Baltic and Nordic identity. Sometimes this searching for identities, which might be characteristic of nation-building phases, appeared confusing. After having emphasised European identity in general during 1995 and 1996, the policy-makers tended to refer to the Baltic Sea region in 1997 (Tarand, 1996; Ilves, 1997a, 1997d).

There were several arguments in favour of a close Estonian relationship with European countries in the middle of the decade, for example: 'We are a European people and we are able to keep our identity only by belonging irrevocably to Europe...' (Kallas, 1996b; Tarand, 1996). Moreover the Nordic neighbours were referred to in terms of 'our common history and cultural background,' whereas the view of Baltic integration was somewhat more restrained, albeit the three countries had achieved 'significant progress in practical cooperation' (Tarand, 1996).

By using the historic analogy of *Hansa* in a 1997 speech on international trading, Foreign Minister Ilves stressed 'Baltic identity,' focusing on the Baltic Sea region, in contrast to European integration:

> The strengthening of economic links will also encourage the development of a distinct Baltic identity in Europe, which will be an important counterbalance in the EU (Ilves, 1997d).

When the same foreign minister some two years later talked about identity, it concerned something different. In this speech he identified a new group of countries, so called 'Yule' countries, whose common denominator was in a combination of factors such as etymology, religion and national character—allegedly a geographical area in which one and the same word signifies both the birth of Christ and the solstice.

The distinction between 'we and them' was now clearly expressed. Not just Russia was excluded from this group, but also the neighbouring Baltic countries. Baltic identity was thus far out of use:

> The Yule-swath that extends from Iceland and Britain through the Scandinavians to the Finnic lands that include Estonia, ends there. In Latvia Yule is Ziemastvetki, in Lithuania Kaledos, in Russia Rozhdestvo [...] *There is no Baltic identity* with a common culture, language group, and religious tradition. For almost four years now, Lithuania has been correctly pointing out that it is a Central European country. Its Catholicism, architecture, history all link it to Poland and the other Visegrad countries. Estonia was and as I will try to point out is, if anything, a member of Yuleland (Italics added; Ilves, 1999e).

When Ilves places his country on an equal footing with Britain, Sweden, Finland, and so forth, rather than Latvia and Lithuania, in terms of ranking in high-tech development and ethics, it becomes clear that he is focusing on an Estonian EU membership in the near future. According to Ilves, Estonia belongs to the group of states that is ranked 'highest in the world in Internet connections and in mobile phone penetration, lowest in the world in corruption. Within the European Union a northern identity is emerging. Yuleland will clearly be a major player' (Ilves, 1999e).

Identity, History and Adaptation

In spite of these sudden changes in aspiration for some sort of regional affiliation, we may discern a general trend during the decade. Estonia wishes to an increasing extent to belong to Europe in general, and to the North Atlantic Community in particular, as 'after all, the Alliance (NATO) is a family of democratic nations for the defence of common values' (Ilves, 1999a).

If one has the intention of defending common values that were fundamental in the creation of identity, it is implied that these values might be threatened. The question is then: what is threatening and who is it that threatens? The conclusion thus far is that the 'Russian threat' has been removed from the official agenda of the EMFA. Instead we have found a long list of *new* threats. How could this disparate threat image be explained in the light of defending values and developing identity? We need to know how threat images can be connected to identity.

Theoretically this could be done in several ways. According to Social Identity Theory there are two partly contradictory propositions (Schafer, 1999). On the one hand, it is suggested that the stronger the collective identification among the members of a group (the 'in-group'), the more negative values they develop vis-à-vis another group (the 'out-group'). In a worst-case scenario such antagonism may lead to open conflict.

On the other hand, there is the proposition that a strong feeling of identity among the members of a group is 'healthy' for individuals, not only in respect to the 'in-group' but also in relations to 'out-groups.' Conflicts and instability are thus, according to this proposition, not positively correlated with a strong perception of identity within a certain group, but rather with a weakly developed perception of identity.

This is not the place to test any of these propositions, but we may nevertheless conclude that the philosophy behind the latter proposition corresponds better to Estonian-Russian relations during the 1990s than does the former. Concurrent with the development of a strengthening sense of identity among Estonians is a strengthening of self esteem, and there is accordingly, no reason to make things more negative than they are through worst-case analyses concerning potential Russian military threats. Estonian decision-makers could instead, in their own words 'devote more energy to other issues,' even in cooperation with the former occupier. This might appear surprising, especially when we look back at the history.

Decades of Soviet annexation might have influenced not only the inner beliefs of policy-makers but also their official vocabulary. There were indeed references to the Second World War, and the Cold War, as well as the Soviet era. But history was often used in order to emphasise a dramatic development in a positive sense. In 1997, Foreign Minister Ilves identified two phases after the Cold War. The first post-Cold War phase, which succeeded the dangerous but stable Cold War, allegedly was characterised by 'unpredictability, potential chaos and instability' (Ilves, 1997a). However, Ilves saw some clear signs of a second phase in the post-Cold War era. There was nothing negative to say about the new phase. The European 'architecture' of international organisations and institutions would be consolidated as a base for a stable and peaceful development within the fields of economy, politics and security. In this respect the second phase of the post-Cold War era was a continuation of the years after the Second World War, characterised by the newly born 'architecture,' of NATO and the European Community (Ilves, 1997a). Thus even in an historic perspective, Estonian policy-makers stressed the development of which they so eagerly wanted to be a part. However, Estonia had a history of its own; the history of the Estonian republic. All these identities—the Estonian, European and North Atlantic—were synthesised by Ilves:

> As Estonia restores and surpasses the statehood enjoyed in the era 1918-1940, a new Estonian is being born: knowledgeable, proud and self-confident, European in outlook, and hungry for achievement in a pioneer kind of way typically associated more with America than the continent. The new Estonian

will shape the Estonia of tomorrow; his attitudes will become the national attitude, his sensitivities will become the national sensitivities (Ilves, 1997a).

Here we might add a pragmatic aspect that connects identity to a process of socialisation. The parallel processes of searching for identities, as well as trying to integrate within the Western organisational structures, also included a process of adapting the official Estonian language to the language of the west. Frank Schimmelfennig elaborates on this theme as he stresses that 'the Western community of states socialises the former Communist states' through organisations such as the EU and NATO (Schimmelfennig, 2000, p. 109; Wennersten, 1999).[9]

A case in point was the language of security. In Western Europe, and especially in Scandinavia, one can discern a shift in the vocabulary concerning security policy issues. What is most striking in this respect is that Russia is not characterised as a potential enemy, as was often the case during the Cold War. A motto for this way of reasoning is that security must be maintained not against, but in cooperation with Russia. During the 1990s, concepts such as 'comprehensive security,' 'civic security' and 'cooperative security' have slowly been integrated into the official vocabularies of Northern European countries. In particular, the Nordic countries have developed this language of international security. According to Clive Archer and Christopher Jones, 'during the years since 1991, the Nordic states have undertaken a process in relation to the Baltic states that could be called socialisation, tutoring, or more modestly, cooperation.' They argue that 'the Nordic countries exported some of their own security concepts to the Baltic states' (Archer and Jones, 1999, pp. 172-174). However, in this study the authors never scrutinise how this exportation might have been performed; it is an interesting problem that remains to be explored.

Conclusion

The construction of threat images could be illustrated as a process in several stages. Firstly, threats can be constructed in our consciousness; we think about something as a threat. This is the cognitive point of departure; threat is not necessarily expressed in language or texts, it is rather a 'think act' in analogy with a 'speech act.'[10] The next stage is thus the 'speech act;' people talk about something as a threat. We are now moving from the individual level of cognition to the social sphere of language and communication. Threat takes on *societal* salience in that it is debated in media and other public forums. It is however not until the next stage that threat takes on *political* salience, when it is moved onto the political agenda. Political actors on all levels are now discussing threat and may also develop a strategy to meet or prevent threat.

It might be emphasised that the suggested process is ideal typically, which means that the process must not follow this (theoretical) logic in practice (Weber, 1962). Hence, one does not necessarily have to analyse the entire process. The process may nevertheless briefly be applied to the threat image trend in Estonia during the last decade of the millennium. We might then observe that the image of the Russian threat plays a prominent part when it concerns the cognitive starting point of the process. Opinion polls support this conclusion. Moreover, within a societal context, the Russian threat image comes out strongly in the media as well as the interviews.

However, when we move to the political arena the picture becomes more complex. On the one hand, the Russian threat is tuned down by the EMFA, while other treats are emphasised. In addition, the NATO membership issue is not connected to assessments of eventual threats from Russia, which is in line with the westernised security language of the 1990s. Estonian policy-makers are thus reframing security as well as their identity and historical experience. We may thus far conclude that what is at issue is a process of socialisation. It concerns a reciprocal process, which has to do with the creation of a new language of international security, not only for Estonia and the Baltic states, or for Northern Europe, but also for the whole European continent, the North Atlantic, and other democracies of the world.

On the other hand, we presume that Estonian policy-makers have action plans for worst-case scenarios of politico-military tensions between Russia and the Baltic states. Thus, it might not be too far-reaching to conclude, that the apparently steadfast belief in the benefits of an Estonian NATO membership could be placed in this context. In order to show this we need to know how the decision-makers are discussing in the inner circles of the Cabinet office and the Ministries. But that is another story.

Notes

Special thanks to Toomas Riim, Tartu University, for valuable comments and helpful assistance in translating articles and documents, and arranging interviews in Tallin.

1. Rose (2000, p. 36-37), *Eesti Päevaleht* (25 March 2000). According to The New Baltic Barometer's opinion poll based on 650 interviews with Estonian citizens in February 2000, 78 percent of the respondents believed that the Russian state was 'definitely' or 'possibly' a threat to 'the peace and security' of Estonia. On another question—'How much of a threat does Russia represent to Estonian independence?'—60 percent responded 'a great deal' or 'some.' A similar question put to 1000 citizens and published by the Estonian paper *Eesti Päevaleht* about the same period, showed 80 percent of the respondents were in the affirmative ('Does Russia represent a threat to Estonia's independence?').
2. Doris Appel Graber has explained the philosophy behind verbal politics some 25 years ago, as she suggests that '[a]n understanding of politics depends heavily of verbal symbols which lack extra-verbal reality.' And she continues by arguing that '[w]e see the world primarily through the words of others. Once word-based images are formed, they serve as mould for the flow of subsequent direct and indirect experiences' (quoted in Winnerstig, 1996, p. 27). Moreover, the approach is connected to discourse analysis rather than cognitive belief system analysis or other similar approaches. While the latter focuses on individual beliefs, the former deals with 'intersubjective beliefs.' It is accordingly also related to 'collective intentionality,' albeit intentionality that remains in an individual's head. But, as John R. Searle stresses, 'within those individual heads it exists in the form of 'we intend,' and 'I intend' only as a part of our intending' (quoted in Ruggie, 1998, p. 20; cf. Larsen, 1999, p. 455).
3. Some of the most important explanatory concepts within the Realist framework are power relations, often expressed in terms of balance-of-power, capabilities and resources, which determine whether the actor is a small state, a medium, or a great power; and last but not least, interests. States' interests are 'exogenously given and stable,' (Schimmelfennig, 1999, p. 200) meaning, for example, that a small state always has an interest in being protected, preferably within an alliance, to avoid being perceived as a power vacuum by a neighbouring great power. Similarly, a great power is always concerned with counterbalancing another great power, and may do this at the

expense of a neighbouring small state's independence. This is the iron law of Realism. (See also Wayman and Diehl, 1994.)

4 Velliste had an even more sophisticated argument in that he stressed that the member states of NATO could take advantage of Estonia's role as a watch dog vis-à-vis Russia (Velliste, 1993d).

5 Personal interviews conducted in April 1999: Gert Antsu (European Integration Bureau); Aksel Kirch (Institute of International and Social Studies, Tallinn); Aap Neljas (former member of the Foreign Policy Committee in Riigikogu), in April 1999 a freelance journalist; Kristina Ojuland (Vice Chairman of the Council of Europe's Parliamentary Assembly); Einar Rull (expert on defence policy, Ministry of Defence); Rein Ruutsoo (Institute of International and Social Studies, Tallinn); Sander Soone (Director of Division, Political Department, Ministry of Foreign Affairs); Enn Tupp (former Defence Minister, in April 1999 the Estonian military attaché to Finland); Trivimi Velliste (former Foreign Minister). One example of this way of reasoning, in which one should note the actor's discussion of alternative security policy options, is Liberal MP Aap Neljas' statement in the leading Estonian newspaper *Postimees*:

'It is obvious that no matter how much money we spend on defence or how many men we can mobilise, we cannot on our own, or even together with other Baltic states, resist a serious Russian attack. That's why we don't have any other options than to seek some help from another power who could balance Russia's influence in our region. NATO and the EU are the only reasonable alternatives, because all the Central European countries feel insecure and are seeking NATO's protection [...] There is, of course, the possibility of starting to improve relations with Russia and the CIS. Although it is economically necessary to improve relations with Russia, an orientation to Russia would hardly maintain our competitive market economy in the long run. In addition, it is impossible to separate economic cooperation from political demands, which are clearly unacceptable to the majority of Estonians' (*Postimees*, 13 May 1994).

6 There is an approach within the field of cognitive studies that would lead us to assume that Baltic policy-makers in the 1990s would accept NATO as the one and only solution to their respective states' security problems, referring to history rather than current military threats. Decision-makers may use past events as guidelines to help them to find the 'right' policy direction. They may, for instance, draw analogies to events from earlier periods, determining a course of action on the basis of the imperative: 'never again will we make the same mistake' (cf. Larson, 1985; Khong, 1992; Reiter, 1994, Reiter, 1996; Houghton, 1996). To put it simply: small states react to lessons from history rather than to current military threats. One of the examples Reiter uses to illustrate his findings is 'the Scandinavian checkerboard of alliances' that started to emerge only a few years after World War II (Reiter, 1994, pp. 522–526). Although all the countries in Scandinavia were exposed to the Soviet threat, Sweden did not join any alliance, indicating that the countries of this region reacted to historical lessons rather

than to any Cold War assessment of military threat. Or, more precisely, in Sweden policy-makers decided to continue the policy of neutrality, a policy that was perceived as successful because it kept Sweden out of the Second World War. In Norway and Denmark, the policy of neutrality was assessed as a failure. Five years of German occupation had thus caused a complete change of policy, with both Norway and Denmark deciding to join NATO in April 1949 (cf. Noreen, 1994, 1997).

7   Risse-Kappen elaborates on this theme in his analysis of identity formation within NATO during the Cold War. Like most of the Constructivists, he distinguishes his position from Realism: 'Threat perceptions do not emerge from a quasi-objective international power structure, but actors infer external behaviour from the values and norms governing the domestic political processes that shape the identities of their partners in the international system' (Risse-Kappen, 1996, p. 367).

8   This was a significant relative increase, in spite of the total increase of the amount of documents during the period in question.

9   Schimmelfennig (2000, p. 111-112) defines international socialisation in the following way: 'the process that is directed toward a state's internalisation of the constitutive beliefs and practices institutionalised in its international environment.'

10 Drawing a parallel between a 'think act' and a 'speech act' presupposes that we consider the thinking as something that is intended, and not something that just happens. (cf. Lübcke, 1997) According to Ole Wæver the 'speech act,' within the framework of 'language theory,' is equivalent to 'the utterance in itself that is the act: by saying it something is done.' I stress this point since Wæver and the so-called Copenhagen school tend to overlook the process that is outlined here. Moreover, Wæver and his colleagues do not make any principal distinction between securitisation within a general societal context, and securitisation within a political context (Wæver, 1997, p. 221). The principal sources to find out how individuals think about threat are opinion polls and interviews.

5 Threat Politics and Baltic Sea Business
MICHAEL KARLSSON

The Copenhagen Declaration signed in March 1992 by the Ministers for Foreign Affairs of Denmark, Estonia, Finland, Germany, Latvia, Lithuania, Norway, Poland, Russia, Sweden, and a representative of the European Commission established the Council of the Baltic Sea States (CBSS).[1] In the declaration, the signatories expressed their determination to 'strengthen the cohesion among these countries, leading to greater political and economic stability as well as a regional identity' (The Copenhagen Declaration, CBSS, 1992). The Council, which could be characterised as a traditional intergovernmental cooperation, entered into somewhat of a new phase in 1996 when it began to hold recurring Summit meetings, including the eleven Heads of Government and the President of the European Commission. The first two Summit meetings, in 1996 and 1998, were on both occasions lobbied by an exclusive transnational group of big business leaders (Karlsson, 1999). The group appeared under the name of the Baltic Sea Business Summit (BSBS) and included 16-17 leaders of major corporations from the eleven CBSS member states. The message that was delivered by this group was that the Baltic Sea region had a considerable potential for economic growth, but that there was a serious *risk* that this would be jeopardised if companies and politicians did not show strong leadership.

The case of the BSBS is but one example of a trend among major European corporations to establish informal transnational collective action with the purpose of influencing intergovernmental cooperation (Greenwood, 1997, pp. 126-128). In this respect the BSBS very much resembles the European Round Table of industrialists (ERT), which was established in 1983 and which has been characterised as a rich-firm club (p.

104) and a 'strategic player' (p. 112) aimed at shaping the European agenda. The ERT was for instance very active in lobbying for the Single European Act in 1986 and the Treaty of Maastricht in 1991 (Green-Cowles, 1995).

The literature on transnational collective action of major corporations has not primarily been linked to security, risk or crisis management.[2] The purpose of this chapter is therefore to apply the threat politics approach—as presented by Eriksson in the introductory chapter—to the case of the Baltic Sea Business Summit (BSBS), with particular emphasis on threat politics at the intergovernmental level. Four research questions are addressed. First, what threat images guided the risk analysis of business leaders? Was it because threats such as bureaucracy, protectionism, or organised crime that they thought there was a serious risk to regional development? Second, what type of referent were the threat frames of the BSBS composed of? Was it events, structural conditions, or actors that were framed as threats? Third, what characteristics did the various frames have? Could they be described as elaborated or restricted frames? Fourth, how successful were the business leaders in their efforts to stimulate threat politics at the intergovernmental level? How was the risk analysis of the BSBS received by the governments in the Baltic Sea region?

The chapter begins with an overview of two fields of research, which are of particular relevance for an analysis of transnational business and threat politics. The first of these concerns theories of international political economy and their images of threats in a market context. The second type of research deals with transnational relations, and especially with strategies for exerting transnational influence. The subsequent section is devoted to a case study of the Baltic Sea Business Summit. This section includes, apart from an introduction to the BSBS (the framing actor), a deeper analysis of the threat frames and the lobbying of the intergovernmental level. Finally, the main findings are summarised in part four.

Contending Perspectives on International Political Economy

Threat Framing in a Market Context

Threat framing in a market context implies a focus on international political economy. Thus, it is the interaction between market and state, or between economics and politics, rather than between market actors per se that will be considered here. This distinction is important since risk-taking is a normal condition of a market, i.e. an efficient market by definition must impose continuous threats of bankruptcy to inefficient actors (Buzan, 1991, p. 123-24). However, leaving such threat frames aside, the issue to consider here is what type of threat frame the transnational business community may be interested in bringing to the attention of governments and peoples.

Table 5.1 Three perspectives on international political economy and the type of threat frames that may be derived from them

	Statism	Liberalism	Marxism
Entity	States	Companies, households	Classes
Environment	Anarchic, conflict	Anarchic, harmony	Stratified, conflict
Entity-environment relationship	Environment constrains	Entities have significant freedom of choice	Environment constrains
Threat frames	All that may decrease the power and welfare of the state	Governmental interventions, protectionism, corrupt and inadequate institutions	Imperialism, domination, exploitation

Sources: Gilpin (1987), Caporaso and Levine (1992), and Frieden and Lake (2000).

The academic literature on international political economy distinguishes between three perspectives: Statism, Liberalism, and Marxism (Gilpin, 1987; Caporaso and Levine, 1992; Frieden and Lake, 2000). Since these perspectives have different views on what constitute the normal condition of the international political economy, they can also be associated with rather different conceptions of threat. Table 5.1 is an attempt to briefly summarise the essence of these perspectives with respect to the 'ecological triad' and the type of threat frames that may be derived from them. The ecological triad is composed of three elements: (1) an actor, or entity, of some sort, (2) an environment that surrounds the entity, and (3) the entity-environment relationship (Starr, 1999, p. 11).

Statism The statist perspective assumes that states are the primary actors in the international political economy. Other actors, such as companies, are of secondary importance and are largely constrained by the activities of the states. The main concern of states is to protect the national interest since the systemic environment is perceived as anarchic and conflictual. Thus, the economic goals of states focus very much on how to increase power and welfare in competition with other states. If other actors can help states to realise these goals they become of interest also to statist analyses. It follows from these assumptions that any activity or event that may decrease the autonomy, power and welfare of a state should be regarded as a threat. For example, the present wave of transnationalisation among companies is partly perceived as a threat by states since they fear that this will lead to a movement of production and technology and thereby weakens the economy and the power base of the state. Considering this threat perception, it is not surprising to find that states increasingly bargain with national firms not to leave home as well as with foreign firms to locate their activities within the territory of the state (Strange, 1995, p. 65).

Liberalism The liberal perspective assumes that the international political economy is mainly composed of non-governmental units such as companies and households. The interaction among these actors takes place in an anarchic environment in which harmony is perceived as the natural order. Thus, the normal condition of the international political economy is when it is guided by the logic of the market economy. The primary threat to a well functioning market economy is according to non-Keynesian liberals believed to come from states and politics, including governmental interventions, protectionism, corrupt and inadequate social institutions. For example, the economic stagnation in Western Europe in the 1970s and

1980s was according to the business community very much caused by the interventionist and protectionist policies of the governments. The business community therefore lobbied actively for the implementation of the Common Market as a way to remove remaining obstacles to a free movement of goods, services, capital, and people.

Marxism The Marxist perspective assumes social classes to be the basic units of society and describe the relations between them as a class struggle or a struggle between capital and labour. The expansion of capitalism has made the systemic environment highly stratified and conflictual. Thus, international exchange is perceived as highly unequal and peoples, especially in developing non-Western countries, live under a constant threat of imperialism, domination, and exploitation. Even though this order developed during former colonial periods, it is generally believed among Marxist scholars that these conditions still prevail in the international political economy. For example, a threat image that has received increased attention in recent years is the exploitation of women from the third world and Eastern Europe by the 'sex industry' in Western countries (Pettman, 1996). It has been estimated that this 'trafficking' has brought some 100,000 women only from South East Asia to prostitution and pornographic related industry in Western Europe.

It is reasonable to expect that the view of the business community in the Baltic Sea area should come very close to the liberal perspective. Thus, we should expect the threat frames of the big business leaders to be focused on the activities of states and show very little concern about state autonomy or possible exploitation of the transitional economies on the Eastern rim of the Baltic Sea.

Transnational Influence Strategies

Considering that threat politics largely is a struggle about the continuity and change of frames implies that the framing process is highly strategic. This means that a framing actor who is attempting to increase the societal salience of a certain frame not only has to look at the characteristics of the frame. It is also important to consider how to attain this goal in competition with other framing actors (Tarrow, 1998). In the market context, the competing framing actors may be, for example, states, trade unions, environmentalists, and international nongovernmental organisations (INGOs). These actors may operate with more or less different views on what is to be conceived of as a threat. Thus, in the framing process the business actors may be confronted with threat frames that come closer to the Statist or Marxist perspectives.

There are a number of different strategies that transnational business actors can use when they want to influence framing processes at the international level. For instance, Karen Mingst (1995) has made a distinction between four transnational strategies that non-state actors can use to influence intergovernmental cooperation. In *the power approach* actors 'attempt to target top decision-makers' (p. 238), for instance by lobbying members of government or high-level civil servants. Considering that democracy reigns in all CBSS member states since the early 1990s, this is a highly plausible strategy because transnational actors usually find it easier to get access to democratic than non-democratic governments (cf. Risse-Kappen, 1995). On the other hand, the outcome of the power approach run the risk of being rather limited since there often are numerous other actors trying to influence these governments. In *the technocratic approach* actors 'use knowledge of procedural mechanisms as well as the legal system' to influence decision-makers (Mingst, 1995, p. 239). For example, knowledge of the rules and principles of an international regime can be used to warn governments to pursue a certain policy. This strategy is equally conceivable, especially since the BSBS operates within an issue area (trade) where international regimes has shown to be more frequent compared to many other areas (Keohane, 1993, p. 38).

In *the coalition-building approach* transnational actors 'utilise domestic actors to build coalitions, forging domestic policy consensus' (Mingst, 1995, p. 240). For instance, by building coalitions with important interest groups a transnational actor can hope to loosen up governmental opposition to international cooperation. Finally, in *grass-roots mobilisation* actors 'try to build widespread public involvement in several countries,' e.g. by mobilising public opinion to activities such as letter writing and demonstrations decision-makers can be put under extra pressure (p. 240).

However, it is often believed, as noted by Justine Greenwood, that 'the less public an interest makes its affairs the more successful it tends to be, because it is able to get its needs met on the 'inside track' of public policy-making' (Greenwood, 1997, p. 16-17). In other words, an increasing use of the grass-roots mobilisation strategy may be interpreted as a loss of such a status. The conclusion of this is that we should expect the BSBS to find the power approach, perhaps in combination with the technocratic and the coalition-building approaches, to be more fruitful than the grass-roots mobilisation strategy.

Threat Politics: The Case of Baltic Sea Business

The Baltic Sea Business Summit[3]

The Baltic Sea Business Summit (BSBS) is an informal round table group of prominent big business leaders in the Baltic Sea region. It was established in April 1996 following an initiative of Peter Wallenberg, a leading industrialist in Sweden. The BSBS should be seen as something more than a 'dining club' since there is a common intent for collective action, seen in the production of action programs and lobbying efforts. On the other hand, it is not a formal organisation, having no steering committee, no secretariat, nor a separate budget. So far it has been able to draw upon the administrative resources of the Stockholm Chamber of Commerce, who has organised the meetings and assisted in the distribution of documents (declarations, press releases etc.).

The BSBS practice a policy of membership by invitation only. A full list of members, as of January 1998, is given in Table 5.2. A closer look at the list reveal some distinguishing qualities of the BSBS. First, it comprises only major corporations, while small and medium-sized companies are excluded. Second, it should be emphasised that the members are corporations rather than individuals. This means that Leif Johansson replaced Sören Gyll when he took over as Chief Executive Officer (CEO) of Volvo. Third, the BSBS is truly regional since the members come from all eleven-member states of the Council of the Baltic Sea States.

Geographically, however, the BSBS has not a strict proportional representation. Eleven corporations have their base in the market economies in Western Europe, while five corporations comes from the transitional economies in Eastern Europe. It is also clear that the initiative originates from a Swedish industrialist since four members comes from Sweden. Finally, it should be noted that the BSBS has a cross-sectoral character, i.e. it is not built around one specific business sector. Among the sectors represented are, for instance, banking (UNEXIM), car industry (Volvo), investment (Investor), oil (Statoil), provisions (Danisco) and telecommunications (Ericsson).

Table 5.2 Members of the Baltic Sea Business Summit, January 1998

Peter Wallenberg	Chair of BSBS, Chairman Emeritus Investor AB (S),
Percy Barnevik	Chairman ABB Asea Brown Boveri Ltd, Investor AB (S)
Georg Ehrnrooth	President Metra Corporation (SF)
Mogens Granborg	Executive Vice President Danisco A/S (DK)
Hans-Dieter Harig	Chairman PreussenElektra AG (D)
Jukka Härmälä	President Enso Oyj (SF)
Leif Johansson	President AB Volvo (S)
Viktors Kulbergs	Managing Director Auto Riga (LAT)
Bronislovas Lubys	President/CEO Joint Stock Company 'ACHEMA' (LIT)
Toomas Luman	Chairman EE Group (EST)
Harald Norvik	President and CEO Statoil A/S (N)
Vladimir Potanin	President UNEXIM BANK (RUS)
Lars Ramqvist	President and CEO Telefon AB LM Ericsson (S)
Friedel Rödig	Executive Vice President Lufthansa (D)
Hördur Sigurgestsson	Managing Director HF. Eimskipafélag Islands (ICE)
Cezary Stypulkowski	President Bank Handlowy W Warszawie SA (P)

Key: (D) Germany, (DK) Denmark, (EST) Estonia, (ICE) Iceland, (LAT) Latvia, (LIT) Lithuania, (N) Norway, (P) Poland, (RUS) Russia, (S) Sweden, and (SF) Finland.
Source: Baltic Sea Business Summit, 1998.

Although the BSBS only comprises major corporations, it claims to be looking after a wider business interest. Thus, the big business leaders have

108 *Threat Politics*

stated that they 'argue for conditions that are mutually good for all businesses, small or large, in all countries' (BSBS, 1998, p. 1). Furthermore, while general associations of business interests tend to focus at an operational level, the BSBS has shown to be interested mainly in strategic issues. This means that they choose to concentrate on 'structural measures' for economic development (e.g. the legal framework, investments, and transports), while avoiding getting involved in the detailed everyday practices of regional affairs.

At the first BSBS meeting in 1996, the business leaders adopted an action program, which specifies the measures needed to stimulate regional growth (BSBS, 1996). The action programme contains in all some eighty concrete recommendations, summarised under the following nine headings: (1) Rule of law, (2) Less bureaucracy and better public administration, (3) Free trade, (4) Integrate Europe, (5) Stable monetary systems and prudent economic policies, (6) Greater flexibility, (7) Links in the Baltic Sea Region—improve infrastructure, (8) Sustainable development, and (9) Human Capital—a natural resource. The recommendations in the action programme are not only with reference to conditions in the transitional economies (1-2, 5, 9), but deals also with conditions in the western economies (6) and in the region as a whole (3-4, 7-8). At a 1998 follow up meeting the big business leaders concluded that '[a]lthough much has been done during the last two years it is less than we hoped for, less than is needed and less than could have been done' (BSBS, 1998, p. 2). They therefore declared that, even though they still held the 1996 action program as a relevant 'check-list,' they now wanted to give extra attention to measures with respect to (1) the legal framework, (2) other obstacles to foreign direct investments, and (3) transports.

Threat Images of Big Business Leaders

The business leaders of the BSBS believe that the Baltic Sea region has a potential for economic gains from market exchange that is considerably above the present level. Thus, they have estimated that intra-regional trade within a 15-20 year perspective ought to grow by up to ten times (BSBS 1996, 1998). Considering this, the chairman of the BSBS Peter Wallenberg argued in his opening address in 1996 that there now exists 'a window of opportunity' for the region (Wallenberg, 1996, p. 1). However, as was also emphasised by Wallenberg, just to perceive a window of opportunity is not enough for growth and development to realise. He therefore called for 'strong leadership,' i.e. a willingness among companies and politicians to take action (Ibid., p. 3-4). The former was urged to increase their foreign investments and the latter to create a climate that promotes investments and trade. As far as companies were concerned, it was also noticed: 'This strategy implies uncertainties and risks, but the rewards for those who dare and handle it professionally are potentially great' (Ibid., p. 4).

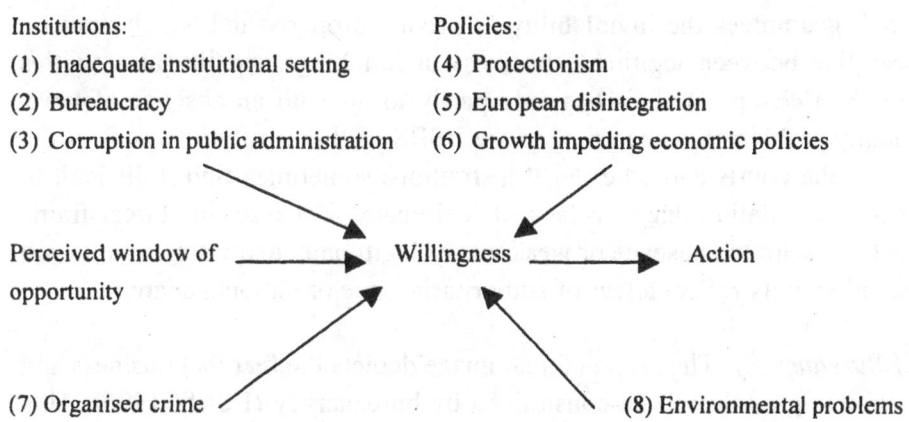

Figure 5.1 Eight threat images framed as affecting the willingness of leaders of major corporations to seize a window of opportunity

A closer reading of available BSBS documents reveal that the expected uncertainties and risks are related to a number of different threat images. It can be observed that all threat images addressed by the big business leaders are framed as jeopardising the goal of regional growth are explicitly linked to notions of threat, risk, fear, or danger. As can be expected, the threat images reveal a general *liberal* frame. At large it seems possible to identify four more or less interrelated clusters of threat images among the business leaders. These clusters are related to governmental institutions, policies, organised crime, and the environment. As is shown in Figure 5.1, these threat images are framed as affecting the willingness of major corporations to take action (e.g. foreign investments) following a perceived window of opportunity. Willingness refers to the motivations that lead the business community to avail itself of the economic growth opportunities in the Baltic Sea region and is basically dependent on their perceptions of the world.[4]

(1) Inadequate institutional setting The frame of the first threat image focuses on the difficulties of establishing rule of law in some of the transitional economies, i.e. a legal framework for commercial activities which guarantees the inviolability of private property and which draws a clear line between legitimate business undertakings and illegal activities (BSBS, 1996, p. 2). This has only partly to do with an absence of laws. Equally problematic, according to the BSBS, is that institutions such as the police, the courts and other legal institutions sometimes find it difficult to enforce legislation due to a lack of legitimacy. Because this threat frame has to do with the absence or weakness of legitimate institutions and laws it may ultimately reflect a fear of authoritarian rule or national anarchy.

(2) Bureaucracy The second threat image depicts the fear that business and economic growth will be constrained by bureaucracy (BSBS, 1996). This image is basically the opposite of the first because it is framed as implicating too extensive legislation, including different national legislations, will complicate administrative procedures for transnational business. To avoid this, the BSBS stress the need to make East European legislations compatible with the 'acquis communautaire' of the European Union and established legislation in the EU countries. Considering that many rules within the 'acquis communautaire' are thought to be very complicated the BSBS also emphasise the need to have these simplified.

(3) Corruption in public administration The third threat image is about the problem of corruption in public administration, which is said to be quite widespread in some of the East European countries (BSBS 1996: 3). Corruption is not only framed as destructive of legitimate business, but also

as a serious threat to the economic growth of the individual countries. To fight this the BSBS asks for measures such as prosecution and competitive wages for public servants.

(4) Protectionism The fourth threat image is concerned with the risk of increasing protectionism (BSBS, 1996, pp. 3-4). The threat of discriminatory rules and procedures for import and marketing of foreign products and services is not connected to any specific country, but is framed as a more general threat. This means that all governments in the Baltic Sea region are urged by the BSBS to work for further trade liberalisation within the framework of WTO and to conclude Free Trade agreements. In addition to this, the BSBS also believes that the EU could promote further trade liberalisation in the region by offering better market access for products from the countries that are not EU members.

(5) European disintegration The fifth threat image is about the risk of European disintegration (BSBS, 1996, p. 4). The business leaders are here above all concerned with the development of the European Union. The fears that are explicitly mentioned are that the enlargement process will run into difficulties and that the EU will not be able to develop its relation with non-member states. It is particularly emphasised that the three Baltic States and Poland must be given the opportunity to become EU-members as soon as they fulfil the requirements and that the EU must build close and solid links with Russia.

(6) Growth impeding economic policies The sixth threat image expresses a fear that regional growth and development may be jeopardised by growth impeding economic policies in the individual countries. The business leaders present a list of recommendations stressing the importance of, for example, stable monetary systems to keep inflation low, prudent fiscal policies, balanced public finances, modernised labour legislation, dismantled monopolies in business, and securing quality in infrastructure and in the educational system.

(7) Organised crime The seventh threat image brings up the problem of organised crime. On this point, however, the business leaders also try not to exaggerate the threat. This means that the BSBS on the one hand acknowledge that there is a problem. For instance, crime is said to 'cause legitimate business very large losses and in some cases even prevent the existence of legal firms' (BSBS, 1996, p. 11). On the other hand, the business leaders make an effort to distance themselves from some of the exaggerations they think can be observed in Western Europe:

> But we want to emphasise that among ordinary people, as well as businessmen, in Western Europe the perception of crime in the countries in transition is often exaggerated. Organised crime severely affects some parts of business-life and especially SME's are likely to suffer from various forms of extortion. But many foreign companies operate without being severely affected by crime.
>
> While governments determinedly should fight crime, we believe that it is at the same time important to improve the image of the countries and try to convey a more accurate picture of the situation. (BSBS, 1998, p. 7).

The BSBS believes that even though the problem with organised crime may change as economic development takes place, it may never be condoned. The business leaders therefore stress the importance of increasing national efforts as well as intensifying regional cooperation between the police forces to combat crime (BSBS, 1996, p. 2).

(8) Environmental problems The final threat image frames the difficulties of securing a sustainable regional development. In contrast to how the other threat images are framed this frame is less specific about the nature of the problem (the diagnostic function) and more concerned with the measures (the prognostic function)—see the introductory chapter and Snow and Benford (1992). For example, the business leaders emphasise that national legislation must be designed for sustainable development, that environmental levies can provide an efficient method to reduce pollution, that environmental assessments should be made before major investments are embarked on, and that safety must be improved in some of the nuclear power plants in Eastern Europe.

Having identified the individual threat images, we can now turn to the question of how they are framed and what type of referent issues are identified. As regards the former question, it can be concluded that the business leaders exclusively have framed structural conditions as threats. Thus, although threat frames such as 'corruption in public administration' or 'organised crime' easily could be linked to other types of referent issues, it is equally clear that they in this case are not referring to any specific event or any specific actors. Furthermore, considering that the business leaders only refer to structural conditions does not mean that the threat frames should be seen as less dramatic. On the contrary, one could very well argue that some of the structural conditions, such as organised crime or environmental problems, also give dramatic associations and therefore have every chance of succeeding in the framing process. On the other hand, if this assumption is valid it also means that it should be relatively more difficult to push some of the other threat images onto the intergovernmental agenda.

As regards the question of frame characteristics, a particularly interesting feature of Figure 5.1 is that the four clusters of threat images vary considerably with respect to how elaborated their frames are. On the one hand, the threat images that are related to governmental institutions and policies are rather detailed in character, which makes it possible to discern several sub-categories of threat frames. This means that governmental institutions are framed differently depending on whether inadequate institutional settings, bureaucracy, or corruption in public administration are highlighted. In a similar way various governmental policies are assumed to produce threat frames about regional growth, including increased protectionism, European disintegration, and growth impeding economic policies. On the other hand, the threat frames that are related to organised crime and environmental problems appear to be rather vague and less elaborated. Thus, the business leaders perceive that there is something wrong with the environment and that there is a problem with organised crime, but they do not go into any details about what exactly these threats consists of.

The described variation in how elaborated different threat frames are can be interpreted in many ways. Following Jerel Rosati (1995), this may for instance be a reflection of the business leaders' interests, knowledge or information about the phenomena that the threat is linked to. The fact that most threat images (1-6) are framed in correspondence with the liberal view of international political economy, suggests that this perspective can account for much of the observed pattern. It is also of interest that the remaining two threat images do not seem to fit any of the three IPE-perspectives as clear as the others. The threat image of 'organised crime,' which in this case is framed in a way that gives associations to anarchy in the meaning of chaos, could probably be derived from all three perspectives. This also has a notable correspondence with the 'hierarchical culture' discussed by Bjereld in chapter two. On the other hand, the threat image of 'environmental problems' seems to suggest the possibility of a fourth complementary perspective, which corresponds to the 'egalitarian culture' addressed by Bjereld.

Threat Politics

The outcome of the business leaders' efforts to shape threat politics at the intergovernmental level has been rather mixed, despite access to the highest political level. In political rhetoric, the Baltic Sea states address basically the same threats as those identified by the big business leaders. There has been considerable progress in cooperation with respect to environmental issues. Furthermore, in 1996 a 'Task-Force on Organised Crime in the Baltic Sea Region' was established. On the other hand, cooperation with respect to institutional problems and flawed policies (threat images 1-6) has been more difficult. For instance, the governments have so far not shown any willingness to establish a Free Trade Area in the Baltic Sea region.

As regards transnational influence strategies, the business leaders have above all focused on *the power approach*. They have on two occasions had the opportunity to personally present their views to the Summit of the Council of the Baltic Sea States, i.e. the eleven Heads of Government and the President of the European Commission (Karlsson, 1999). At the first Summit, in Visby in May 1996, the view of the BSBS was presented by Mr. Wallenberg personally and at the second Summit, in Riga in January 1998, the lobbying was carried out by a small group of three BSBS representatives (Peter Wallenberg, Mogens Granborg, and Viktors Kulbergs). On both occasions the BSBS presented extensive declarations, or 'check-lists,' on the conditions for growth and development in the Baltic Sea region. These 'check-lists' reflected, among other things, the eight threat images discussed above. In addition to these lobbying efforts, the BSBS in 1996 also invited the Swedish Prime Minister Göran Persson, who then worked as the chairman of the CBSS, to present his view on the regional development. It should be emphasised that the business leaders have only used the power approach to target the highest political level, i.e. the Heads of Governments, while ignoring bureaucrats and policy-makers on lower levels of government. As a comparison it could be mentioned that the Baltic Sea Chambers of Commerce Association (BCCA), whose 52 members (chambers of commerce) represent more than 400,000 companies in the Baltic Sea region, has approached the latter level considerably more. The BCCA is for instance regularly invited to the Working Group for Economic Cooperation of the CBSS.

In addition to the power approach, the BSBS has also employed *the technocratic approach*. The 1996 and 1998 memorandums contain references to international regimes within the issue-areas of trade, human rights, and environment. First, it is established that '[t]he trade regimes in the region are centred around the EU. ... In this perspective there is no need and no time for vague designs about trade cooperation in the region' (BSBS, 1998, pp. 7-8). In this case the major corporations not only put pressure on the Eastern countries to liberalise trade, but also reminded the EU to, among other things, abolish remaining restrictions on products from applicant countries. In connection to the free trade issue the BSBS also urged the Russian government 'to remain committed to WTO membership and to take the appropriate steps to qualify for membership' (p. 8). Second, the business leaders also found support in the Convention on Human Rights, in which the Council of Europe prescribes a minimal level of protection for individual freedoms. Thus, in the 1998 memorandum the BSBS reminds the countries that they have all ratified the Convention and 'thus undertaken to uphold and protect those liberties' (p. 12). It is also emphasised, with special address to the transitional economies, that the Convention 'has given arguments for provisions of the right to appeal authorities' decisions' (p. 20). Third, as regards environmental problems, the BSBS stress the importance of eliminating the 'hot spots' on the HELCOM list (Helsingfors Commission on Environment Protection) and that all countries should ratify The Vienna Convention on Civil Liability for Nuclear Damage (BSBS, 1996, p. 6). Finally, as regards the remaining two strategies there is no evidence that these played any significant role. Although the BSBS arranged a public seminar in Riga in January 1998, this was a single event in connection to the Summit meeting and was not intended to mobilise the grass roots.

The transnational lobbying of the business leaders has been successful in so far as the Heads of Government at the Riga summit in 1998 decided that the CBSS should follow-up the proposals of the business leaders. Thus, in response to the Riga decision, the CBSS Working Group on Economic Cooperation decided in December 1998 to do a survey on the progress on implementation of the recommendations in the BSBS memorandum of 1998. The survey, which was presented in January 2000, concluded that: 'The results seem to justify some optimism as they indicate considerable progress in many of the topics under consideration. However, as the reader will see, many of the recommendations are still only partly implemented, i.e. a lot more needs to be done' (CBSS Secretariat, 2000). Thus, although the concerns of the business leaders clearly have been put on the intergovernmental agenda, it appears as if the outcome of their lobbying so far has been rather mixed. In other words, the threat frames of the BSBS have not caused the governments to make any far-reaching changes in the direction of their cooperation.

The outcome of the business leaders' transnational lobbying can partly be explained by the orientation of the CBSS cooperation. The founding document of the CBSS reveals that the Council should 'serve as an overall regional forum to focus on needs for intensified cooperation and coordination among the Baltic Sea States' (CBSS, 1992). Six areas of cooperation were singled out for special attention, namely: (1) Assistance to new democratic institutions; (2) Economic and technological assistance and cooperation; (3) Humanitarian matters and health; (4) Protection of the environment and energy cooperation; (5) Cooperation in the field of culture, education, tourism and information; and (6) Transport and communication. To this should be added that the CBSS countries might decide to include other areas of cooperation as well. For instance, following a decision of the Heads of Government in May 1996 a 'Task-Force on Organised Crime in the Baltic Sea Region' was established.

An analysis of these areas of cooperation indicates that some of the threat images of the BSBS are well known to the governments in the Baltic Sea region. For example, the threat images concerning inadequate institutional settings, environmental problems and organised crime, concern issue-areas that already had the attention of the governments when the BSBS began its lobbying activities in 1996. The environmental cooperation began already in the 1960s and has, according to some, even reached the stage of a regime, i.e. the states have agreed on principles, norms, rules, and procedures for dealing with these problems (Efinger, Mayer and Schwarzer, 1993, p. 259). As regards cooperation to fight organised crime, it should be noted that the actual decision in 1996 to establish a Task force was taken prior to the BSBS lobbying. In these cases it seems reasonable to expect the influence of the business leaders to be more a matter of emphasis than substantial policy change. In addition, it should be obvious that framing organised crime and environmental problems as threats, hardly could meet any serious resistance from other framing actors.

Furthermore, it is obvious that the principle of sovereignty set clear limits to what the intergovernmental cooperation can achieve with respect to the perceived threats of bureaucracy, corruption, and growth impeding economic policies. On these issues the BSBS cannot be expected to have an influence on anything else than recommendations. Finally, the lobbying that has been directed against tendencies of protectionism and European disintegration clearly cover issues of interest also to the CBSS. However, it is equally clear that the governments so far have not agreed on establishing a Baltic Sea Free Trade Area. There is also reason for the BSBS to be disappointed about the enlargement process of the European Union and the fact that the three Baltic States and Poland still, more than one decade after the Cold War ended, have not received membership status.

Conclusions

This chapter has been devoted to a case study of the big business leaders of the Baltic Sea Business Summit (BSBS) and their efforts to shape threat politics at the intergovernmental level. The BSBS claims that the Baltic Sea region has a considerable potential for economic growth, but that there is a serious risk that this will be jeopardised if companies and politicians do not show strong leadership. The case study showed that the risk analysis of the business leaders was based on eight threat images. Six of these were about governmental institutions and policies, which is in accordance with a liberal framing of international political economy. The additional threat images, on organised crime and environmental pollution, are not the sole domains of any the three major IPE perspectives (Statism, Liberalism and Marxism). On the other hand, as Bjereld shows in chapter two, emphasis on organised crime corresponds to a 'hierarchical culture' and environmental problems to an 'egalitarian culture'.

To get governmental attention for these threat images, the business leaders used the 'power approach' by targeting the Heads of Governments at their Summit meetings of the Council of Baltic Sea States. This strategy was supplemented by the 'technocratic approach,' including for instance references to international regimes. The transnational lobbying has been successful in so far as the CBSS Working Group on Economic Cooperation has done a survey on the progress on implementation of the recommendations of the business leaders. However, since the governments already are cooperating with respect to institutional setting, environmental problems, and organised crime, it can be argued that threat politics was established before the BSBS began its activities. As regards the threats of bureaucracy, corruption, and growth impeding economic policies, it should be stressed that the principle of sovereignty set a clear limit to the possibility to establish an intergovernmental threat policy. Finally, the lobbying to reduce the threats of protectionism and European disintegration has so far not achieved the stated goals. The governments have not agreed on establishing a Baltic Sea Free Trade Area and the three Baltic States and Poland have, at the time for this writing, still not received EU membership.

Notes

1. Iceland joined the CBSS in 1995.
2. Though there is an emerging body of literature on economy and security (Blanchard, Mansfield and Ripsman, 2000; Andersson, 2000; Cable, 1995; Buzan, Wæver and de Wilde, 1998, ch. 5; Buzan, 1991, ch. 6; Luciani, 1989; Sjöstedt, 1987), it is focused on 'economic threats' to national security and the welfare of national economies, rather than the threat politics of transnational business agents.
3. Unless otherwise stated, this section draws on Karlsson (1999, pp. 17-21).
4. On the concepts of opportunity and willingness, see Starr (1999, pp. 11-16).

Part III
Issues in Focus

Part III
Issues in Focus

6 Securitising Submarine Intrusions

FREDRIK BYNANDER

When in 1982, depth charges and mines were fired in the small archipelago bay of Hårsfjärden outside Stockholm, Sweden; the whole world seemed to be in the audience. Around 400 journalists from media organisations around the globe reported the event. Approximately two years earlier a very similar submarine hunt had taken place in the vicinity. Eight journalists, none of whom visited the site more than twice, covered that incident. What had happened in between was that the U137, a Soviet whiskey-class submarine had hit land in the inner archipelago in southern Sweden and remained sitting impotently on a reef. This illustrates the enormous turn in attention and perceived severity that the submarine issue took in that period.

This chapter is about Sweden's problems with repeated and protracted underwater intrusions during the 1980s and how those problems became the gravest security threat of the decade. Evidence of the intrusions took the form of repeated indications by submarine defence equipment such as sonar, magnetic mine barrages, and by observers seeing periscopes and other submarine-related phenomena all of which gave rise to prolonged submarine hunts. This study investigates the political implications of these incidents turned national crises, and how people in charge dealt with them, or failed to deal with them. It sees the issue as pertaining to security, especially politics of framing. It analyses how the interaction between bureaucratic organisations (here the military), party politics, and the media combines to evoke public fears and concern, thereby determining the public agenda.

The Securitisation Process in International Relations

In the post-Cold War world, the logic of the bipolar structure in world affairs is losing in interest, and the particular problems facing individual states during that time has rapidly become irrelevant to how most scholars in international relations and security studies view the problems they face today (Lebow and Stein, 1994; Wendt, 1999; Baldwin, 1996; Betts, 1997; Keohane, Nye and Hoffmann, 1993). On many of the complex security issues of the Cold War, however, no bookends have been achieved, and in dealing with many protracted and serious problems, the decision-makers of that era were saved by the proverbial bell that was the dissolution of the Soviet Union.[1] Studying those issues anew can certainly add to our historical understanding, but it can also tell us something about security policy today and in the future (Keohane et al, 1993; Lebow and Stein, 1994; Khong, 1992; Bynander, 2000).

Some may argue that the submarine issue constituted core 'security' long before troubles began in the 1980s–that maritime military activities are securitised by definition. Thus, existential threats are identified, and extraordinary measures such as secrecy and the use of military means are legitimated (Buzan, Wæver and de Wilde, 1998; Introduction to this volume). The approach championed here is quite different. Threats (or issue areas containing threats) do not acquire security status by objective means—they are placed there (or removed) as results of political processes. The analysis will show that early on, the peacetime submarine issues were ranked in the 'naval nuisance area' on the defence agenda.[2] From there it rapidly assumed the massive proportions it would have for the remainder of the decade.

Even though U137 was an important turning point, the process of moving submarine intrusions to the security core goes further back than 1981. To show this, one only has to recall the sigh of relief from Chief of Staff, Bengt Schuback, when the submarine was discovered: 'At last!' (Hellberg and Jörle, 1984, p. 96). Border violations had mostly been regarded as 'peacetime squabbling'—playing games to keep the armed forces on their toes. As the submarine problem emerged two new aspects became apparent: 1) Not being able to protect ones territory from intrusions on a systematic basis damages the credibility of the defence, and 2) These vessels must have a stronger motive for their actions than playing games, considering the substantial risks that the intruders run of loss in men and diplomatic difficulties/humiliations (Agrell, 1985; Bynander, 1998).

This qualitative change of perceptions of the submarine problem is accompanied by an incremental and quantitative change—the budget decisions made in conjecture with incidents and revelations in the policy area. The table below is meant to give a tentative picture of this process.

Table 6.1   Events and actions in the submarine defence, 1980-1984

Event	Period	Action
Utö-Huvudskär	September 1980	Temporary submarine analysis team
	Fall 1980	'The SEK 49 million package'
Whiskey-on-the-Rocks	October-November 1981	
	Spring 1982	'The SEK 200 million package'
Hårsfjärden	October 1982	Permanent submarine analysis team
	November 1982	The establishing of the Submarine Defence Commission
The Commission's Report, SOU 1983:13	April 1983	'The SEK 250 million package'
Sundsvall	May 1983	
Töre	July 1983	IKFN rule change. 'Force to surface'
Scuba-divers in Stockholm archipelago	September 1983	The Steen Commission
Karlskrona	February-March 1984	'The SEK 50 million package'

Source: The Swedish Submarine Commission (SOU 1995:135), p. 53.

Table 6.1 shows that a perceived insufficiency of available resources for submarine defence became increasingly present and constantly pressed onto the cabinet's decision-making agenda. Specific incidents triggered budget increases and reinforcements of operative capabilities. Another tentative measure of securitisation is the indications reported by the Supreme Commander (SC) in his annual report.

Figure 6.1, which depicts the period 1981-94 (no report was made in 1980), gives us another clue to the legitimacy situation. Quantifying a phenomenon is to make it more concrete in the perceptions of the potential audience. It also means concealing or simplifying important problems of categorisation and reinforcing the legitimacy for the actors who count.[3] In this case the defence establishment maintains its policy monopoly by defining the phenomenon at issue and by being the information producing entity for media and for the political level.

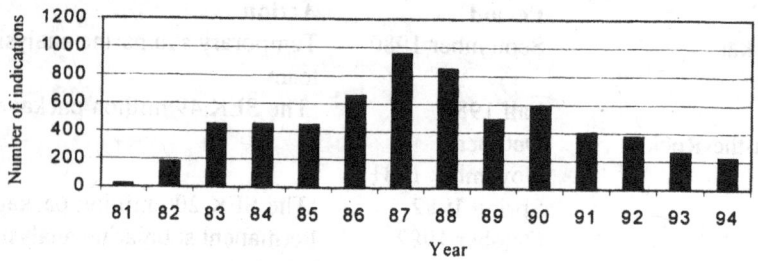

Source: The Swedish Submarine Commission (SOU 1995:135, p. 33)

Figure 6.1 Number of indications cited in the Annual Submarine Commission Report, 1981-1994

Traditionally, foreign policy in Sweden has been presented as 'consensual,' meaning that the main political and organisational actors have officially agreed on the political ends and means in this area. Neutrality coupled with territorial integrity has been seen as desirable values both across the party spectrum and within the relevant organisations (Sundelius, Stern and Bynander 1997; Molin, 1991; Bjereld, 1992; Andrén, 1996). In the Swedish submarine example, on several occasions bureaucratic politics (and party politics) feed into the securitisation process. The competition between different policy objectives, organisationally incorporated into different intersubjective frames, is often camouflaged and kept in closed rooms using soft voices. The organisational promoters, or political entrepreneurs, often stand to gain more if their influence passes undetected or if their true motives are cloaked in other guises.

Determining the Growth of the Submarine Threat

So, how do we know security when we see it? What thresholds should we establish to decide for us the level of salience and threat framing where an issue moves from non-security to security? Salience is easier to observe than framing. If, during an incident, there are major news articles in both of the analysed national newspapers *Dagens Nyheter* (DN) and *Svenska Dagbladet* (SvD), and after the incident there are more than one article a week covering aspects of the submarine problem it is considered salient.

Framing is a more complex and qualitative analytical concept. The main issue will be if submarine intrusions as a phenomenon are presented as a threat in news articles and editorials. The threshold for 'securitisation' is arbitrarily set to a majority of the coverage where a qualitative statement regarding the nature of the submarine problem is made. The framing aspect has wider implications, however, as to who is setting the frames, and whether journalists accept them or not.

What and who causes issues to become security in the way described above? A complete answer to this question is naturally to complex to answer in full; so three main suspects will be rounded up here in accordance with the expectations derived from agenda-setting and framing theory. Bureaucratic political modes of explanation (e.g. Allison and Zelikow, 1999) and politics of problem definitions (Rochefort and Cobb, 1994; cf. Douglas and Wildavsky, 1982) will also be consulted in order to describe the actors targeted, and to form credible ideas about their actions and interactions.

The Main Actors

Since politics is the game here, politicians should definitely be the players. And to one extent they are: they have the formal decisions on 'security' in their hands, and they evidently sometimes use that power. Successful political rhetoric gives short-term power and influence over the issues of the day, but also longer-term effects such as credibility and popularity. Indeed, finding representations of potentially dividing issues that can form compromise and bring opposing views together can be seen as the 'most subtle form of power.'[4] In agenda-setting theory, the political level is attributed great importance, though it is often exercising influence through complex interaction with other spheres of society. Both regarding the level of societal salience of an issue and the frame it is represented in across society, the nature of the media-policy relationships is crucial (Kingdon, 1995, pp. 57 ff; Cobb and Ross, 1997; Cohen, 1963).

The importance of politicians for agenda setting lies in their roles as newsmakers. Their daily input to the media organisations is vital, and that gives the political sphere of society a disproportionate influence of what is put on the media agendas (Dearing, 1996; Wood and Peake, 1998). These results often hold true for the situation in the United States, but it is harder to have a clear idea of politics-media influence in Sweden. It is probably safe to assume that the Swedish media organisations have roughly the same role conceptions vis-à-vis the political sphere as their US colleagues.

What role do civil servants and military officers play in the formation of policy? This is a question that public administration scholars have researched for years, and developed a literature that only reluctantly has been adopted in international relations and security studies (Wilson, 1989; Lipsky, 1980). Beginning with the works of Graham Allison (1971) and Morton Halperin (1974) the influence of the bureaucratic complex on the outcomes of foreign policy decisions became a significant area in security studies.

The scheme with which to approach the impact of bureaucrats is to assess the different roles of these actors in different stages of the threat framing and salience making processes. For example, the navy experts were throughout the studied period in possession of an information monopoly regarding central areas to the submarine issue (such as sonar analysis, intelligence analysis, submarine defence measures, etc.). This put them in a position to define and assess the technical problems fin relation to the political level and the media. How this position was capitalised is central to our analysis of the securitisation process. Also, the universally observed and locally present, problem of military in-fighting—'the battle of the branches'—relates to this analytical aspect. What difference did it make that the controversies inside the military at times were severe, and that public (media-oriented) strategies were sometimes used to gain the upper hand in these disputes?

Both with regard to societal salience and threat framing, media seems to be in the dead centre of the developments that securitised the submarine problem. News coverage first temporarily peaked with the 'whiskey-incident,' and then reached the level it would maintain for several years with the Hårsfjärden incident. This extreme media attention was certainly reflected in public opinion polls, and the pressure on politicians and military officers alike was mounting.

The scope and process of attaining societal salience for the submarine issue is researched in order to get an idea of how the media agenda is manipulated, and what intentional and unintentional forces are moving it. A role theory approach of agenda setting to this problem would suggest that resources for agenda-setting towards the media could shift substantially in case of a crisis or a very dramatic event. Policy-makers with greater social power can be sidestepped in rapidly unfolding events to the benefit of lower social power officials, perceived to be closer to the events and thus more informed of the situation (Berkowitz, 1992, p. 98 f). In bureaucratic settings this tendency is reinforced (Graber, 1984).

Another justifiable question in this context is how media organisations respond to different strategies of damage control that bureaucrats or politicians might instigate once a credibility issue has arisen. One such strategy is 'agenda-denial', the act of refusing to address or recognise a problem that other actors are pushing for a position on the formal decision-making agenda (Cobb and Ross, 1997). The press is central in this respect, sometimes acting as the referee, ultimately deciding the credibility of the opposing claims. This process is a version of what Bovens and 't Hart (1996) has labelled the 'construction of political fiascos,' where media is the main player and a number of defensive techniques can be distinguished. In our setting, this kind of disputes repeatedly came to the fore, forcing official policy representatives to apply techniques of agenda denial and to bid for time in situations of legitimacy challenges.

The Framing of Three Incidents. Stage I: Utö-Huvudskär

The Swedish ordeal with over ten years of repeated submarine intrusion started, in political perception if not in broader public, on 18 September 1980. An unidentified underwater indication was made in the outskirts of the Stockholm archipelago during exercises between Swedish submarine forces and the coastal navy. A second, similar, indication was made on 23 September. A massive naval operation escalated over the following week, but the vessel slipped away. So far, the events did not cause much concern. But the indications returned. This time further inside the archipelago, outside Huvudskär. The apparent consistency in this behaviour, to remain in Swedish waters despite discovery marked in the eyes of the operative personnel something qualitatively different from the usually cautious behaviour of foreign underwater vessels in the contact with Swedish navy close to, or sometimes within, Swedish waters. The hunt lasted for an additional 12 days, before the coastal navy had to admit its failure to effectively counter the intrusions that had occurred.

This incident marked something new in the field of peacetime border control. This is illustrated by the out-of-the-ordinary remarks of the minister of defence, Erik Krönmark, who demanded of the defence staff 'a more active performance' (Diary of Lennart Ljung, 24 September 1980). The call was made from several actors, in politics and the media, to deal with the problem decisively.

Setting the Stage

1980 was a year of intense defence debate, primarily fuelled by the Soviet invasion of Afghanistan during the last weeks of 1979. The apparent anomaly of defence budget cuts in the midst of a renewed cold war led several defence analysts and part of the national media corps to advocate rearmament of the Swedish defence. Young and coming MP for the Moderate party, Carl Bildt, asked rhetorically 'What Conclusion Should Sweden Draw?' in a June article in *Svenska Dagbladet*. He argued that The Swedish defence needed considerable reinforcements (SvD, 12 June 1980, p. 4).

This line of argument was pervasive as superpower relations worsened, and the problems within the Swedish defence structure had worsened. The matter was brought further into focus by the unstable parliamentary situations. The parliamentary period 1979-82 is known as the 'lottery parliament' from the fact that the two parliamentary blocs were equally divided and that the luck of the draw had to decide issues on the floor.

Emphasising the 'weak defence' debate, a Foreign Ministry memo outlining foreign government assessments of Swedish defence capabilities was leaked in July of 1980. The memo was intended for the ministers of defence, foreign affairs, foreign aid and trade. It reflected diplomatic dialogue with West Germany, USA, Finland and the United Kingdom, and the message was one of worries in these capitols over the state of the Swedish defence. The Foreign Ministry warned of consequences for the security balance of northern Europe if the credibility of the Swedish defence deteriorated further (DN, 21 March 1981).

The Nationality Genie Escapes its Lamp

On September 25, navy sources leaked the story to morning daily *Svenska Dagbladet*, that at least on one occasion had an intruding submarine been identified as Soviet. The defence staff or the Foreign Ministry did not officially confirm the information, but permanent secretary to the Foreign Ministry 'admits that the nationality [of the intruding vessel] is known, but wants the operation to be over before deciding whether to issue a protest to the embassy in question.' This is harsh diplomatic language. To further mark the gravity of what had happened, the commanding officer of the hunt stated that 'it is, at this point, impossible to say what is the intent of this submarine. I have never experienced such a prolonged incident.' (SvD, 25 September 1980, p. 13.) The Eastern military area Commander, General Eklund, made another unprecedented remark in the same news article:

> We are considering bringing up helicopters from the West Coast to finally get a hold of this submarine. This time it is really acting audaciously and it is therefore important for our defence to be able to deter it. A submarine is a perfect platform for intelligence activities and there are sensitive military installations in these waters. I also believe it is important to emphasise the fact

that both NATO and the Warsaw pact are violating our borders. Accordingly we need a satisfying preparedness along all of the Swedish borders. (SvD, 25 September 1980, p. 13.)

These statements are followed by an appeal, by the reporter, to increase the capacity for simultaneous submarine hunts, and a reminder that decisions on these matters 'soon comes before the minister of defence, Eric Krönmark.' Taken together, the remarks and the reporter's sympathetic appeal are attempts to push the issue up the security agenda and to allocate more resources to the coastal navy.

On 26 September, an editorial in *Svenska Dagbladet* asks 'Why is there a submarine continuously violating Swedish waters from the—repeatedly self-stated—peace-loving Soviet union, far into Swedish territorial waters? And why is it that the submarines just happen to be discovered close to Swedish defence installations as secret naval exercises are underway?' The appeal for additional resources is renewed in clearer language and the minister of defence is told to seriously consider the coordination of the navy and air force helicopters for future in submarine hunts. 'The weakening of the navy cannot be allowed to continue' (SvD, 26 September 1980, p. 1).

In SvD, Navy officers had found a true ally in their ambition to bolster their own view. SvD's editorial can be compared with earlier statements made in the Navy's own journal *Marinnytt*. In a 1979 issue, a review article is headlined 'Is the Navy becoming the weak link in Sweden's defence?' It cites a debate article in a southern Sweden local daily by a coast artillery officer: 'for the navy, the situation is serious. [T]he demand for preparedness in naval operations even in peacetime has increased. Simultaneously, a forceful strengthening of the eastern Baltic Sea naval forces has been undertaken' (*Marinnytt*, 1979, No. 4, p. 1; cf. *Marinnytt*, 1980, No. 2, p. 3). A list of the cutbacks in naval capacity is presented and these quotes are essentially left uncommented.

'Securityness' at Issue

The quoted articles were the first attempts from parts of the navy to push neglected naval problems on the defence policy agenda. An agenda that through the planned development of a new domestically engineered fighter aircraft (JAS Gripen) and reinforcements to the army seemed to marginalise the entire naval branch—something that went against the development in most surrounding states. Submarine hunts would provide the vehicle to do the job (SvD, 7 October 1980, p. 6).

Another theme that would prove pervasive surfaced on October 5. A news article in SvD was entitled: 'Defence Staff vs. Marine Staff: Internal Disagreement on the Submarine Hunt' (SvD, 5 October 1980, p. 6). The article reveals that the marine staff claims to have identified the nationality of the submarine, while the central defence leadership in the defence staff discredits their evidence. This illuminates a wish to force the notorious genie back into the lamp after its release in the widespread comments on nationality by marine authorities.

Yet another concern raised by the incident was the implementation of international law—an issue that would continue to be controversial and that had clear implications for the 'securityness' of the submarine problem. On the one hand, as the SC initially pointed out, the navy was required to reject a surfaced submarine rather than detain it. On the other hand the increased pressure applied by the political leadership and the media made this option increasingly embarrassing. Consequently, the 'what if'-issue became a major concern for the SC while the political level was divided on it and avoided it as best they could (Diary of Lennart Ljung, 25 and 27 September 1980).

Salience and Framing

The hunt in Utö/Huvudskär was the first one to be taken seriously by Swedish media. It is apparent that what was reported was decided by the press relations department at the defence staff, and by more or less authorised comments by operative commanders. The information regarding the incident were under control of the authorities, and that the comments on the funding situation for the navy were considered within the limits of good taste. The salience of the submarine threat was modest, and the incident never quite became 'front page news' (the two major morning dailies had short texts on their front pages).

Also with regard to framing, the Utö hunt was interpreted hesitantly. The inability to monitor Swedish territory was considered worrisome, but no public debates can be found regarding the motifs behind the violations. Moreover, there was no debate on the commonality of violations, an issue that would later heat up the perceived severity of submarine hunts. The comments by Commander Eklund on the appropriateness of submarines as intelligence platforms can be seen as a rare declaration of threat framing. What were present in the aftermath of the incident were the pressing realities of the Cold War that would later be recalled in assessing the seriousness of the submarine threat.

Stage II: Whiskey-on-the-Rocks

The international crisis triggered by the grounding of the U137 on 27 October 1981, was an attention grabber. As national and international media realised the volatility of the situation for the small neutral, and knowing the sensitivity of the eastern superpower in matters of naval weapon systems, the media organisations pilgrimaged to the site of the grounding. The hotels in the small harbour town Karlskrona where crammed with reporters only two days into the crisis. Everybody involved, including Soviet decision-makers, could feel the pressure mounting, as more eyes turned to the little bay Gåsefjärden in the southern Swedish archipelago (Hellberg and Jörle, 1984). From a submarine violation salience perspective, this was the touchdown—it was widely represented as a deliberate intrusion in the most important military safe zone along the Swedish coast.[5]

In framing the problem that faced Swedish policy-makers on the morning of October 28, the media immediately echoed the official harsh stance and suspicious attitude towards the intentions of the leadership of the submarine called U137. SvD opened its editorial on 29 October with a legal expression: 'The statement of the defendant does not deserve credit'

(SvD, 29 October 1981, p. 2). SvD also quoted the first Swedish officer who came onboard the vessel, Karl Andersson as saying: 'It is technically impossible to misnavigate that far into the Swedish archipelago.'[6] It was also clearly stated that the Swedish navy had orders to stop any attempt of rescuing the submarine. The Soviet ambassador was promptly called to the Swedish Foreign Ministry where he received a sharp protest. The next day, the SC stated that he cancelled a trip he was scheduled to make to the Soviet Union, claiming 'inappropriate timing.' (SvD, 30 October 1981, p. 1) It became obvious that Swedish authorities would not play down the incident in order to appease the Soviets.

Raising the Stakes—Whiskey Goes Nuclear

When on Thursday the 5th of November, it was announced that the submarine carried nuclear arms underwater intrusions became a prioritised security issue. A number of cognitive factors contributed to that impression. Consider first the reaction of the SC on October 28 in learning of the stranded submarine; he immediately decided to detain the vessel. This decision, which has not widely been questioned retrospectively, was by no means obvious. In fact it is possible to argue that had not the prehistory of violations (most prominently Utö) constituted the most readily available cognitive scheme a major alternative would have been to help the submarine off the rock and expel it. At the time, some international law experts in the Foreign Ministry favoured this alternative. However, the political dynamics forced that view into the background as detainment advocates where given exclusive access to the government level (Sundelius and Stern, 1992; Sundelius, Stern and Bynander, 1997).

The decision to test the submarine for weapon grade radioactivity was made ad hoc and without reaching the political level. The initiative came from an expert group from the Defence Research Establishment (FOA) and was cleared by the SC. The conditions were to keep the operation discrete, and to give the SC the possibility to cover up whatever would be the findings. As the preliminary results came back positive, however, the political dynamics again took priority and the cabinet had to act on the new information. The Prime Minister shared this information with the media as he announced that the submarine was to be released on 5 November (Sundelius, Stern & Bynander, 1997).

One concern that strongly affected the dynamics of securitisation in the submarine issue was the asymmetry of the strategic situation. As many small states could witness, taking on a superpower could prove extremely costly (North Vietnam, Afghanistan, Hungary). The Swedish tactics had consisted of balancing a strong stance on national defence with cordial relations bilaterally. When it became obvious that Whiskey-on-the-Rocks meant a considerable humiliation for the Soviet Union, the Swedish strategy was to expose the events as much as possible. International media became the main weapon in this war of words. The asymmetry in force was to be balanced in world opinion as a restriction on aggression. From a securitisation perspective, this meant an emphasis on Sweden as the western outpost against the east, in need of a strong defence and recognition of its neutrality status (Stern and Sundelius, 1992).

The peaceful and victorious resolution of the crisis was reassuring to the Swedish leadership. 'David beating Goliath' became a prominent theme in the media after the acute phase of the crisis was over. Then minister for Foreign Affairs, Ola Ullsten, stated years later 'taken together, from the perspective of the Swedish public, U137 never turned into a crisis' (Stefenson, 1993).

Salience and Framing

Seen as an isolated incident, the Whiskey-on-the-Rocks can only be compared to the greatest media stories of the half-century, such as the assassination of Olof Palme (see Stern and Hansén, this volume), and the sinking of the M/S Estonia. What this study needs to consider, however, is whether this enormous coverage touched on the submarine threat, or if it merely played on the relations towards the Soviet Union? Before the crisis commenced, several allusions to the commonality of intrusions and Swedish inability to properly defend its borders had been made. However, during the incident, comparisons to other submarine incidents or the submarine threat as a whole were rare, sweeping and never explicitly related to the submarine defence capacity of the Swedish navy. In fact, many editorials expressed the reassuring view that violations now should cease to occur—that the Soviet navy for the time being had suffered enough embarrassment and probably would think twice before sending submarines into the Swedish archipelago.[7] A realisation of the submarine threat required a manifestation of a concrete external pressure (U137) as well as evidence of a Swedish impotence in countering that pressure. In the public relief that the incident had had a peaceful resolution, and the widespread interpretations of the outcome as a Swedish 'victory' the second part of that equation did not protrude in the debate, even though some warnings were voiced with regard to future violations.[8]

Stage III: Hårsfjärden

The year following Whiskey was one of substantial debate, regarding security policy in general and regarding submarine intrusions in particular. On 30 July 1992, in a period usually with little news, defence Chief of Staff Bengt Schuback was interviewed in *Svenska Dagbladet*. The front page of the paper is headlined: 'Top brass officer on the submarine alerts: Enemy prepares war with Sweden.' The implied intent behind the intrusion by U137 is also referred to: 'some nations are prepared to accept the risks of undertaking war preparations on other nation's territories. This is apparent from the submarine incident in Karlskrona.' (SvD, 30 July 1982, pp. 1 and 6). These statements are supported by editorials in *Svenska Dagbladet*, and a statement by Moderate party defence expert Carl Bildt (Ibid.).

When Air Force Chief Sven-Olof Olsson, played down the significance of violations, the tensions within the defence were exposed again. The Chief of the Marine, Per Rudberg, counters Olsson's statement and also criticises the SC, saying '[a]ll the submarine violations, and the thought of what they might be doing prior to discovery, give me nightmares. One of the reasons for the poor results of the hunts is the invasion defence composition of the armed forces that the SC is pushing' (SvD, 3 August 1982, pp. 1 and 6).

The Hårsfjärden incident started with an indication on 29 September 1982 in the heart of the Stockholm archipelago. Helicopters and patrol ships were increasingly dispatched to the site and the hunt escalated and moved southward over the following two days. On October 2, the submarine was located inside the bay of Hårsfjärden—the location of one of Sweden's two main naval bases. The operative assessment was that the submarine was now trapped in the narrow bay, and procedures to safeguard the only navigable exit pass way was rapidly undertaken. During this time, a considerable gathering of media reporters had been building up around the Berga naval academy, adjacent to the bay (Bynander, 1998).

A decision was made in consultations between the newly appointed Chief of Staff, the naval base Commander, and the Press Officer to create a media centre in the naval academy gymnasium in order to contain media and not have them all over the area of operations. That night the gates were opened and media personnel were rapidly installed in the new press centre.[9] At the site of the submarine chase, no results were reached despite a massive escalation of the efforts. Depth charges, mines and other weapon systems were used at an unprecedented rate, closer to the presumed target than the interpretation of the rules had allowed for earlier. The lack of results was obvious to everyone, especially the media representatives that now had been installed on bleachers at the shore, overlooking the operations.

Politically, Sweden was in a period of transition. The new Palme cabinet, after being out of power for six years, was reclaiming the helm on September 7. Before that time, the interim liberal-liberal coalition was very reluctant to do anything about the developments at Hårsfjärden. A decisional void was created in which the SC had to ad lib any action out of the ordinary. On the explicit urging of the SC, the Cabinet prepared a resolution for the event that the navy would be able to surface the vessel (Diary of Lennart Ljung, 5 October 1982). The Palme cabinet was also preparing a chock devaluation of the Swedish Krona that occupied most of the Cabinet members' time.

This was the almost chaotic environment in which the Hårsfjärden submarine hunt took place. Decisional paralysis on the political level, and great difficulties in handling the media on the military leadership level, led to a deterioration of the decision-making process. In the midst of this, clear attempts at securitisation were made. These attempts were made within the context of strong organisational tension, militarily and politically.

Battle of the Branches

A fundamental controversy within the military leadership had become apparent as the submarine threat excelled on the security agenda. The Swedish naval forces were at the outset of the incident pattern already in a phase of rapid downgrading and modernisation, most significantly manifested by the deactivation of its three destroyers. The modernisation meant that helicopters came into focus (Agrell, 1984, p. 35; Bynander, 1998).

Helicopters and smaller vessels seemed more cost-efficient, creating a 'smaller but sharper' Swedish defence. However, as the inner water submarine intrusions started to show a more persistent pattern of prolonged operations, closer to the major naval bases, some of these arguments seemed less valid. By the time the helicopters arrived to the site, the indication had ceased, whereupon the former would burn large amount of fuel trying to regain contact. This problem was to complicate virtually all of the operations during the 1980s.

The restructuring resulted in bureaucratic rivalry within the defence staff. It offered good arguments for a multitude of costly shifts into expensive spending on new and 'vital' weapon systems, especially for the navy. However, a majority of the naval experts thought otherwise, for example the Chief of Staff (Diary of Lennart Ljung, 12 October 1982; Interview, Adm. Bror Stefenson). It is important to note that the opinions in these matters differed strongly even within the defence staff, and the rift was clearly between navy personnel and the other two branches. A vivid example of this is the navy position stated by Adm. Stefenson: 'as a submariner I was not as convinced [as Ljung] that stationary equipment would help' (Interview, Adm. Bror Stefenson). Though it was a technical issue it revealed bureaucratic rivalry.

A diversity of messages was communicated to the press concerning the severity of the threat, the conduct of the navy, the security interests at stake, etc. (DN, 1-14 October 1982; SvD, 1-14 October 1982). Not only did politicians and the public get a scattered picture of the events, they did not know what to think of the means necessary to improve the situation, or indeed what the reasonable ambitions of submarine defence were. In the words of Ljung:

> This is naturally hard to explain to the Swedish public—that we cannot be in control of every square meter of the Swedish territorial water. In saying that, one has to admit that it is pitiful that the marine has not been willing to devote more interest or funds to the surveillance system. The marine attitude to the submarine defence issue has been completely fixed to the chances and opportunities to obtain additional helicopters. The truth of the matter is that the helicopters can be used at the earliest when the existence of the submarine in a wider area has been established. And this takes other technical equipment than helicopters. The Chief of the Marine and his aids for tactical reasons have however, denied this so far (The Diary of Lennart Ljung, Oct. 28, 1982).

Arguably, the different branches saw each other as the true rivals regarding budget issues, and that the defence purse was virtually the same regardless of the perceived security threat. This would explain the propensity to disregard the fact that public statements such as these hurt the defence on the whole.

This environment increased the pressure on the mid-level officers, who generally tried to make their organisation and personnel look good without creating the impression that their capacities were quite sufficient for their mission. It is natural to engage in placing the blame when failure seems likely (Bovens and 't Hart, 1996). Furthermore, this phenomenon strikes the defence in its weakest spot—media management. With an incoherent organisational response to operational events, the role of the leadership becomes extremely difficult. Failure is certainly demoralising, as is the knowledge that you do not get the full picture of what is happening.

The process described can be labelled: 'controlled securitisation gone wrong.' The navy strived for a higher priority for its core missions, using peacetime submarine intrusions as a concrete vehicle in this project. Securitisation as a conscious exercise is risky business, it seems, since other dynamics—fuelled by the media, and political conflicts—can kick in. Coming to grips with the submarine defence problems and creating a picture of resolute and responsible actions were demanding tasks that were never really completed.

Salience and Framing

The Hårsfjärden submarine hunt was the missing ingredient in the securitisation of the submarine threat. It completed the equation by putting the spotlight on the Swedish inability to counter grave violations, and it underscored a pattern to the intrusions. Whiskey had made clear what the threat might be—submarines on Swedish territory carrying nuclear arms. The failure in Hårsfjärden uncovered the difficulties in archipelago submarine defence, and escalated the feeling of vulnerability that was fuelled by the media. The Submarine Defence Commission legitimised the media interpretations of the situation, and further claimed the intruders to originate from the Soviet Union. Moreover, it firmly rooted the problem among the prioritised national security issues. Consequently, it was the combination of the two highly salient incidents that finalised the submarine threat as a securitised problem by introducing both a concrete sense of what the threat was and the realisation that the Swedish navy might not be able to counter it.

Conclusions

The analysis has revealed a process of securitisation, generated by the sequencing of previous, mostly unresolved, experiences of threat and uncertainty. We are dealing with a rather complex chain of events of which decision-makers and operative personnel had to make sense under severe media pressure and difficult operative conditions. The initial precautions that submarine defence is a tricky thing and should be handled with low expectations went largely unheeded and were silenced by the massive public demands for results.

As in other cases of securitisation under pressure, the submarine threat seemed to acquire a 'life of its own.' The political dynamics of the widely publicised incidents implied a strong incentive for the actors involved to move policy towards a public image of decisiveness and increased efficiency, operationally and diplomatically. Displaying a united political front remained a priority in the face of escalating pressure from the media and the public. The picture, however, is devious because of the ambiguity of the problem and the advocacy that so clearly took place. The claim put forth in the introduction to this book, that threat politics involves the framing and salience making of influential actors is central to understanding the growth of the submarine threat.

This argument should not be confused with the partisan claim that the navy invented its own 'budget submarines,' knowingly devised to deceive the public and further the navy's position in the budget negotiations vis-à-vis the other branches of the defence. A more reasonable interpretation is that the navy furthered a threat frame that it had publicly harboured for decades—that there was a systematic pattern of underwater intrusions of Swedish waters that represented a real military threat under conditions of increased tension in the region. The fact that the realisation of this threat contained budgetary opportunities probably constituted a 'bonus effect' that was too sweet to remain unattended.

Moreover, the dilemma of receiving political pressure in an area so dependent on technological and operative factors caused the political leadership to sit back and do nothing for long periods (most notably during the Hårsfjärden incident). The other preferred strategy was to simply react to public and military demands and temporarily increase the funding of submarine defence capabilities. Importantly, the 'epistemic community' (Haas, 1992) of navy officers and experts had the privilege of framing the threats. That the politicians were bound by what these experts told them was perceived for instance by Ingvar Carlsson, who succeeded Palme as Prime Minister. In the words of Carlsson (1999): 'We had no one else to listen to but the navy officers.'

Our assessments of the salience and level of threat framing after each of the three incidents gives the impression of a three-step process. Whereas the Utö/Huvudskär incident spread unease over Swedish submarine defence capabilities within the Stockholm security elites, the crucial events came later. Whiskey-on-the-rocks put submarine intrusions on the media agenda, creating an extreme level of salience for a military threat under comparatively peaceful conditions, and setting the stage for the public fiasco one year later. Hårsfjärden, the pièce de résistance, provided credible grounds for the argument that there is a systematic activity of foreign underwater intrusions, and that the Swedish capabilities for countering it are insufficient.

Although it is clear that the main mode of political behaviour was adaptive, this picture needs elaboration. The political level was acting under a great level of uncertainty. The cross-pressure of media and events in the archipelagos forced the decision-makers under the mercy of the area experts, the shady interpretation of evidence from sonar equipment and sea floor investigations. Simultaneously, they were playing their game on two different levels—domestic demands for a strong stance against the Soviet Union needed mitigation and a touch of diplomatic caution not facilitated by the submarine commissions report or public statements by the securitisation agents. In the intersection between domestic and foreign policy all actors but the two governments were secondary, and therefore less liable to take this intermediate view. In fact, the intermediate logic was constantly under suspicion of being less than caring for the 'national interest.'[10]

Politically, the handling of this reorientation was troublesome. For the social democratic party in general and for Palme in particular, this was a time for initiatives aimed at relieving tension between the superpowers, not for picking this David against Goliath fight. Much evidence suggests that this troublesome rift between diplomatic ambitions and political 'realities' caused lasting frustration for the policy-making elites, especially after the period here studied.

Actors involved in a securitisation process regularly find themselves in situations of great uncertainty. The discrepancies between perceived 'objective' threat evaluation and the dynamics of organisational interests in the securityness of threats produces modes of decision-making other than the traditional strategic one. This has been clear throughout this study, which has shown policy elites stuck with a problem they did not predict, battling political consequences often disproportional to the operative difficulties.

Notes

1 Examples of such issues are the war in Afghanistan whose logic changed after 1991, the conflict in the Middle East, U.S.-Cuban relations, and the position of 'rouge states' such as North Korea.
2 Wilhelm Agrell, in his 1985 study of the submarine problem, states: 'Before October of 1981 there is no discernable debate as to the purpose of the intrusions. The 'normal procedures' that had been developed during the 1960s and 1970s in the Baltic Sea area was generally considered—also in military circles—unproblematic. Incidents could arise from carelessness, accident and the will to 'test' preparedness, but all this was seen as security policy routine procedure, and not containing serious risk during peacetime' (Agrell, 1985).
3 Stone (1997).
4 Adler (1997). As Michael Focault puts it: '...as psychoanalysis has shown, discourse is not simply that which manifests (or hides) desire—it is also the object of desire; and since, as history constantly teaches us, discourse is not simply that which translates struggles or systems of domination, but is the thing for which and by which there is struggle, discourse is the power which is to be seized.' Foucault (1984).
5 Lately, this has been a point of contention (Bergström and Åmark, 1999). It is clear that the Supreme Commander settled the issue for the duration of the crisis, when he ordered detainment on October 28 (Stern and Sundelius, 1992).
6 Karl Andersson has later restated his view on this and is now a firm believer of the Soviet explanation (SvD, 20 October 1981, p. 6; Bergström and Åmark, 1999, p. 104).
7 *Svenska Dagbladet*, 7 November 1981; *Dagens Nyheter*, 8 November 1981.
8 A large number of articles in *Dagens Nyheter* and *Svenska Dagbladet* expressed fears that the violation pattern would not change with this incident, yet many editorials seemed to recommend a cautious approach to this—to 'wait and see.' See for example *Dagens Nyheter*, 7-8 and 11 November 1981; *Svenska Dagbladet*, 7, 11-13 and 27 November 1981.
9 This decision is controversial. The Chief of Staff, Bror Stefenson was under the impression that the issue was put on hold for the next morning. When heard of the establishment of center and the demands for information that was building there, he was surprised (Interview with Bror Stefenson).
10 Several news stories (as we have seen) were skeptical towards any secret negotiations with the Soviet side, and the view that any dealings with the soviets should be in the open strongly restrained both governments.

7 Securitising IT
JOHAN ERIKSSON

The revolutionary development of information technology (IT) is increasingly considered as one of the most salient concerns in contemporary social and political discourse (Castells, 2000). In the late 1990s, Sweden was internationally recognised as a leading IT society. In 2000 about seventy percent of Swedish households had computers, and almost as many regularly used the Internet (SCB, 2001). Sixty percent of the Swedish population had mobile phones. It was expected that within a few years Sweden would have the most developed broadband network in the world. Stockholm was seen as one of the booming IT capitols of Europe, attracting financial investments and IT professionals from all over the world. Several international reports and investigations held that Sweden was at the forefront of IT development. The previous pessimism about the declining Swedish welfare state and the fallback of Sweden in global economic competition faded away, as the 'new economy' emerged, and with it new hopes and dreams.

Though the optimistic scenarios and hopes invested in the development of IT prevail, warnings and fears have accompanied it, as is often the case with new technologies implying structural change. In this study, however, focus is not on the much-debated 'dotcom' death of overrated IT firms, but rather on IT as a source of security threats. In the case of IT, it is noteworthy that decision-makers have been aware of the vulnerability of computer systems since the first computers were constructed. But it was not until the 1990s that IT got onto the agenda as a source of security policy threats.

Why was IT securitised? Why did it so rapidly get a top position on the security agenda? In answering these questions, the framework presented in the introductory chapter will be applied. That is, after the securitisation of IT has been described, the analysis will consider: What were the framing agents behind this development—including policy networks and international policy diffusion? What are the characteristics of IT as an object of securitisation—is it about events, structural conditions, or hostile agents—and in what ways have these factors contributed to the securitisation of IT? What are the frame characteristics of the securitisation of IT? What patterns of continuity and change can be discerned with regard to the securitisation of IT?

The swiftness of the securitisation of IT, and its considerable political impact, makes it a particularly fruitful case for analysing threat politics— how and why some threat images but not others take on societal salience. Importantly, the framing of IT as a security problem is observed as a case of 'securitisation,' as defined by the Copenhagen school of security studies (see the introductory chapter). This implies specific connotations that are not applicable to every thinkable security concept: that the issue is perceived as an existential threat to the core values of a collective unit, particularly the sovereignty and identity of a state (Buzan, Wæver and de Wilde, 1998, ch. 2; Wæver, 1995; Eriksson, 2000). In addition, it is argued that this conception legitimates the use of extraordinary measures such as secrecy or the use of violence. Hence, securitisation implies moving the issue into a rather traditional military-bureaucratic security policy realm, even if the issue itself is conceived of as a non-military threat. It will be argued that that though 'IT security' represents a widening of the security concept beyond the traditional military focus, the policy establishment in which this issue has been framed and pushed onto the agenda is basically the same as for the traditional Cold War threats. This observation sheds light on bureaucratic tenacity and adaptability. In addition, this case considers aspects of security agenda setting that previously has been neglected, especially international diffusion of images.

IT on the Security Agenda

In 1996 IT appeared as a security problem on the government's agenda—as a separate issue in the very first Swedish IT bill, as well as in a defence bill proper (Government of Sweden, 1996a, 1996b). Though it was presented as something entirely new on the agenda, a governmental commission noted already in 1978 that the computerised society had become unacceptably vulnerable, which required immediate countermeasures (Karlsson and Sturesson, 1995, p. 221). However, not much happened at this time, and the issue soon faded away from the security agenda, being squeezed out by the new Cold War of the early 1980s and the reemergence of 'hard' military threats, including the 'submarine threat' (see Bynander's contribution to this volume).

Since the mid 1990s, the government has increasingly paid attention to and dramatised IT as a security problem, as observed in defence bills and reports from the Defence Commission—a policy preparatory body with members from the political parties represented in the national parliament (Government of Sweden, 1996a, p. 91; 1999a, 1999b; Defence Commission of Sweden, 1996, p. 35; 1999, 2000, 2001). Now the issue was framed in different ways, but primarily under the title of 'information warfare' (IW) and with concerns for the 'vulnerability of computerised systems' of societal importance. The government noted that the revolutionary development of IT implies on the one hand the emergence of new means of warfare, including 'hacking,' virus attacks, electronic espionage, deception etc., and, on the other hand, a broader range of potentially hostile actors, including states as well as countless non-state actors, such as terrorists and criminal organisations that can take advantage of the increased vulnerability resulting from the dependency on IT. The government decided that an interdepartmental working group—including both civil and military expertise—was to be set up with the task of monitoring and coordinating IT security and 'information warfare' (Government of Sweden, 1996a, 1999a, 1999b; Defence Commission of Sweden, 1999, 2000).

The government considered the 'IT revolution' as a major determinant for the development of 'information warfare' as a new security threat. However, though the vulnerability of computerised information systems was seen as particularly important, 'information warfare' was seen as covering much more than merely 'IT security.' It was noted that governmental analyses of 'information warfare' demanded expertise not only on IT, but also security policy, intelligence service, criminality, and psychological warfare (Government of Sweden, 1996a, p. 91; Government of Sweden, 1999a, p. 145).

In a number of reports and policy documents, it was noted that the concept of 'information warfare' was very difficult to define (Government of Sweden, 1999a, p. 145). If there was any consensus about meaning of it, it was that it was a very broad concept, incorporating a great variety of perceived threats and risks related to the use and abuse of information. Various governmental actors have suggested a general definition, including the Ministry of Defence, the National Defence College, and the Agency of Civil Emergency Planning. These definitions emphasise that 'information warfare' is both offensive and defensive, and more specifically about 'activities aimed at getting access to, destroying or delaying other actors' information, and countermeasures for preventing such attempts' (Working Group on Information Warfare, 1997, pp. 8, 61).

It is noteworthy that the frame 'information warfare' (IW) is being replaced by 'information operations' (IO). Of this an instance is how the interdepartmental Working Group on Information Warfare (AgIW) recently changed the latter part of its name to Information Operations (AgIO). With direct reference to the debate in the U.S., the National Defence College (1999, p. 59) argues that the term IO is more 'neutral' than IW. In addition, the Government holds that IO incorporates a broader variety of threats and risks. However, the explicit definition of 'information operations' is basically the same as that of 'information warfare' (National Defence College, 1999, p. 61). Nevertheless, in contrast to 'information warfare,' the frame 'information operations' does not necessarily have the same connotations of hostility, threat and war. Speaking about something as 'warfare' is much more constraining and aggressive than 'operations' might be. Moreover, 'warfare' is a military term, thus indicating a responsibility for the military defence. 'Operations,' on the other hand, is not limited to this categorisation, and is more easily defined as a responsibility for civil administrations.

That the governmental apparatus for managing IT security and 'information warfare' is yet to be settled indicates that a bureaucratic turf battle is going on. What authorities are to be responsible for this 'new' and allegedly growing 'security threat'? The concern for finding institutional solutions has been discussed in a report by the IT firm Mandator (Lindén, Posacki and Wallström, 1999), and has been addressed by the National Defence College (1999, pp. 47-49), and the Defence Commission:

> *Threats against the information society*
> The Defence Commission emphasises the need for continued and deeper work on issues concerning protection against information operations and IT-security. Society's vulnerability in this respect is of great importance to security policy. An attack could be undertaken, for example, by a criminal actor, some individual or organisation with political motives or by a state or an actor supported by a state, something that makes the question of who should handle an acute threat even more difficult. An integrated grasp of this new area is needed and responsibility at authority level must be defined and established very soon (Defence Commission of Sweden, 1999, p. 9).

At this time of writing, however, the notions of IW and IO were used simultaneously, often interchangeably. In addition, a few other terms were also introduced, though not to the same extent as IW and IO, such as 'critical infrastructure protection' and 'information assessment.'

Originally mentioned as a subheading under the title of 'command and control'—often presented last in reports and defence bills—the issue is later on treated in separate chapters presented earlier in the documents. In 1999, 'information warfare' was discussed for the first time under a separate subheading in the summary of a defence bill—a sign of the increasing salience of the issue (Government of Sweden, 1999b). Furthermore, the government and the Defence Commission have argued repeatedly that 'information warfare,' 'information operations' and 'IT related threats' are becoming more and more important security threats, requiring significant and immediate countermeasures. (Government of Sweden, 1999b, pp. 186-191; 1999a, pp. 145-148; 1998, pp. 67-69; 2001; Defence Commission of Sweden, 1999a, pp. 101-103; 1999b, pp. 93-100; 2001).

Who Made IT a Security Problem?

Before IT got onto the government's agenda as a source of insecurity, a broad consensus on the salience of the issue emerged among several institutions within and beyond the traditional security policy realm. An interesting observation is that the framing of IT as a security problem simultaneously emerged from separate policy realms. On the one hand, the Ministry of Communication, the Government's IT Commission, the National Police Administration (including the security police), the Agency for Administrative Development, and the Business Delegation on Security raised concerns about the vulnerability of IT systems, electronic crimes, and 'hackers'—but from a strictly civilian viewpoint. These themes were also increasingly addressed in the media. On the other hand, the Ministry of Defence, the Agency of Psychological Defence, the Defence School, the Agency of Civil Emergency Planning, and the Defence Research Establishment were all deeply concerned about IT as a source of potential *security policy* threats. A few years before the issue was put on the agenda, it was discussed in seminars and conferences with participants from both policy areas, and several reports were presented—a development that has intensified since then (Friman, Sjöstedt and Wik, 1996; National Defence College of Sweden, 1999). The analyses and suggestions provided by the various commissions have had a notable impact in the defence bills, increasingly so as time has passed by.

Governmental experts and analysts working in the military-bureaucratic security establishment have been highly influential in putting the issue onto the agenda. This observation stands in contrast to the argument made by John Kingdon (1995), who argues that the 'policy primeval soup' may be influential in formulating policy options, but less so in putting problems on the agenda. On the other hand, studies of 'epistemic communities' (Haas, 1992) show that these 'knowledge elites' can be very influential also in formulating problems. What the securitisation of IT demonstrates is that after the end of the Cold War a major reorientation of security policy was initiated throughout Europe and the former Cold War powers. Suddenly the old security problems declined, and the government demanded analysis not only of policy proposals, but also above all of the emerging and largely unknown security landscape. Instead of monitoring well-known problems, such as counting Soviet tanks and navy vessels, experts and analysts were asked to *find out* what were the security problems in this new situation. Suddenly the government turned to advisors, specialists, analysts and researchers not only for getting advice on policy alternatives, but also for identifying new challenges and problems.

Decision-makers and their advisors went looking for new problems to put on their suddenly empty threat agendas. Not surprisingly, the government set up special units that were assigned the task of analysing these 'new' threats. This situation gave experts and analysts a new freedom and opportunity to formulate and even construct 'new' threats they considered being of vital importance for national security. With this observation in mind, there is reason to elaborate Kingdon's agenda setting theory, and emphasise the agenda setting options that can be seized by governmental policy analysts and experts, given that a major policy window is opened, such as that represented by the end of the Cold War (Eriksson, 2000).

From the beginning in the mid 1990s, the issue has been treated as a cross-sectoral security problem. As the process has continued, however, the traditional security establishment has seized a dominant position in the securitisation of IT. Information security is now considered belonging to the realm of defence policy, and thus the Ministry of Defence. Yet this includes the Agency of Civil Emergency Planning, which is responsible for coordinating 'civil' IT security. The interdepartmental Working Group on Information Operations (AgIO) consists of participants from the Ministry of Defence, the Military Headquarters, the National Defence College, the Defence Research Establishment, the Agency of Psychological Defence, the National Police Administration, and the Ministry of Communication. Importantly, however, the AgIO is set up under the auspices of the Ministry of Defence. In addition, the government has decided that the responsibility for research and analysis of this security problem stays with traditional security institutions, that is the Defence Research Establishment, the National Defence College, the Agency of Civil Emergency, and to a lesser extent the Agency of Psychological Defence.

Thus, despite the widening of the security concept, the security establishment remains basically the same (cf. Hart, 1976). The depoliticisation of traditional military threats has resulted in huge cuts in the defence budget and the closing down of more than half of Sweden's regiments and military bases. But the military-bureaucratic security establishment in Stockholm has remained intact. It has demonstrated a remarkable ability to adapt to changing threat images. This corroborates an observation made in security studies: that the ability of framing security effectively is not enough, but that it is also necessary to hold a social or political position from which this can be made—which usually but not necessarily is held by state elites (Buzan, Wæver and de Wilde, 1998, pp. 32-33). Such a position is obviously held by the traditional security establishment.

Furthermore, there is a noteworthy consensus about IT security and information warfare not only among the experts, but also among the political parties. Thus, in terms of agenda setting theory, the circumstances in the 'political stream' have been unusually beneficial (Kingdon 1995; Eriksson, 2000). All parties agree on the importance of analysing and preparing for these allegedly 'new' threats. This is revealed when studying the 'deviant comments,' which party representatives attach to the Defence Commission's reports. There is disagreement and a lot of complaints about Swedish policy towards Russia, NATO, the EU, and the Balkans, but almost nothing about the official policy on IT security and information warfare. On one brief occasion, MP Lennart Rhodin (the Liberal party) argues that countermeasures against information warfare must be coordinated and organised much quicker and more efficiently than he thinks has been the case (Defence Commission of Sweden, 1999, p. 117). But the other political parties represented in the national parliament also regard this as very important parliament (Defence Commission of Sweden, 2000, 2001). The absence of critical voices, i.e. attempts to desecuritise IT, is a most striking observation.

International Policy Diffusion

It will now be argued that the securitisation of IT largely is a result of international policy diffusion. Indeed, it can be argued that international policy diffusion is characteristic of IT policy more generally (Karlsson, 1996; Mörth, 1998), and is not only a feature of IT security.

The literature on policy diffusion has not addressed images of security threats specifically, but has been more focused on solutions (Karvonen, 1981) and issues with positive connotations, such as democracy (Uhlin, 1995). Intuitively, however, the perspective of policy diffusion can also be applied to threat images. International policy diffusion may occur either as a result of attempts to actively influence policy in another polity, or because of imitation. It will be argued that the present case is one of imitation. However, recent contributions to the study of policy diffusion have criticised the somewhat trivial notion of fixed policy packages travelling around the world, arguing instead that ideas are constantly changed and adapted to the demands and circumstances of agents in domestic and international policy networks. This process is referred to as 'translation' and 'editing,' implying an active role for the 'receiver' (Czarniawska and Sevón, 1996; Mörth, 1998). Thus, policy diffusion entails a process of communication involving the travelling of both ideas and organisational change.

Policy diffusion is a neglected aspect in studies of agenda setting as well as in the securitisation literature. Notable exceptions are a few agenda setting studies that deal with foreign policy and international organisations (Durant and Diehl, 1989; Jönsson et al, 1995), and a brief discussion of securitisation in the EU (Buzan, Wæver and de Wilde, 1998). The combined importance of domestic, international and transnational forces are increasingly being emphasised in international relations theory in general, and foreign policy theory in particular (Risse-Kappen, 1994). International actors are probably more important for agenda setting in the security realm than in others (cf. Hermann, 1990, p. 15-16). That security agenda setting is becoming an increasingly international or even supranational activity is most notable within the complex 'European security architecture' of NATO, EU, WEU, OSCE and their institutional offsprings. It is high time the diffusion of ideas, or indeed the importance of international agenda setting in its own right, are incorporated in theorising on agenda setting and securitisation.

IT security, IW and related frames are not something invented in a Swedish context. Swedish experts, analysts and policy-makers have been inspired and influenced by conceptual and organisational development in the U.S. Indeed, it can be argued that this is not specific for information security, but that for a very long time Sweden and most other Western countries have been generally influenced by U.S. military terminology and acronyms. In several Swedish policy documents, bill and reports, there are many direct references to what has been said and done in the U.S. with regard to IT as a security problem (National Defence College, 1999; Swedish Agency of Civil Emergency Planning, 2000, p. 7; Mortensen, 1999). It is repeatedly and explicitly argued that IT security as discourse and practice is of U.S. origin. Though notions of 'electronic warfare' and 'information security' had been floating around among experts and policy-makers for some twenty years, the breakthrough for the framing of 'information warfare' came in the early 1990s (Schwartau, 1996; Molander, Riddile and Wilson, 1996; Agrell, 2000, p. 98). The policy window that made this possible was the U.S. involvement in the 1990-1991 Gulf War against Iraq (Denning, 1999, pp. 3-11; Demchak, 2000; Agrell, 2000, pp. 25, 97).

Swedish experts have described the U.S. development of both *framing* and *organisational* solutions to the perceived threats to information security. The framing of IW, IO etc. is directly imported from the U.S. context. The official definitions are almost exactly the same. In many cases the terms are not even translated into Swedish, even when the discussion is in Swedish. A 1996 directive from the U.S. Office of the Secretary of Defense defines IO as 'Actions taken to affect adversary information and information systems while defending one's own information and information systems' (quoted in Denning, 1999, p. 10; cf. National Defence College, 1999, p. 59-60). Apparently, the official Swedish definition approximates the U.S. definition: 'Activities aimed at getting access to, destroying or delaying other actors' information, and countermeasures for preventing such attempts (Working Group on Information Warfare 1997, pp. 8, 61). Though this definition is being replaced by a joint proposal from the National Defence College and the Agency of Psychological Defence, even the new one approximates the U.S. definition: 'Collective and coordinated activities in peace, crisis and war in support of one's own political or military objectives by affecting or using an adversary's or other foreign actor's information and/or information systems while using or defending one's own information and/or information systems' (National Defence College, 1999, p. 61).

Importantly, this is not a case of conscious policy diffusion on behalf of U.S. agents trying to influence Swedish security thinking. Swedish agents have carried out this policy diffusion, implying that the *active* agent has been the *receiver* rather than the sender. This has occurred partly because of a general awareness and active monitoring of U.S. security thinking, and partly through direct contacts. On several occasions, Swedish experts and policy analysts from the Defence Research Establishment, the Agency of Civil Emergency Planning, and the National Defence College have visited the U.S. and returned with new ideas, concepts and solutions (National Defence College, 1999, p. 7; Swedish Agency of Civil Emergency Planning, 2000, appendix 2, p. 3). That the agents of this policy diffusion are mostly bureaucrats is in accordance with observations made in other studies (Haas, 1992; Mörth, 1998, p. 39; Karvonen, 1981).

Not only the framing but also U.S. *organisational solutions* for managing information security have inspired Swedish policy-makers (cf. National Defence College, 1999, pp. 31-37, Working Group on Information Warfare, 1997, 1998; Lindén, Posacki and Wallström, 1999). Of this an example is how the Swedish government has imitated the U.S. method of testing its own IT security by having so-called 'Red Teams' making controlled attempts to penetrate information systems. The government has set up its own 'Red Teams,' and is planning to imitate a U.S. information warfare exercise called 'Eligible Receiver' (Government of Sweden, 1999a, pp. 145-148).

It is noteworthy that while the Swedish *framing* of IT security is an almost perfect imitation of the U.S. model, imitation of U.S. *organisational solutions* involves a lot more 'translation' and 'editing' (cf. Czarsniawska and Sevón, 1996; Mörth, 1998, p. 41). Though for instance 'Red Teams' have been set up in Sweden, and coordinating organisations resembling those in the U.S. have been developed, the size, build-up, resources and responsibilities of these units are not the same as in the U.S. The reasons for these differences can be looked for in the differences between Sweden and the U.S. as countries of very different size and with very different political and administrative systems. Sweden is a small country with a unitary parliamentary system, while the U.S. is a superpower with a federal presidential system. Put simply, it is easier to *talk* about a problem in the same way in two different contexts than to imitate *organisation*.

The Substance of IT: Events, Structural Conditions, and Agents

Is there something about the very substance of information and IT that makes this issue susceptible for a position on the security agenda? Information as a security problem fits very well into traditional security thinking. 'Information warfare' including espionage, subversion, concealing or distorting information for tactical purposes, intelligence service, military deception, strategic surprise, command and control and so forth have always been a part of warfare. More than 2000 years ago, Chinese general and strategist Sun Tzu, author of *The Art of War* (1963), put down his thoughts on 'information warfare' (though this term is anachronistic), especially concerning deception. In this sense, the *substance* of IT security and information warfare is nothing new, but these particular frames are very new. This helps to explain why IT security and 'information warfare' so rapidly and seemingly without any resistance has become a favourite topic among military analysts and security experts, whose traditional expertise has been the 'hard' issues of military strategy and armed conflict. 'Information warfare' relates to something very familiar within the military-bureaucratic establishment. Traditional and established knowledge about warfare, security policy, strategy and existential threat is still required in this perspective (Hart, 1976), though the traditional knowledge has to be updated or complemented with knowledge about new technology and new, non-state actors operating on a transnational basis.

In addition, the military-bureaucratic establishment has always been among the first to adopt and even invent new technologies. In military studies, it is generally observed that there have been three revolutions in military technology. The first was the mechanisation of warfare, shown by the development of machine guns, indirect artillery, tanks and aeroplanes. The second was the development of nuclear weapons, and the third was the development of electronic means of warfare, including radio communication, radar, battlefield sensors, satellites and computer-based information systems (Agrell, 2000, pp. 21-25). Indeed, the Internet—sometimes seen as *the* symbol of a *civil* world society—was originally developed by the U.S. Department of Defense Advanced Research Projects Agency as a means of *military* communication (Denning, 1999, p. 74). Hence, the framing of IW and IT security might be seen as old wine in new bottles—the traditional military concerns about information and technology put into new, virtually real bottles.

As suggested in the introductory chapter, the substance of problems can be classified as events, structural conditions or agents. All three are applicable to IT as a source of securitisation. A great many *events* have illustrated the vulnerability of IT systems and thus helped pushing the issue onto the security agenda. The increasing numbers of 'hacker' attacks, and electronic virus pandemics such as the infamous 'Melissa' and the global 'Love letter,' have made decision-makers increasingly aware of the downsides of IT. It is argued that as information systems are increasingly computerised and connected to global networks, attacks and security leakages will increase, especially with the development of broadband networks that connect information systems online at all times. Consequently, in cooperation with the Business Delegation on Security (NSD), the Swedish government has set up a unit that is monitoring and making statistics on 'hacker' attacks (Lindén, Posacki and Wallström, 1999; Working Group on Information Warfare, 1998; Mortensen, 1999).

One of the most salient IT events of all was the so-called Y2K or millennium computer bug. This was a policy window that opened up for securitisation of IT on a global scale. Once again, it was a case of international policy diffusion of North American origin. Canadian computer expert Peter de Jager omitted the first public warning of the bug already in the 1960s. It was not until the early 1990s however, specifically after a doomsday article published in *Computer World* (Morrison, 2000, p. 4), that the issue was securitised and got onto the agendas of states (Morrison, 2000, p. 4). In Sweden the dramatisation of the Y2K bug had an enormous impact. The Agency of Civil Emergency Planning coordinated a huge campaign of preparing Swedish Government and society for the perceived crisis (Year 2000 Delegation, 2000; Lones, 1998, ch. 7-8). Politicians and experts feared all possible disasters, ranging from breakdown of supply of electricity to riots and even nuclear catastrophes. Between January 1997 and December 1999, the Swedish Government issued 21 major decisions regarding the Y2K bug. A temporary 'crisis command central' was set up. On New Years Eve 1999, Sweden was prepared almost as for war. Indeed, Sweden was one of the most well prepared countries of the world. However, though the bug was real, the expected consequences were exaggerated. Only minor incidents were reported (Price, Morrison and Chaffin, 2000; Morrison, 2000; Year 2000 Delegation, 2000).

Incidents such as 'hacker attacks' also demonstrate the vulnerability of IT as a *structural condition*. This was recognised as early as the late 1970s, and was occasionally discussed during the 1980s. The continued development of and dependency on IT will most likely imply an increased fear of this structural vulnerability. That the problem is not only about sporadic events, but also about a general and increasing weakness of the emerging network society provides an important push for the securitisation of IT. This is why it is being perceived as an existential threat.

The securitisation of IT is also about specific *actors*. In discussions about IW and IO, it is usually assumed that a *hostile actor* is behind the threat—an official requirement for the posturing of *security policy* threats, according to the Swedish Government (Defence Commission of Sweden 1999; Government of Sweden, 1999a). Importantly, these potentially threatening actors include not only foreign governments, as has been the tradition in security policy analysis, but also a wide range of non-state actors. Denning (1999, p. 26-27) suggests a taxonomy of five different types of actors: insiders, hackers, criminals, corporations, governments, and terrorists.

That anonymous adversaries may attempt to penetrate information systems from anywhere in the world breaks with the traditional understanding of security—that the identity, location and goals of the enemy are known (cf. Government of Sweden 1999a, p. 30; Working Group on Information Warfare, 1997, p. 8). Understandably, this increases the sense of fear and insecurity. The introduction of *non-state enemies* in security thinking implies opening up Pandora's box, as the number of potential enemies in 'cyberspace' is virtually unlimited. Of course, this helps pushing IT onto the security agenda. In addition, these 'new' potential adversaries dissolve the distinction between *internal* and *external* threats, as well as between the *private* and *public* spheres of action—two of the most basic distinctions in traditional security thinking. A single offensive 'information operation' may involve a network of insiders, hostile governments, corporations, criminals and terrorists. The Swedish Working Group on Information Warfare (1997, 1998) gives several examples of this.

Taken together, the combination of series of events, structural vulnerabilities and actors perceived as threats strongly contribute to the securitisation of IT. If, for instance, some actors were perceived as potential adversaries but very few incidents had occurred, it would obviously have been more difficult to securitise the issue. Indeed, the securitisation of IT is sometimes far too exaggerated. All computer problems, bugs, data diddling, spamming, and break-in attempts are hardly existential threats to a sovereign state. This was particularly obvious with the Y2K bug, which had far less consequences than generally expected. As argued in the introductory chapter, it is not always the damage as such that provides the pull for dramatisation, but perhaps even more so the perceived inability to control events (cf. Johnson, 1997, p. 11-12).

Elaborated or Restricted Frames?

In one particular sense, the various frames of IT as a source of security threats are *restricted* frame, since they present the issue as something that endangers core values. This is about the 'diagnostic' function of frames, i.e.

blaming or identifying the cause of a problem (Snow and Benford, 1992, p. 137). Indeed, even a high degree of IT security is often seen as implying serious costs, with regard to individual integrity, freedom of opinion, and access to information (Cate, 1997; Flaherty, 1989).

Despite this, the frames are relatively *open* (elaborated) with regard to specific content, as almost anything may count as IW, IO or IT security. A lot of time and energy as been invested in trying to define more precisely what IW, IO and IT security are about. But the Swedish Government has also emphasised that these concepts covers a broad range of specific threats and risks with implications for almost every sector of society.

However, the conceptual confusion is not only a technical problem, but also an expression of contending views on IT security, IW, IO and related frames really are about. According to a more restricted interpretation, it is about the development of the automated, electronic battlefield—electronic means complementing or supporting armed attacks on physical objects. In contrast, a more elaborated perspective holds that it is about an entirely new type of 'cyberwar,' in which physical destruction is replaced by digital, and in which enemies are subdued by information superiority and psychological control rather than brute force (cf. Harshberger and Ochmanek, 1999, p. 162; Agrell, 2000, p. 98; Denning, 1999). These contending frames are part and parcel of the politics of threat, and will not disappear simply because official definitions are suggested. In practice, it is difficult to conclude which of the competing frames will gain the upper hand.

In sum, the securitisation of IT is a combination of being a restricted, negative and threat-oriented frame, and a more elaborated frame open for application to a variety of specific issues. The restricted (negative) nature of the frame is necessary or perhaps even defining of the securitisation of IT. The elaborated nature (open ended application), on the other hand, has facilitated the emergence of a cross-sectoral and cross-party consensus on putting the issue on the security agenda. This makes it possible for specialised institutions, as well as different political parties, to make their own specific interpretation of what it means and what particular threats are to be dealt with, without letting one particular authority dominate the issue-area. Both civil and military institutions are involved, as well as governmental and nongovernmental actors. The latter, nongovernmental institutions, however, are mostly specialised business organisations; such as the IT firm Mandator, and the Business Delegation on Security (operating under the Swedish Association of Employers, SAF). However, the traditional security establishment seems to be getting a more dominant position, especially when the issue is interpreted more narrowly as a *security policy* problem, rather than as a more general vulnerability problem for the information society.

Conclusion: Continuity and Change

Why, then, have issues framed as IT-related security threats emerged on the political agenda? The explanations suggested above can be summarised as follows. First, the end of the Cold War opened up a general policy window for redefining and broadening security beyond the traditional focus on nuclear threats and conventional war between states. This became an opportunity for securitising IT, in addition to a great many other 'new threats' of a political, economic, environmental or societal nature.

Second, this coincided with the breakthrough for IT as a revolutionary development in modern society. Not surprisingly, entering the 'information age' implies not only hopeful expectations, but also uncertainty and fear. This is understandable in consideration of the rapid pace and fundamental structural change that is implied by the revolutionary development of IT.

Third, information and technology have always been core elements in military affairs. The framing of 'information warfare,' which originally took on societal salience in the U.S. in the 1990s, can be seen as the major breakthrough for the third revolution in military affairs, following the mechanisation of warfare and the development of nuclear weapons. This helps to explain why the military-bureaucratic establishment embraced the framing of IT as a new source of threats, and indeed contributed to putting information security on the agenda.

Fourth, the military-bureaucratic establishment has shown a remarkable ability to adapt to changing circumstances, including new political priorities. While defence budgets and armed forces generally are being downsized, the military-bureaucratic institutions have been maintained and sometimes even strengthened. Indeed, both in the U.S. and in Sweden, IT and information security has become a booming market. The institutions of the military-bureaucratic security establishment have seized the shares of this market. New units for analysing and preparing for these newly framed threat images have been set up, such as 'Computer Emergency Response Teams,' and 'Red Teams,' sometimes popularly referred to as 'hacker platoons'. As Defence Minister Björn von Sydow puts it: 'We have to get our computer nerds into the military defence' (Älmeberg, 1999, p. 6). In the Swedish case, this has developed by way of imitating the framing and organisational solutions that originated in the U.S.

Fifth, there has been no serious opposition to the securitisation of IT. In Sweden, there is a notable cross-party consensus on this. If there has been any criticism, it has rather been that governments do not take this issue seriously enough. That the frames of IW, IO and the like are relatively broad and open to various interpretations might have contributed to this consensus.

Finally, the discovery and attention paid to the Y2K computer bug helps explaining why IT was securitised during the 1990s. This bug became a major boost for IT security corporations and obviously caught the attention of governments and public administrations, not least in the U.S. and in Sweden. Indeed, the framing of the Y2K was a case of international policy diffusion that had a noticeable global impact.

These explanations also shed light on the question of continuity and change. The rhetoric of IT in general and information security in particular gives the impression that society is being fundamentally transformed, and that nothing will ever be the same in the new information age. This is obviously a rather sweeping and somewhat misleading depiction. To be more specific, it should be noted that the framing of information warfare, information operations, information assurance and indeed the notion of IT began taking on societal salience in the early 1990s. This development has continued, for instance by the reframing from 'information warfare' to the allegedly more neutral and comprehensive frame of 'information operations'. In addition, the organisational solutions for dealing with these threat images are also new, as they have been devised in the mid to late

1990s. On the other hand, much of the substance and partly some of the thinking behind this originated much earlier. Of this the best example is how the U.S. Department of Defense already in the 1960s developed the Internet as a means of military communication. Furthermore, as argued above, much of the success for the securitisation of IT can be explained by the continuity of the military-bureaucratic establishment. Thus the institutional setting for the framing of IT threats is basically the same as during the Cold War. This is not changed by the add-on of some new units and organisational schemes. The security establishment maintains its framing power.

8 Framing the Palme Assassination

ERIC K. STERN AND DAN HANSÉN

On Friday 28 February 1986, the Swedish Prime Minister Olof Palme and his wife Lisbet attended the nine o'clock performance of the film 'Bröderna Mozart' (the Brothers Mozart). The Palmes were unescorted; Palme had dismissed his bodyguards and told them that they would not be needed any more that weekend. The film ended at a few minutes past 11 p.m. Olof and Lisbet Palme began strolling down Sveavägen, a main thoroughfare in Stockholm. A few hundred meters from the cinema, a man stole up to them and fired two shots. The first bullet hit the Prime Minister between the shoulder blades, smashed his spinal cord, aorta and windpipe. The second bullet grazed Lisbet Palme's back. As she leaned over her dying husband, she saw the killer jogging calmly down Tunnelgatan.

The shots rang out at 11:21 p.m. The first police patrol arrived a few minutes later. They found a man lying in a pool of blood, surrounded by some ten people. When the head of the patrol, Chief Inspector Söderström, asked the victim's wife to identify herself, she cried to him: 'Can't you see who I am? I'm Lisbet Palme, this is my Olof, Prime Minister of Sweden!'

This tragic event is, of course, not unique. History provides us with numerous examples of crises triggered by the assassinations of heads of state or government. The conspirators' murder of Julius Caesar, the assassination of Archduke Francis Ferdinand, the sniper's strike on John F. Kennedy, the killings of Egyptian President Anwar Sadat and Israeli Prime Minister Yitzhak Rabin are cases where states, even international systems, were plunged into turbulence by a well-timed blade or bullet. The assassination of a leader can shake a polity to its very core, provoking struggles over the political succession, shaking elite and mass senses of security and political order, and widening political cleavages in society. As such, this type of contingency offers a rare opportunity to study the political psychology of threat framing under crisis conditions.[1]

This chapter will focus on the initial governmental response to the Palme Assassination crisis and the management of the murder investigation during the first few months after the deed. Such an analysis provides us with an opportunity to explore the rapid succession of threat frames (of varying degrees of elite and societal salience) that emerged during this period. The analysis will be based on the cognitive-institutional process tracing strategy outlined in the following section. A series of acute decision problems will be described and a number of threat frames identified for further analysis. The chapter concludes with some reflections on the political psychology of threat framing based upon our empirical findings.

The Cognitive Institutional Process Tracing Strategy

Exploring the nexus between crisis decision-making and the psycho-politics of threat entails studying processes that take place across levels of analysis. The crisis managers (and mis-managers) are embedded in complex institutional settings that enable and constrain their responses to the crisis. To identify and illuminate those settings, we will apply the cognitive institutional process tracing strategy developed by Sundelius and Stern (Sundelius, Stern and Bynander, 1997; Stern, 1999) as means of dissecting the critical first two months after Palme's death. The crisis is divided into decision occasions—a series of urgent 'what to do now' problems perceived by the participants and identifiable in a narrative reconstruction of the case.[2] Particular attention is devoted to tracing political-administrative escalation and de-escalation processes. At what point or points do relevant participants located at various sites in the system under study perceive themselves to be facing acute, stress-inducing problems? In this fashion, crisis problems can be traced through the political-administrative system over time.

Decision occasions are identified on the basis of three complementary criteria. First, the analyst focuses on the most important and attention consuming problems perceived by the participants. These may be complemented by a look at issues which may not have been emphasised by the participants but which—in hindsight—proved to have had a major impact on the course of events (Rosenthal, Charles and 't Hart, 1989). Finally, the analyst may wish to focus some attention on decision problems depicting phenomena of potential practical/prescriptive value—even if they do not quite meet either of the first two criteria. For example, occasions which seem to clearly illustrate best or worst practices—e.g. strategic innovations or pathologies—are often worth further study and can help to flesh out the analysis of a particular case.[3] The results of the crisis dissection are then subject to thematic and comparative analysis. In this case, we will emphasise the theme of threat framing—which should be seen as belonging to the broader category of *problem perception and framing* (Sundelius, Stern and Bynander, 1997; cf. Snyder, Bruck and Sapin, 1963; Vertzberger, 1990; Sylvan and Voss, 1998). Let us now take out our scalpels and begin the dissection.

Critical Decision Problems (28 February – 1 May 1986)[4]

Olof Palme Is Shot Dead![5]

This first dramatic impetus generated frantic activity all over Stockholm. The most prominent actors during the night of the murder were the police, the cabinet, the military and the media. The communication centre of the Stockholm police came to be the hub of the network. The Stockholm police headquarter, the headquarters of SÄPO (the security police) and the National Criminal Division were all located on the same premises.[6]

The murder took place on the Friday night of the last weekend of the winter holidays. A large part of the Swedish population, including vital decision-makers, was on vacation and difficult to reach.

At 11:30 p.m., less than ten minutes after the murder, Chief Inspector Hans Koci and his staff at the Stockholm police communication centre knew that the Prime Minister of Sweden was the victim at Sveavägen. It was not an 'ordinary' crime. They had to find out whether the shooting was an isolated event, if other persons needed protection and if any countermeasures had to be taken.

The initial manhunt was marked by deviations from standard operation procedures. The roped-off area around the scene of the crime was much too small and technical evidence was compromised. Within ten minutes after the shooting, some ten police patrols were searching the surroundings, but not systematically. Moreover, neighbouring police districts were not alerted and thus could not assist in the hunt. Off duty policemen, who volunteered, were not used. Possible escape routes were not secured. The Deputy Commissioner of the Stockholm police, Welander, turned up at about 12:30 a.m. He took charge, but did not change the organisation of the manhunt.[7] He prepared a nation-wide alert that was sent out at 2:05 a.m., which indicated that there were two perpetrators, probably belonging to the Croatian 'Ustasja' movement. At 3:07 a.m., Welander and the head of SÄPO, Hjälmroth attended a meeting of the cabinet.

Had it not been for curious journalists, the information processing would probably have been slower at the onset of this affliction. The Stockholm police communication centre did not inform the security police (SÄPO). An operator at SÄPO, alerted by journalists, called the Stockholm police communication centre for a briefing.

At Rosenbad, home of the Cabinet Office, the situation was no less chaotic.[8] Contrary to existing contingency plans, neither the cabinet office nor the police informed the military. The Defence Staff was apprised of the murder at 1:15 a.m. when the Swedish Military Attaché in Washington called the headquarters in Stockholm and asked the surprised operator if the rumours about Palme's death circulating in Washington were true. Later, the Supreme Commander as a precautionary measure ordered a limited military alert.

A central question in the Cabinet was whether or not the government was constitutionally authorised to govern. Legal expertise was required. However, the Cabinet Office's constitutional adviser, who also was its head of security, had recently passed away and had not yet been replaced (Eklundh, 1999). Vice Prime Minister Ingvar Carlsson took charge of the interim government.[9] In addition to the constitutional issue, the government discussed general and personal (e.g. bodyguards) security issues. Welander and Hjälmroth briefed the government on the police efforts. The highest available police command was thus removed from supervision of the manhunt for several critical hours.

After having driven like a 'car thief,' Stockholm Police Commissioner Hans Holmér returned from his interrupted holidays at 10:50 a.m., Saturday March 1. He then took charge of the police efforts (Holmér, 1988). With Holmér's arrival a new phase of the crisis began.

Getting Down to Business

As the dramatic dust of the first night's events settled, the cast of characters managing the crisis began to change. Some of the actors active during the night, like the military, were no longer part of the crisis management by the next morning. The problem increasingly came to be defined as an isolated murder by person or persons unknown and the Stockholm police took centre stage.

A police managerial group was set up quite spontaneously during the first weekend of March. Besides Holmér, it contained a number of other senior staff from the Stockholm police force and the National Police Board. Two officials from the Department of Justice were assigned as observers to the managerial group. Within this group, Holmér created an inner circle, the Brain Trust, consisting of himself and three other senior police chiefs. The idea was to have a forum to formulate tentative thoughts and to help each other criticise favourite hypotheses (Åsheden, 1987).

The growing amount of information, tips and witness accounts seemed to the Brain Trust to indicate that the deed had been carefully planned. In order to encourage anyone with knowledge of the murder to come forward, Holmér and Wickbom (the Justice Minister) decided to offer 500,000 Swedish crowns for information leading to the capture of Palme's murderer.[10]

In the political arena, the way back to normalcy was fairly smooth. The succession issue had been resolved and the new regular cabinet worked from 12 March. Carlsson had been Palme's shadow for his entire political career and was known to be the trouble-shooter of the party, internally nicknamed 'Crisis-Carlsson.'

Holmér's managerial group was now firmly in control. The 'normal' murder investigators and the prosecution authority were positioned at the periphery of the decision-making hub. To some extent, this was also true regarding the national police's representatives in the managerial group.

How to Carry Out Palme's Funeral Safely?

On March 15, a solemn last farewell to the late Prime Minister was arranged in the City Hall of Stockholm. Statesmen and women from all over the world came to Stockholm to pay their respects. Given that Palme's assassin had not been captured, the Stockholm police were under heavy pressure to provide top-level security for the event. Well over a hundred eminent guests were expected, each of whom were a possible target for the malefactor(s). Sweden had already received a violent shock when Palme was gunned down in the open street of Stockholm, which was only reinforced by the subsequent criticism directed at the police force. It was seen as essential for Sweden to demonstrate its capacity to carry out the funeral safely.

Sune Sandström, in his capacity as head of the police department in charge of public order, organised the police effort during the funeral. Together with a team consisting of police officers and representatives from the Social Democratic Party, he orchestrated the event, closely supervised by Holmér himself. Meticulous preparations left nothing to chance. There were 2000 policemen on duty in Stockholm that day (Holmér, 1988; Åsheden, 1987). Once the funeral ended without a hitch, there was a collective sigh of relief from the Stockholm police leadership.

The Failed Line-up

Since the beginning of the investigation, the police had made use of underworld contacts and followed up on a wide range of tips. A 33-year-old man without previous convictions attracted interest from the beginning. Different witnesses stated that they had met him not far from the scene of the crime just a few hours before the murder. The man had then very explicitly aired his hatred for Olof Palme. On 12 March, Chief Prosecutor Svensson decided to take him into custody.

One witness reported the day after the murder that he had been driving his car at a street off Tunnelgatan, at around 11:30 p.m. on the night of the murder 28 February. A man had stopped his car and offered whatever the driver wanted if he could ride with him. The witness got scared and drove away. When the 33-year-old was behind bars, two working groups within the police headquarters without each other's knowledge received orders to confront the suspect with the witness. On 14 March, the first group gave the witness a stack of photographs, one of which depicted the 33-year-old. The witness did not recognise 'his man' from the pictures. This news was not forwarded upwards or laterally in the police hierarchy.

Two days later, the second group called the witness in and arranged a line-up with the 33-year-old. The witness pointed out the arrested man and another man in the line-up (Interview with K-G Svensson, 1998). The positive identification of the suspect was reported upwards and strengthened the circumstantial evidences against the 33-year-old. The next day, the Chief Prosecutor submitted a detention order for the suspect and started to prepare for court proceedings.

During these preparations, Svensson found out about the separate photo identification, which cast doubt on the evidence from the line-up. Svensson decided to set the suspect free. Holmér was informed of Svensson's decision just when he was about to enter a press conference. He then was forced to announce this sensational news, and he supported the decision before the press corps. However, this incident was the deathblow to the working relationship between Holmér and Svensson. The following day, Holmér and Wranghult visited Claes Zeime, the Director of the Stockholm prosecution authority, and asked him to replace K-G Svensson. Zeime refused (Åsheden, 1987, pp. 59-67).

The Investigation under Scrutiny

As time passed and the investigation did not seem to produce any substantial result, voices were raised calling for a commission to scrutinise the investigation. On 5 March, an editorial writer of the influential daily

Svenska Dagbladet already called for a commission like the Warren commission (SvD, 5 March 1986: 2). The Attorney General, Bengt Hamdahl, proved susceptible to this signal of public dissatisfaction (SVT, Rapport 5 March 1986). Party leaders found the idea of appointing a commission somewhat rushed; the police needed to work in peace. But some kind of commission, they agreed, would be needed in the future (DN, 6 March 1986, p. 8).

Although the investigation was exposed to these sporadic expressions of distrust, the bond with the government remained intact. The Minister of Justice met regularly with Holmér and was very well informed as to the proceedings of the investigation. He also received information via the observers in the managerial group. But on 16 April, Wickbom used the tabloid *Expressen* to hint that the search team might become the subject of a commission's scrutiny. This news came as a shock, at least to Holmér. Though another month passed before the Cabinet decided to set up a commission, Holmér felt that this statement caused a rupture in the mutual confidence between the team and the government. The police in the field felt increasingly isolated in their efforts to bring the case to an end (interview with Holmér, 1998; Åsheden, 1987, p. 130).[11]

The Sour Relation between Police and Prosecutor

In the month of April, the investigation proceeded quite calmly. The police had still doubts regarding the whereabouts of the 33-year-old on the night of 28 February. When the suspect's alibi could not be confirmed, the managerial group requested additional line-ups for a large number of people. On April 25, the police handed Svensson a list of 74 witnesses. Svensson found the number of people to be in violation of the suspect's rights and selected 11 witnesses from the list.[12] Holmér was furious and tried to reach Zeime in another effort to eliminate Svensson from the investigation.

On 27 April, the Prosecutor General explained to Svensson, that he might have to overrule his decision about the number of line-ups. Svensson decided that an additional 11 witnesses would be called in for line-ups; mostly because he wanted to avoid a confrontation with the managerial group. On 28 April, Holmér, Svensson and Magnus Sjöberg (the Prosecutor General) were asked to attend a meeting at the Ministry of Justice. At the meeting, Holmér and Svensson reported on their different points of view with regard to the number of line-ups. Svensson found them rather useless and stated that the 11 additional line-ups would be the last ones, as far as he was concerned. That was his final decision. Holmér stressed the importance of exhausting this 'main lead' and argued for additional line-ups. The Justice Minister expressed sympathy for Holmér's view. The following day, Sjöberg studied the material on which Svensson had based his decision and overruled him. Svensson was present, but did not object (interview with Sjöberg, 1998).

Holmér found the situation intolerable and together with Wranghult, visited the Director of the prosecution authority, Claes Zeime, on 1 May. After having discussed the matter, Zeime decided to replace Svensson and to take over his duties. Svensson would remain prosecutor of the 33-year-old (Government of Sweden, 1987b). However, before this, on 29 April, when Sjöberg officially handed in the decision to overrule Svensson's decision regarding the line-ups, Svensson explained to Sjöberg that he was not able to fulfill the duties of the prosecutor under the prevailing circumstances. He found that the way Holmér had organised the investigation was not realistic; in fact, he wanted the managerial group to disband and be replaced by the regular police, i.e. qualified homicide specialists, and ending the dominance of the police jurists. It was not until 5 May that Svensson was informed that he had been discharged from the case and that Zeime had taken his post (Parliament of Sweden, 1987, p.152).

Analysis: A Succession of Threat Frames

The Palme Murder confronted the Swedish authorities with a crisis situation. The polity had already suffered a great loss, from which it had to recover. However, the murder, which as we have seen came as a shock to the relatively 'innocent' Swedish polity was (and to this day remains) a fundamentally ambiguous act. It was obvious to all that the heinous act posed a threat, but the question remained: what kind and to whom? In other words, information regarding who was responsible, why the act was perpetrated, and whether or not it was the first move in a more extensive campaign was lacking. Efforts to remedy this information deficit were launched immediately (although, as we have seen, not always in an organised and professional fashion). Soon, the crisis actors would face the typical double problem—shortage of certain types of vital information and an excess of other kinds. Decision-makers and analysts were forced to cope with the rapidly increasing flow of crisis related information—necessitating selectivity—and at the same time finding ways of 'going beyond the information given' in order to create a basis for action (Dror, 1986).

In the section below, we will describe the succession of threat frames (and the actions/inaction linked to them) which were considered and in some cases discarded by the crisis managers in the early stages of the Palme Murder crisis. For each frame, we will describe the relevant framers—those who emphasised (or actively ruled out) a particular threat frame. Finally, we will reflect upon the patterns revealed, drawing upon psychological, organisational, and political (scientific) theories.

Table 8.1 Overview of threat frames and main framing actors

Threat frames	Main framing actors
1. Croatian separatists	Stockholm Police/Government
2. Strategic Assault/Terror Campaign	Military headquarters/Government
3. Sugar Lump Theory/Terror Campaign	Social Democratic Headquarters
4. 33-year-Old: Right Wing Extremism	Police's Managerial Group

Croatian Separatists

Although none of the witnesses could provide a distinct description of the culprit, the Stockholm police sent out a (nation-wide) all points bulletin indicating that Croatian separatists were likely to be involved in the shoot-out (Government of Sweden, 1987a, p. 47-48). Lisbet Palme had expressed an allegation directed toward the Croatian Ustasja movement when interviewed at Sabbatsberg's Hospital (interview with Tommy Lindström, 1998). One of the policemen who talked to Lisbet forwarded this allegation to Gösta Welander, the Deputy Police Commissioner, who ordered the nation-wide alert to be sent out before joining them at the hospital. In a second nation-wide alert that was sent out a few hours later, the connection to Ustasja was deleted.

However, the possibility of a Croatian terrorist involvement was not discarded by all of the key decision-makers. Even when it became clear that Miro Baresic, Lisbet Palme's prime Croatian suspect had spent the night of the murder behind bars, elements within SÄPO (the security police), the Stockholm police and even the Government clung to this lead. Against the wishes of the prosecutor and by order of the Cabinet, Baresic's telephone was secretly tapped for several months (Government of Sweden, 1999c).

With the benefit of hindsight, the Croatian separatist hypothesis seems to rest on some pretty thin evidential ice. Pursuing a cognitive-institutional analysis may however enable us to provide some explanations to why the 'Croatian threat' took on an apparently disproportionate degree of salience for the crisis managers. Where did this threat frame come from?

As noted above, the supposition of a Croatian involvement derived from information given by Lisbet Palme. Ustasja, the Croatian separatist movement in question, seemed to be a possible perpetrator in Lisbet's mind.[13] Miro Baresic killed the Yugoslavian ambassador to Stockholm in 1971. Even though that murder had taken place fifteen years earlier, Baresic and his companions were not forgotten by the leading Social Democrats. First of all, up to that point the crime was unparalleled in modern Swedish history. Secondly, the terrorists remained in Swedish custody, which was seen as creating a chronic security risk.[14] Moreover, Miro Baresic had repeatedly turned to the Government with a request to have his lifetime sentence commuted, but in vain. However, only a few months before the Palme murder, the Government had changed its mind and decided to commute his sentence, but he was still dissatisfied and had communicated his contempt for Palme and his Government to the media (Government of Sweden, 1999c).

Furthermore, Croatian terrorists linked to HDP (Ustasja) had also been responsible for another spectacular episode in the short history of terrorism in Sweden—the Bulltofta Hijacking of 1972. The hijacking was a sequel to the ambassador murder. Three Croatians managed to force a domestic flight to land in the south of Sweden (Bulltofta airport). Their aim was to have seven of their countrymen released from Swedish prisons, where they were serving time for the ambassador murder and an occupation of the Yugoslavian consulate in Gothenburg (Karlsson, 2000).[15] While we have not uncovered direct evidence that the decision-makers explicitly referred to this case, it should be noted that Olof Palme himself was intimately involved in the Bulltofta crisis management. This case was highly publicised in Sweden, making it very likely that it was available to Lisbet Palme, other members of the Social Democratic leadership and not least the police—for whom it would have stood out vividly as one of the most spectacular crimes in modern Swedish history. Finally, it may have contributed to the plausibility of this hypothesis that the Yugoslavian Chief of Staff was scheduled to visit Sweden on March 9—just eight days after the murder. Thus, the Croatian terror schema was both vivid and highly available to the Swedish decision-makers (cf. Nisbett and Ross, 1980, Khong, 1992), who were able to use it in an initial attempt to make sense of the Palme killing.

But why was it that this threat frame persisted in spite of the complete absence of any manifest evidence?[16] Why did Lisbet Palme's intuitive utterance in a state of shock not just fade away from the picture, when the prosecutor found nothing to substantiate the initial suspicion? Even the operative head of SÄPO, P-G Näss, proved incredulous of the Ustasja lead, dismissing it as 'originating from Hans Holmér and his managerial group' (Government of Sweden, 1999c, p. 557). Apparently a rumour had it that a person in the circles around Baresic had been spotted close to the scene and time of the murder. However, neither the origin of the rumour nor the identity of the concerned suspect has been traceable in subsequent scrutiny (Ibid., p. 557-8). Nonetheless, the acting Prime Minister (Ingvar Carlsson), the Justice Minister, and six more ministers found the Baresic lead salient enough to overrule Svensson's decision and to have Baresic's prison telephone tapped by Cabinet order. The reason given for this undertaking was the risk for future actions of similar nature (Ibid. p. 558). This persistent focus on the Croatian separatists arose from a small but influential group consisting of at least parts of the Government and parts of the police managerial group, which refused to abandon this frame.

From a rationalist perspective, this behavior seems puzzling indeed. However, from a cognitive perspective, it seems rather less surprising. A substantial body of social psychological laboratory experiments as well as field observations has documented the human tendency to allow beliefs or theories to persevere in spite of a lack of supporting evidence and even in the face of disconfirming evidence (Nisbett and Ross, 1980, pp. 167-192; Fiske and Taylor, 1991, p. 150-151). People tend to frame problems and formulate 'theories' on the basis of scanty evidence and have great difficulty in updating such beliefs. As two leading social psychologists put it:

> Belief perseverance sometimes occurs because people have an emotional commitment to the belief. Perseverance is even likely when there is no such investment, however, because (a) people tend to seek out, recall, and interpret evidence in a manner that sustains beliefs, (b) they readily construct causal explanations of initial evidence in which they then place too much confidence, and (c) they act upon their beliefs in way that makes them self confirming (Nisbett and Ross, 1980, p. 192).

From this (rather pessimistic) perspective on human information processing, the behaviour exhibited regarding the Croatian scenario seems less puzzling.[17] Finally, it may be interesting to consider the role of stress in encouraging perseverance, as stress has been suggested as a factor creating tendencies towards cognitive rigidity (e.g. Staw, Sandelands, and Dutton, 1981; c.f. Stern and Sundelius, 1998).

Strategic Assault/Terror Campaign

The Cold War had just begun to thaw in February of 1986. In defence circles, the scenario of a strategic decapitation strike by a powerful neighbour was frequently discussed at the time. A team of well known 'hawkish' defence analysts working under a pseudonym (Winter, 1988) would publish a controversial fictionalisation of the politically incorrect scenario, *Operation Garbo*, based on these discussions. Not only fiction but also a number of Cold War incidents inside and outside of Sweden fuelled this threat image during this period. In one troubling development, the Soviet Union suddenly invaded the neutral Afghanistan in late 1979, an action promptly condemned by the Swedish government. Furthermore, Sweden had what was thought to be a series of territorial incursions by foreign submarines (the most spectacular of which was the 'Whiskey on the Rocks' incident of 1981) during the six years prior to Palme's death (Bynander, this volume; Stern and Sundelius, 1992). Thus this threat frame was in circulation at the time of the murder. But did it play a prominent role in the threat framing debates to follow?

During the mid-1980s, the Swedish armed forces maintained constant reconnaissance over the Baltic Sea in order to monitor the developing military threat constellation. On Fridays, the Supreme Commander held intelligence briefings with representatives from the different branches of the armed forces. A typical briefing was held on Friday, 28 February 1986, the day of the murder. The finding was that there were no indications of increased threat against Sweden that weekend (Government of Sweden, 1987a). When the news of Palme's death reached the military headquarters, there was thus no particular reason to interpret the killing as a sign of an impending strategic assault on Sweden.

Apparently, the military had enough confidence in their intelligence capabilities so as not to be unduly alarmed by the news. The Supreme Commander was informed at 1:30 a.m. (following the call from the Defence Attaché in Washington described above) and arrived at the headquarters at about 2 a.m. (2½ hours after the shooting). He immediately contacted the Defence Ministry, the Chancellery and the National Police Board for consultations. Thereafter, a limited military alert was implemented in the Eastern Military District. The Supreme Commander also ordered flags flown, mostly as way of letting the news percolate through the military organisation.

At six o'clock in the morning of March 1, Supreme Commander Lennart Ljung met with Defence Minister Roine Carlsson and discussed the situation. The Defence Minister did not think that any additional military security measure were necessary. Roine Carlsson declared that there were no indications of terrorism related to the murder of Palme (Lennart Ljung's diary 3 March 1986). The interpretations supplied by the Defence sector actors thus runs counter to the Croatian hypothesis.

It is striking to observe how quickly the leading Defence sector actors dismissed the strategic decapitation hypothesis. Many decades of relative calm (and nearly two hundred years of unbroken peace) seems to have dampened the military threat sensitivities of many of these actors.[18]

Similarly, it is striking that most members of the Government acted in a manner which suggests that they were relatively unconcerned about their own personal security—making their own way (by ordinary taxi), unescorted, to the Chancellery in the small hours of the night of the murder. At that point, they had little or no information regarding the circumstances of and motives for the assassination.[19] Like the Defence Minister, most of the other Cabinet Ministers did not consider, or quickly dismissed, the possibility that a strategic decapitation or terror campaign might be in progress. It might be that a phenomenon that we elsewhere have referred to as 'Swedish exceptionalism' (Hansén and Stern, in press) can help us understand their behaviour. For non-Swedish readers and even contemporary Swedes disillusioned and shaken by a decade and a half of crises and scandals, it may be difficult to imagine the 'innocence' and sense of civil invulnerability, which prevailed at the time of the killing. The few serious domestic crises of the seventies, such as the Bulltofta hijacking of 1972 and the West-German Embassy Siege of 1975 had not been directly targeted at Sweden, had not claimed Swedish lives, and had relatively (and perhaps undeservedly) happy endings (Hansén, 1998). Sweden was seen by leaders and citizens alike as a place largely spared from the spectre of political violence. This pervasive sense of innocence and crisis optimism goes a long way in explaining the lax security measures prior to and immediately following the assassination. Ironically, though, this profound sense of invulnerability had just cost the Prime Minister his life. To sum up, the evidence suggests that both military and civilian decision-makers were initially strongly disinclined to take the strategic decapitation and terror campaign scenarios seriously at the outset.

The Sugar Lump Theory

As the shock of the first night wore off, some of the crisis managers did become more inclined to think in terms of the murder having been planned as part of a wider conspiracy. Though the motives of and circumstances surrounding the murder remained shrouded in uncertainty, actors began to hypothesise and speculate about the causes and security implications of the murder. For example, the Police managerial group emphasised the likelihood that the murder had been part of a carefully orchestrated plan at the press conferences held during the first days of March 1986 (DN, 3 March 1986, p. 1; SvD, 3 March 1986, p. 6). Many actors found it difficult to believe that an act so devastating in its consequences could have been a random and spontaneous act by a lone madman. This tendency fits well with a number of lines of psychological research which suggest that people expect causes to resemble effects (Fiske and Taylor, 1991, pp. 58-60; Levy, 1997, pp. 111-115; cf. Lebow and Stein, 1993). These theories suggest that people seek to produce a cognitive 'balance' (Heider, 1958) between dramatic events and the causes which produced them.

For the committee at the Social Democratic headquarters in charge of organising Palme's funeral, the possibility that Palme's murder might have been part of an even more diabolical plan was taken very seriously indeed. It was clear that the funeral would attract hundreds of prominent guests from around the world, and that socialist leaders would be heavily represented. This could provide a unique opportunity for an anti-socialist terrorist or group. In this scenario, Palme might have actually been killed for the express purpose of drawing these statesmen to the slaughter—an interpretation which was quite in keeping with the previous history of terrorism on Swedish soil (which up to that point had been directed primarily at non-Swedish targets)—and with the general notion of Swedish exceptionalism. This notion was linked to an evocative metaphor—a sugar lump placed out in the open to attract flies—which probably made the hypothesis more vivid, emotive and compelling to some (Vertzberger, 1990, pp. 300, 339-341; Shimko, 1995).[20]

Though little or no specific intelligence available to the police in support of the sugar lump theory, maximal security precautions (2000 police officers were on duty in Stockholm that day) were taken to ensure that the funeral could be held without incident, as described above. In retrospect, police leaders emphasise the symbolic importance of the funeral and the credibility issues at stake to explain these expensive precautions, rather than the substantive threat estimation (interviews with Holmér, 1998, and Wranghult, 1998). Whether these accounts accurately capture the threat assessments at the time or have been distorted by hindsight bias is difficult for the post hoc researcher to say.

The 33-year-old: Right Wing Extremism

After Baresic, the so-called 33-year-old was the first in a line of prime suspects under scrutiny in the Palme investigation. Although he consumed a great deal of the investigation team's time and energy and triggered the rift between the prosecutor and the police described above, this suspect was never definitively linked to the crime. Why was this suspect taken so seriously?

The 33-year-old initially was perceived as fitting the mould of a potential prime-minister murderer. He was connected to an extreme right-wing party (EAP, the European Labour Party), which had been vocal in its opposition to and bitter criticism of Palme for many years. Not only did the suspect have an apparently appropriate political profile, but his personal demeanour seemed to fit the image of a potentially volatile fanatic—a kind of Swedish Oswald figure who had been overheard making threatening statements about Palme, shortly before the murder.

In understanding why this threat frame acquired and maintained the elite salience it did for so long, phenomena such as motivational bias and wishful thinking may be helpful (Lebow and Stein, 1993; Chaiken, Giner-Sorolla, and Chen, 1996). The managerial group must have been aware that pushing the investigation of the 33-year-old so hard in the face of scepticism on the part of the prosecutors assigned to the case was risky. Why would they continue to push so hard if they had come to regard this suspect as a long shot?[21] Prospect theory does suggest a possible explanation. Prospect theory suggests that decision-makers are more likely to be risk acceptant if they perceive themselves to be acting in the domain of losses (McDermott, 2001, pp. 17-43). Having already bet so much on what was increasingly looking like the wrong horse, they were willing to go even further what would prove a futile hope of saving their credibility by finding the murderer.[22]

As criticism for the lack of progress in the investigation gradually mounted, a parallel threat for the managerial group was of losing face—a threat that would prove quite realistic (the government would transfer the case out of their jurisdiction within the year). As we have seen, Holmér and his staff had pressing 'political' and psychological needs to show progress in cracking this case; they had already raised public expectations by word and body language. Their credibility was on the line and perhaps it is not so strange that they latched on to a suspect and threat frame like this one and refused to let it go despite rising costs and the dearth of non-circumstantial evidence in favour. The police leaders may well have been grasping at straws at that point, torn between an increasingly desperate need to solve the case and their fears of being left without a hot trail to follow.

The right wing 33-year-old was not the last of the threat frames to emerge following the Palme killing although we will end our threat frame analysis with him. The Kurdish PKK terrorist frame, which became the main lead during the summer and fall of 1986 (and which was the main focus of the so-called Ebbe Carlsson affair),[23] the South Africa frame[24] and the Police Conspiracy frame[25] (both variants of right wing extremist scenarios) are among the others which would follow. In fact, the vast array of conspiracy theories, which have flourished in the wake of the Palme investigation over the last fifteen years, is suggestive in the dissonance between police and lay interpretations of the crime. In the post-Holmér era, the bulk of the evidence presented by the police has argued that a lone madman (Christer Pettersson—whose initial conviction by a lower court in July 1989 was overturned on appeal four months later) committed the crime.[26] The conspiracy theorists and a large segment of the Swedish population, like the legal system, have rejected this possibility—although not necessarily for the same reasons. For the person in the street, the lone, deranged gunman theory simply does not seem in balance with the loss not only of Palme's leadership but also of innocence and psychological security caused by the shooting. Here the parallels with the U.S. experience following the Kennedy assassination are obvious.

Conclusions

What can we say about the politics of threat framing (and the framing of threat politics) on the basis of our study of the Palme case?

Psychological Security

To begin with, the murder of Olof Palme—executed in seconds—had a profound effect on the way Swedes (both citizens and elites alike) viewed their society. The bullets which penetrated the body of Olof Palme also constituted a symbolic rape of the body politic—from which it has yet to recover fully. This suggests that psychological security for collectives is fragile and asymmetrical in the sense that it may be rapidly lost—while regaining it may be a long and difficult (if not impossible) process. In this respect, psychological security seems to operate much like credibility and legitimacy.

Fragmented Crisis Response

The Palme crisis clearly demonstrates the multi-dimensional and even fragmented character of acute crisis response (Stern, 1999). Crisis managers generally do not experience crises in a uniform, unitary manner. Instead, they experience crisis differentially (Stern and Sundelius, 1998) depending upon their roles, interests, and psychological states at the time of the crisis (Allison and Zelikow, 1999). The crisis begins and ends at different points in time for various actors and they face different threats (and opportunities) along the way.

Crisis participant Claes Eklundh (1999) pointed us in the right direction when he described the Palme Murder as representing not one but two crises: the crisis that never began and the crisis that never ended. The former referred to initial threat perceptions that the Palme Murder might be the first act in a broader drama such as a strategic decapitation by a foreign power, a coup d'état, or a constitutional crisis. Fortunately, these fears proved unfounded and none of these worst case scenarios occurred. So, in this sense of strategic foreign and domestic threats to the stability of the Swedish polity, the crisis did indeed never really get started.

By 'the crisis that never ended' Eklundh was referring to the psychological and political consequences of the inability of the responsible authorities and institutions to bring the murderer to justice—and the enduring controversy surrounding the motive behind the murder, as well as the organisation and practices of the investigation.

Cognitive-Institutional Approach

If one shifts the focus of attention away from macro crisis conceptions and towards the problems as experienced by the actors, it is clear that involved actors perceived the first months of the Palme murder crisis as a *series* of urgent political and/or operational problems to be solved. Using the cognitive-institutional process-tracing methodology developed in the CM Europe programme (Stern, 1999b), it is possible to dissect and analyse the case and identify the succession of political and operational problem frames, which emerged during the first months of the crisis. Furthermore, elements of cognitive and institutional theory are helpful in understanding *why* given actors framed particular situations in particular ways. For example, we have noted that the initial all points bulletin identified Croatian separatist terrorists as the likely suspects. Why was that the case? The available evidence suggests that a combination of availability and analogical reasoning drove this framing process (Nisbett and Ross, 1980; Vertzberger, 1990; Khong, 1992). The last time a major political figure was assassinated in Sweden (the Yugoslavian ambassador) in 1971, Croatian terrorists were identified as the culprit. Croatian terrorists were also responsible for the Bulltofta hijacking of 1972—another of the most spectacular acts of political violence in modern Swedish history. Thus, the question of why actors perceived and framed a problem in a particular way is empirically researchable.

Framing, Expectations, and Credibility

As has been made clear by others in this volume (e.g. Eriksson, Robertson), framing is not only about how actors perceive problems, but also about how they represent them to others (cf. Charlick-Paley and Sylvan, 2000, pp. 704-705). Our findings, like the more applied literature, suggest that actors have the potential to influence the frames of reference which others use to assess their behaviour. Credibility (and ultimately legitimacy) is closely linked to expectations. Actors and institutions which meet or exceed normative and performative expectations tend to maintain or increase credibility and legitimacy. Actors and institutions which do not meet normative and performative expectations tend to lose credibility and legitimacy (Stern and Kuipers, forthcoming). Our findings suggest that Stockholm Police Commissioner Hans Holmér contributed to raising the expectations of the media, the citizenry, and other elite actors by his words, 'body language,' and actions during the first weeks of the Palme Crisis. When he proved unable to deliver the murderer, he was replaced—the investigation transferred to the national level and Holmér's previously promising career came to an end (Hansén and Stern, in press).

Threat and Opportunity

In the psychological literature on framing, so-called prospect theory (Kahneman, Slovic and Tversky, 1982; McDermott, 2001; Farnham, 1994; Levy, 1997) occupies a prominent position. This theory suggests that individuals (and possibly collectives, cf. Vertzberger, 1997) respond differently to identical situations, depending upon whether they are portrayed as involving gains or losses. Laboratory experiments (and some findings from the field and archives) seem to indicate that individuals tend to be relatively risk averse with respect to gains and risk acceptant with regard to (avoiding) losses. This suggests that differences in problem framing of this kind may have an impact on the kinds of strategies adopted in crisis. Of course, the notion that framing situations as threatening may involve opportunity for certain actors is central to the securitisation perspective as well (Buzan, Waever, and de Wilde, 1998).

Facing this idea has a number of significant implications, not least for the notion of crisis solidarity. In many polities, there are political cultural norms (of varying degrees of strength) towards crisis solidarity and unity. When confronted with a threatening foreign actor or a natural/technical tragedy, political or bureaucratic rivals are often expected to put their differences aside and support the greater good. Yet even in crisis, conceptions of the greater good vary. Problem framing and threat assessments remain contestable; actors will tend to accept frames (and threat assessments) seen as compatible with idiosyncratic worldviews and parochial interests (Ripley, 1995; Stern and Verbeek, 1998). As a result, normative pressures toward crisis solidarity are likely to be at odds with more divisive tendencies. In fact, contrary to some hypotheses (e.g. Rosati, 1981) bureaucratic politics appear to be common in crisis situations (Rosenthal, 't Hart, and Kouzmin, 1991).

The Palme crisis presented both threats and opportunities to actors on the Swedish political scene. Actors also varied considerably in their situational assessments and tactical preferences. Rivalries between various police agencies—SÄPO, the National Criminal Division and the Stockholm police—pre-existed and were manifest in the crisis management. In addition, conflicts emerged between the police chiefs leading the Palme investigation and the prosecutor assigned to the case. Holmér's behaviour and courting of the media suggests that he enjoyed the spotlight and saw the potential to advance his career and the fortunes of his organisation. As it turned out, these hopes were not realised. Subsequently, others were able to exploit the opportunities presented by the case to realise the project of a national SWAT unit—a project which had previously been politically impossible (interview with Welander, 1998). It is ironic that such a force would not have been of any use whatsoever in preventing or coping with the Palme assassination. Similarly, the political and legal scandals which emerged in the wake of the Palme murder were a threat to the social democratic incumbents, but also potential opportunities for the opposition.

If threats and opportunities are inevitably intertwined in the volatile and value-loaded terrain of crisis (and security), there may be reason to rethink our crisis definitions (Hermann, 1963; Rosenthal, Charles, and 't Hart, 1989; Brecher, 1993), which tend to focus on the threat side of the coin.

From the decision-making perspective, perhaps it would be better to emphasise that crises involve situations in which actors perceive that major values are *at stake* (which entails threat, opportunity or both), uncertainty, and urgency. The notion that opportunity (as well as threat) can be a source of stress for individuals and institutions in the face of uncertain and rapidly moving events seems highly plausible.

Notes

1. Following Sundelius, Stern and Bynander (1997) and Stern (1999), we are defining crisis as a situation in which key decision-makers perceive threat to core values, uncertainty, and urgency (c.f. Hermann, 1963; Rosenthal, Charles, and 't Hart, 1989; Brecher, 1993).
2. For reasons of space, the narrative has been omitted from this chapter.
3. Note that it is not uncommon for the same 'case' to contain vivid examples of both 'best' and 'worst' practices.
4. The study draws upon all five reports of the four commissions of inquiry into the Palme slaying. The Jurist Commission started to collect data for its two reports (Government of Sweden, 1987a, 1987b) in May of 1986. They reconstructed the course of events by interviewing no less than 178 people involved in the management of the murder. The transcripts from the 1987 hearings before the standing committee on the constitution (Parliament of Sweden, 1987) have also been used. Interviewing has been used to complement the written record. It is important to keep in mind that these sessions took place almost 13 years after the murder—a salient circumstance from source critical perspective. Three other works heavily used are the memoirs of Holmér (1988) and Krusell (1998), and the documentary by Åsheden (1987). The latter, a journalist from Dagens Nyheter, met with Holmér 30 minutes a day during the three first months, to document the proceedings of the investigation.
5. Information regarding the first occasion for decision derives, if not otherwise stated, from Government of Sweden (1987a).
6. The security police (SÄPO) was responsible for assigning bodyguards. Olof Palme dismissed his bodyguards telling them he would not need more protection that weekend—the Prime Minister typically decided himself what level of security he wished maintained. Palme was supposed to tell the bodyguards whenever he moved outside the 'triangle,' consisting of his home, Rosenbad (which houses the Prime Minister's office), and the Parliament, but this time he did not do so.
7. It should be noted that the head of the National Criminal Division was never called. The task of reinforcing the protection of the police headquarters was thereby not fulfilled (Interview with Tommy Lindström, 1998).

8 The on duty official had been to a restaurant during the night, and when staff from ABAB (the security company that guarded the entrance to Rosenbad 24 hours a day) tried to call him, he was in the subway, where his beeper did not work.
9 The executive committee of the Social Democratic Party chose Ingvar Carlsson as candidate for the post as party leader unanimously on 1 March. The new government was sworn in on 12 March, with Ingvar Carlsson as Prime Minister.
10 An interesting feature of the initial investigation was the decision to tap a certain Miro Baresic's telephone. (Miro Baresic was the assassin of the Yugoslavian ambassador to Stockholm in 1971.) On March 2, two days after the murder, a representative from SÄPO wanted to have Baresic's telephone tapped at Täby prison. He therefore contacted the appointed Chief Prosecutor in this case, K-G Svensson. Svensson did not find a single shred of evidence against Baresic and declined the request. The same night, Svensson was told that the government had decided to tap Baresic's telephone. A meeting had been held at the Justice Minister's home, where Wranghult had been present. The Justice Minister called six other cabinet ministers, including Ingvar Carlsson. Together they made the decision to tap Baresic's telephone anyway (Government of Sweden, 1999c, pp. 557-559).
11 This should, however, be interpreted as a personal disappointment. Both Tommy Lindström (1998) and Hans Wranghult (1998) refer to the political game, which has to be played by the political establishment, given the enormous public pressure. They (Lindström and Wranghult) would not say that Wickbom's initiative affected the police in general at all.
12 According to Svensson, his decision regarding the line-ups with the 11 witnesses was not final (Parliament of Sweden, 1987, p. 149).
13 Lisbet Palme and the Government referred to the terrorist organisation as Ustasja (as did Tito, the Yugoslavian leader), even though Baresic's group called themselves HDP.
14 Captured West German terrorists were summarily remanded into German custody following the spectacular West German Embassy Occupation of 1975 in order to minimise the risk of further actions on Swedish soil (Hansén, 1998).
15 The hijacking succeeded. An unprepared crisis cabinet put a premium on the passengers' safety and let the plane leave for Madrid with six of the prisoners and SEK 460.000. Once in Madrid, however, the hijackers surrendered (Karlsson, 2000).
16 The only evidence with any substance was the fact that Baresic had called unusually many people from the prison in the days after the murder (Government of Sweden, 1999c, p. 559).
17 Of course, people do change beliefs and abandon theories on a regular basis. From a social psychological perspective, the key issue is under what conditions such change is more or less likely (Fiske and Taylor, 1991, pp. 149-154).
18 During the post war period, Sweden had only experienced two major militarised foreign policy crises—the DC 3/Catalina affair of 1952 involving the downing of two Swedish aircraft over the Baltic Sea in close proximity to the USSR (see Karlsson, 1995, 1998), and the 1981 'Whiskey on the Rocks' incident (see Bynander, this volume).
19 Two exceptions were Finance Minister Kjell Olof Feldt and Justice Minister Sten Wickbom, both of whom sought police protection on their own initiative.

20 A classic example of the power of metaphor in policy-making is the so-called domino theory, which guided U.S. policy in South East Asia (and Latin America) during much of the Cold War (Shimko, 1995, pp. 76-79).
21 In an interview with Wranghult (1998) a picture was conveyed, suggesting that he and Holmér did not really believe in this lead by the end of April 1986; they were rather interested in something else that they thought the 33-year old was hiding.
22 Here the predictions of prospect theory dovetail nicely with another phenomenon documented in laboratory as well as in real life, the escalation of commitment (Staw and Ross, 't Hart, 1994) in which people 'through good money after bad.'
23 In the summer of 1988, when the second Palme investigation team had been working for a year and a half, the existence of an illegal shadow investigation run by elements within the security police with the knowledge of the Cabinet was revealed. Ebbe Carlsson, a publisher with close ties to the Social Democratic leadership, had been involved in this group. The new Minister of Justice, Anna Greta Leijon would resign when she was linked to the smuggling of illegal bugging equipment to be used in the secret Palme investigation (which clung to the PKK lead after its dismissal by the official investigation) to Sweden.
24 In 1996, South African national Eugene de Kock stated that the South African intelligence had committed the murder of Olof Palme. As a consequence, the Palme investigators pursued this lead for several months under intense media scrutiny (Government of Sweden, 1999c).
25 The police conspiracy frame was never explicitly considered by the Palme investigation. Journalists and other unofficial investigators have pointed at actions of individual policemen, and suggested possible connections to the murder. This theory has been discussed in several of commission reports, which have examined the investigation (Government of Sweden, 1988, 1999c).
26 A subsequent bid by the prosecution to retry Petterson—submitted just before the statute of limitations expired—was rejected by the superior court.

9 Framing an American Threat: The European Commission and the Technology Gap

ULRIKA MÖRTH

This chapter discusses how the activity of framing legitimises certain interests and actors in EU's political process, but also how frames are important in constructing a European actorness and identity. Emphasis is on how the issue of defence equipment has been framed by the European Commission in the 1990s as part of the classic European discourse on the European 'malaise' towards the U.S. It is argued that even though the political breakthrough for the issue of defence equipment is evident in the ongoing formation of a defence policy and capacity in the EU, it has also for a long time been considered to be a question of Europe's (civilian) economical and technological capacity towards the U.S.[1] This was especially salient in the 1990s—when the need for the EU to address the issue of European economic competitiveness and technological development is articulated—than it has been during any earlier period of EU's history.

The empirical section of the chapter is divided into two parts. In the first it is argued that the perception of the need for strengthening Europe's economic and technological competitiveness towards the U.S is a regular feature in EU politics. Three waves of technology-gap threats can be identified. The first occurred in the mid-1960s, the second in the early 1980s and the third during the 1990s. The second section analyses how defence equipment has been part of this technology-gap threat in the 1990s, and how a market frame on the issue of defence equipment has enhanced a sense of a European actorness and identity.

Frames and Institutional Settings

As argued in the introductory chapter, frames are referents for action and give direction to the political process. Frames legitimise certain decisions and activate different actors. Actors also use frames in order to gain influence in the political process. This means that frames can be seen as instruments for pursuing various interests. Actors can use 'globalisation' and other catchwords in order to promote a specific set of policy solutions to various external threats (Rosamond, 1999). An issue can be framed as a threat to certain values and will therefore be the focus of political attention. Indeed, actors are not merely 'finding' circumstances but are also very much in the making of circumstances (Ruggie, 1998a, 1998b). However, conflicts concerning how to define and conceptualise a policy or an issue are not only about different interests. They are also about constitutive rules—how the rules of the game are shaped (Ruggie, 1998b, p. 871).

> The environment in which actors operate is given meaning through ongoing processes of social construction. This means that there is an inherent connection between the social construction of the 'external' environment and the interests that actors acquire (Rosamond, 1999, p. 658).

I argue that both the power and the identity dimensions are important in frame analysis.[2] The power dimension of the analysis focuses on conflicts between actors pursuing different frames. The identity dimension of the analysis is essential in order to study how an issue is interpreted and how actors organise collective experience. In other words, I am not only interested in why actors compete over how to categorise and define an issue but also in how definitions and conceptualisations direct the political process and determine the rules of the game.

Why does one particular frame appear rather than another? (cf. Foucault, 1972). Why are certain issues framed as threats whereas others take on more positive connotations? Major political and economic events seem to function as important triggers for a certain policy process and make possible policy activities that previously were considered to be political 'dead-ends' possible to pursue (Sandholtz, 1992). The general political development is thus an important factor behind the process of political attention. The end of the Cold War or the War in Kosovo cannot, however, in themselves explain why certain issues are on the European political agenda or why they are framed in a certain way.

I argue in this chapter that how an issue is framed partly depends on the institutional and organisational setting (cf. Powell and DiMaggio, 1991; Bourdieu, 1996). Frames do not come out of the blue. They consist of certain ideas that travel both in space and in time (Merton, 1965). An institutional and organisational approach takes into account that actors strive for influence, but this approach emphasises that they are also part of institutions which consists 'of cognitive, normative and regulative structures and activities that provide stability and meaning to social behaviour' (Scott, 1995, in Peters, 1999, p. 106). Indeed, European political integration can be viewed as a continuous process of institutionalisation—the process by which social processes take on rule-like status in social thought and action (Meyer and Rowan, 1991).

Europe's Competitiveness: Three Waves of Technology-Gap 'Fever'

The First Wave

Since the early and mid-1950s research and technological development (RTD) and industrial issues have been very much at the heart of the European Communities. The first RTD programmes that were launched were not based on any article in the treaties but on the general Article 235 in the Treaty of Rome.[3] This Article provided:

> a range of policy powers which could be used to determine the regulatory framework and market conditions for European industry. Thus, competition policy, freedom of capital and labour movements, the right of establishment, customs union, harmonisation of national laws, and state aids fell within the treaty's competence. But they were not subsumed under a general framework for industrial policy (Sharp and Shearman, 1987, p. 26).

In the mid-1960s technology policy and industrial policy began to be linked to each other, both in national politics and at the EC level. 'At the same time, a panicky debate erupted in Europe over technology gaps that left European industries dangerously behind the American competitors' (Sandholtz, 1992, p. 70). The diagnosis of a technology gap was presented by both national actors, such as governments, and European and international organisations, especially the OECD (Sandholtz, 1992; Mörth, 1996). The well-known book by Jean-Jacques Servan-Schreiber, *The American challenge* (1968), illustrates the general sense of a European 'malaise' towards the U.S. that existed in the late 1960s. National programmes were launched at the national level and the aim was to create national high-tech champions (Ibid.; Mörth, 1996, 1998).

Another policy response toward this perceived American threat was the decision to create a more coherent RTD policy and industrial policy at the European level. An important component in this endeavour was to create the framework programme on RTD in 1983 (see below). This process started already in the late 1960s when the Council adopted RTD plans that were elaborated by the Commission.[4] The Commission advocated supranational RTD and industrial policies, especially by the Commissioner Altiero Spinelli (1970-76), whereas the governments pursued a more intergovernmental policy-making style (Nau, 1975; Hodges, 1983). The Commission and the governments both shared, however, the view that the EC should take a greater responsibility for RTD and industrial issues that were regarded as strategic for the future of Europe. Under the leadership of Pierre Aigrain, French Delegate-General for Scientific and Technical Research, 'over forty projects for European-owned companies (to avoid encouraging further U.S. penetration) were put forward under the sectoral headings already identified' (Peterson and Sharp, 1998, p. 31). In 1971 an outline plan was decided for a European programme of Cooperation in Science and Technology (COST).

The Second Wave

The second wave of technology-gap 'fever' came in the early 1980s and was even more articulated in the period after the decision of the Single

European Act (SEA) in 1986-87. The policy responses this time were more focused on the European level than during earlier periods and one reason for this was the perceived threat from Japan. 'The impetus behind a legal and political mandate for an EU technology policy in the 1980s was the re-emergence of concern about Europe's lagging technological competitiveness—this time not just *vis-à-vis* America, but also in relation to Japan' (Peterson and Sharp, 1998, p. 68).

Three major European RTD programmes were launched between 1982 and 1985. Two programmes were sponsored by the EU: ESPRIT (the European Strategic Programme for R&D in IT) and RACE (R&D in Advanced Communications Technologies for Europe). The then Commissioner for research questions, Etienne Davignon, initiated the programmes for industry, with his close dialogue with the directors of the twelve largest European IT companies (Sandholtz, 1992; Peterson, 1992). They were, together with other high-tech programmes, part of EU's framework programme for research and technological development that was decided by the Council in 1983. The third programme, EUREKA—European Research Coordination Agency—was initiated by the then French President Mitterrand in 1985 as a first response to the American Strategic Defence Initiative programme (SDI) (Mörth, 1996). EUREKA was formally organised and financed outside the framework programme but it 'responded to the same fears about the status of high technology that motivated ESPRIT and RACE' (Sandholtz, 1992, p. 5). The framework programme and EUREKA comprised a European Technological Community and provided an umbrella for the promotion of a technological fortress Europe (Wyatt-Walter, 1995).

The Third Wave

EU's RTD policy can be characterised in the 1990s and in the early 2000s by the continuous building up of Europe's structural base of civilian power—so-called 'soft power' (Nye, 1990; Nye and Owens, 1996). The image of a declining Europe is still vivid but has somewhat changed focus. The framing of Europe's competitiveness is less focused on the technology-gap and more on unemployment 'and the EU's failure to match either the fast growth-rates of South-East Asia or the faster employment creation of the U.S' (Peterson and Sharp, 1998, p. 12). Thus, the inability in Europe to create jobs is considered to be an important symptom of its 'declining competitiveness' (Ibid.). The most comprehensive EU approach towards a common industrial policy emerged out of the White Paper 'Growth, Competitiveness, Employment,' which was published in December 1993 (COM (93) 700). The report identified a number of issues concerning EU competitiveness and aimed to 'lay the foundations for sustainable development of the European economies, thereby enabling them to withstand international competition while creating the millions of jobs that are needed' (Ibid., Preamble). The Commission had already in 1990 presented the so-called Bangemann Report (COM (90) 556), which outlined the major problems that the European industry was facing in an increasingly open and competitive environment. It was argued that Europe's competitive position in relation to Japan and the U.S. had worsened with regard to employment, shares of export markets, R & D etc (Ibid.).

In a 1993 White Paper it was suggested that a solution to the problem of European competitiveness lies in a strong knowledge-based economy. 'In the wake of the globalisation of economies and markets, it is no longer possible to divide industry and geographical areas into clearly identified and relatively independent segments' (Ibid., p. 65). This was, according to the communication, most evident within the fields of telecommunications, information technology, consumer electronics, etc. in which strategic alliances between firms are increasing (Ibid.). The former commissioner for industry, Martin Bangemann, has recurrently emphasised the need for the European nation-states to act as one entity since Europe is competing globally.

> The world is now becoming a global economy, thanks to Information and Communications Technology. In the global economy, wealth will only come from our ability to compete. We are in a race for competitiveness [...] competitiveness is not everything. But without competitiveness, everything is nothing (Speech at the 10th World Congress 'Technology and Services in the Information Society,' Bilbao 3 June 1996).

The problems of coordination between various political levels and policy activities have also been at the centre of various communications during the 1990s. According to the Commission this was especially a problem within the RTD area in which national policies were still developed largely without reference to one another (SEC (92) 682; COM (93) 700). The lack of coordination was 'particularly marked between military and civil research activities in each Member State...' (COM (93) 700, p. 98). The Commission argued that the lack of coordination between various RTD activities and other policy areas was an important factor behind the greatest weakness of Europe's research base, namely its 'limited capacity to convert scientific breakthroughs and technological achievements into industrial and commercial successes' (Ibid.). This European weakness was explicitly contrasted to the case in the U.S., which, according to the Commission, has succeeded in transforming research accomplishments into the commercial market (Ibid.). The diagnosis of Europe's problem vis-à-vis the U.S is also well elaborated in the Commission's Green Paper on Innovation in 1995. In the paper the European paradox is presented—Europe is good at research but not at transforming these skills into a competitive advantage. The reason for this paradox is that the European effort is fragmented. In an interview, the former commissioner for research, Edith Cresson, argues:

> I am afraid that we are wasting resources by spreading them too thinly over too many fields. This is why, together with my colleagues Commissioners Bangemann and Kinnock, I introduced the Task Forces. Their aim is to strengthen cooperation and coordination between research and industry, and to target our research efforts more precisely' (*Innovation & Technology Transfer*, 1996).

What was needed was a 'genuine European strategy for the promotion of innovation' (European Commission, 1995, p. 5).

Clearly, technology policy has thus been closely linked to other policy areas, such as trade, competition and economic policy (Cini and McGowan 1998). Indeed, by the late 1990s, the EU's technology policy had a far clearer and more widely accepted rationale than ever before (Peterson and Sharp, 1998, p. 114). The changed technology policy was evident in the framework programme during the 1990s. The redistributive component of the programme changed in the early 1990s to become more targeted towards the aim of strengthening Europe's competitiveness. In April 1997 the Commission presented a proposal for the fifth framework programme (F5P) for research and technological development (1998-2002, COM (97), 142). The overall theme of the proposal was how to cope with globalisation on a European level by making European research more effective and giving European added value. The programme covered a very broad area, including such issues as the knowledge-based society, employment, economic globalisation, European competitiveness, and foreign policy.

The importance of the information society and Europe's technologic and economic competitiveness has been a concurrent theme in the Presidency Conclusions of the European Council during the 1990s and in the early 2000.[5] There has thus been no disagreement between the Commission and the European Council on how to diagnose Europe's problem. One difference, however, between the Commission's communications and the Presidency Conclusions of the European Council, is that whereas the Commission has underlined the problematic relationship between Europe and the U.S., the European Council hardly ever explicitly mentions the European malaise towards the U.S. This could be explained by the fact that the Commission is more focused on thinking on Europe as an entity and how to transform a 'fragmented' European effort into a more coherent actor in a globalised economy.

To sum up, the three waves of technology-gap 'fevers' in the EU all share the general notion of a technologically declining Europe. The responses to this perceived threat to Europe's prosperity have consisted of various RTD programmes at the European level. The Commission and the European Council have recurrently stressed the importance of coordinated EU activities and that Europe must be seen as an entity. We now turn from this general discourse on Europe's technological and economic competitiveness to the issue of defence equipment and how the future of Europe's defence industry has become part of the classic lagging-behind theme.

The Commission and the Market Frame

In January 1996 the Commission took the unusual step of explicitly discussing the difficulty of separating between civilian and defence-related technology and that this fact had to be considered in various ways in EU policy-making (COM (96) 10). An important argument for the perceived need for increased linkages between the civilian and defence-related spheres was the changed dynamics in the technological and industrial sector. Traditionally it was the military sphere that gave the civilian sphere the technology—the so-called spin off effect—but the spin-off effect has more or less been replaced by the so-called spin-in effect (Ibid.). This meant that defence industry was becoming more dependent on civilian industry and civilian RTD programmes. The interlinkages between the two spheres were especially evident in the space and aerospace sector, which was in a great need for a coordinated approach (COM (96) 617). In the era of information technology and technological globalisation the separation between defence-related and civil technology and RTD activities were perceived as obsolete.

The communication from 1996 showed the Commission's ambition to pursue a more comprehensive industrial policy—an action plan—that not only included the civilian industry in Europe but also the defence-related industry. Although the future of the defence industry had been discussed earlier, the communication was the first comprehensive document from the Commission on the problems of the European defence industry. This was a rather bold initiative due to the fact that this sector has been regarded as an area of exclusive national prerogative. Article 296 (formerly Article 223) in the Treaty of European Union may be evoked by member states in their defence industry deals, which means that rules on mergers, competition and procurement are not applicable. The deals are normally considered within the market rules by the Commission for possible overlaps, which might raise anti-trust concerns. However, so far the Commission has never opposed a defence industrial merger or had the Court try whether a country has broken the rules in not notifying a merger within the defence industry (Interview with senior official in DG IV).

It is clear that the Directorate General on industrial affairs, DG III, pursued a policy of introducing more of industrial policy into the defence industry, meaning that the rules of the internal market could, after necessary adaptations, be used for this industry as well. DG III had close relations with the industry, both bilaterally and with EDIG and AECMA.[6] In order to create a European defence industrial strategy there have been several meetings between DG III and EDIG on the issue of defence equipment (Interviews with officials at DG III and the General Secretary of EDIG). The Commission and EDIG agree on the need to create a collective effort 'to tackle the various sensitive issues leading to the establishment of a European Defence Equipment Market where Defence Industry will survive to remain competitive and capable of catering for the European Armaments needs' (EDIG, 1995, p. 2).

According to DG III the incorporation of the defence industry into the first pillar must be implemented systematically. Although DG III recognises that the defence industry is a very special market, with its close relationship with the state, and therefore differs from other sectors of the economy, it is also obvious that it can be approached from a perspective of cost effectiveness. This is also DG III's task within the Commission. In the autumn of 1997, DG III presented a 'Draft Action Plan for the Defence-Related Industry' outlining measures for the short as well as the long term. A first step is to begin a process of standardisation of European defence equipment, intended to rationalise the different sets of standards currently being used by the defence ministries of the member states. This process of standardisation also entails common rules of public procurement. In a longer perspective, this standardisation process must also extend to differing national export policies with regard to conventional arms (see below). The next step would be to incorporate the defence industry sector into the EU's competition policy and state-aid regulations. During this stage there would also be a need for a European Armament Agency in charge of conducting armament cooperative and R&D programmes.

Clearly, the profile of DG III and its then Commissioner Martin Bangemann was very high on defence industry issues. They organised seminars, informal meetings with representatives of the industries, national administrators and other European bodies (Mörth, 1998, 2000). At a conference in June 1996—The Future of Europe's Defence Industry—Bangemann urged the national administrators to take part in the 'decision-finding process' that the Commission had initiated and that they should tell 'us what are the main problems and priorities' (Opening speech at 'The Future of Europe's Defence Industry' Conference in Brussels, 18 June 1996). The Commissioner emphasised the problems that the European defence industry was facing towards the U.S.

> First, if European defence industry will not overcome its structural problems we may lose the capacity either to compete efficiently or to cooperate on equal terms with the USA. Secondly, we will be challenged with technology gaps and a disappearance of technological skills. As nowadays, dual-use technologies are widespread, this may also have impacts in the commercial sphere. Given the long period of time for developing new technologies and new systems, these gaps could not be filled in a few years. This would have substantial economic and political consequences (Ibid.).

We can thus conclude that the activity of the Commission, especially DG III, and EDIG, was intense during the early to mid-1990s on the future of the European defence industry. In November 1997 the Commission presented another communication on the defence industry and in that communication the market frame is less salient than in the communication from 1996. In fact, in the communication the commission argues that the issue of defence equipment must be conceptualised from both a market and a defence frame (COM (97) 583).

To sum up, the Commission has been very active in framing the issue of defence equipment as a market issue. We now turn our attention to the defence industry, especially to the aerospace industry in Europe, and its activities during the 1990s and in the early 2000s.

European Defence Industry and the Fear of U.S. Competition

There have been major changes in the European industrial landscape during the 1990s and in the early 2000s. National companies—national champions—have been transformed into European and transatlantic companies.[7] The transnational linkages between the companies are multiple and complex (Schmitt, 2000b). Major industrial changes took place in 1999, which of course could be explained by the general development in the European defence policy process (Heisbourg, 2000). It is difficult to imagine that complex cross-mergers between defence industries would have taken place if there were no credible political development of a European defence policy. This being said, it is also quite clear that the industry itself created pressure for political initiatives and that the process towards a strong European defence industry are driven by market factors and not only by the logic within the defence policy process.

The aim in this part of the chapter is to discuss the industrial and the political idea of creating a European aerospace company—EADC—the European Aerospace and Defence Company. The general rationale behind the importance of creating a strong European defence industry has already been partly outlined in the previous section, namely that the borders between technologies are considered to be blurred and that the national protection of the defence industry is an obstacle to a common European effort to strengthening its industrial and RTD base.

Many observers within industry and the European Commission claim that the European aerospace industry suffers from the increasingly acute:

> effects of the continued partitioning of its industrial structures. To adapt the industrial structures to the internal market and to the increasing globalisation of the economy, the priority questions are: do current competition conditions allow the European aeronautical industry to be effective? What suitable measures can be taken to improve European competitiveness? (COM (92) 164:1c).

This diagnosis of the aerospace industry is presented in several communications from the Commission during the 1990s (e.g. COM (96),

617). In contrast to the situation in the U.S., European industry is perceived as fragmented because of national boundaries and separate research and defence policies (Ibid.).

The U.S. is the market leader in both civilian and military aerospace and the recent history of U.S. industry has been one of consolidation (James 1998). In 1993 the then U.S. defence minister Les Aspin invited the defence industry for a 'last supper' in which he made it clear that the industrial defence companies had to restructure (James, 1999). This was not only a rhetorical change by the American government but was followed by a merger wave in the American defence industry—from 20 companies to three prime suppliers: Boeing-McDonnell-Douglas, Lockheed Martin and Raytheon (Ibid.). The European defence industry, and the European Commission, closely monitored the American defence industrial consolidation. One major turning point from the European defence and civil aerospace industry perspective was when Boeing and McDonnell-Douglas merged in 1997. Until then the civil European aircraft project, Airbus, had challenged Boeing but after the American merger the power balance between the American and European companies profoundly changed (Lars Gissler, Vice President, Saab Aerospace Strategy, Saab AB, Conference at SIPRI, 13 October 2000).

The comparison with the situation in the U.S. is striking in various reports from the Commission. 'In comparison with the U.S., the pace of consolidation in Europe has been dramatically slow [...] in recent years the European aerospace industry has lost ground to that of the restructured and revitalised U.S. industry' (COM (97) 466, p. 5-6). Indeed, the European consolidation of the European defence industry must include measures to build in mechanisms that will prevent American companies from buying European companies (Interview with senior official, DG III, September 1999). In a report from the Brussels-based think-tank CEPS (Centre for European Policy Studies)—consisting of representatives from the industry and from the EU, WEU and NATO—it is stated that the 'European defence industry suffers from a widely fragmented 'home market base,' overcapacity and duplication of official procedures and processes. Its ability to compete in the global defence equipment market is threatened by these impediments' (CEPS, 1999, p. 22; cf. AECMA, 1996, p. 55). What is needed is thus 'rationalisation' and 'consolidation' of the sector and the creation of European companies (Ibid.).

Although the market for aerospace products is global, the European branch organisation AECMA holds that 'Europe requires an aerospace industry to support its role in global air transport, to allow an autonomous foreign policy and defence position, to safeguard its access to space and to contribute to technologically driven growth' (AECMA, 1996, p. 23). This means that a favoured way for the restructuring of the European aerospace industry 'is to replace the current loose cooperative arrangements with transnational company structures which have truly European dimensions' (Ibid., p. 51). According to individual branch organisations, Europe should not 'become dependent on third countries in the area of armaments [...]' (EDIG, 1995, pp. 2-3, 14).

The framing of a technology and capability gap between the U.S. and Europe is also presented by several journals specialising in defence industry matters, for instance *Aviation Week & Space Technology*, *Defence News* and *Jane's Defence Weekly* (JDW). Comparisons between the U.S. and Europe, for instance concerning defence budgets or RTD budgets, always show that the U.S. spends more (see for instance JDW 29 March 2000). Implicitly, sometimes even explicitly, these journals present the model for Europe—that of the U.S. The journals also underline the image of a 'war' between the U.S. and Europe on defence equipment matters (see for instance the case of Meteor, *Aviation Week & Space Technology*, 22 May 2000, p. 25).

Hence, the general image of European defence and aerospace is that of fragmentation and that the industry needs to be consolidated in order to compete with American companies. In December 1997 the French, German and British governments issued a statement in which they stressed the vital political and economic interest of restructuring the European defence industry. The political initiative has been interpreted as a reaction to the industry and its demand for political activities to enhance the creation of transnational defence companies (Interviews with officials with the Commission, EDIG and Saab). Until then the European governments had been rather silent on the question of the future of the European defence industry and the most active actor at the European level was the Commission (Mörth, 2001).

In the summer of 1998 the three governments plus the governments in Sweden, Spain and Italy presented the Letter of Intent initiative (LoI), which aimed to enhance the creation of Transnational Defence Companies. In July 2000 a general agreement was signed by the six governments that will bring the national defence industry policies closer to each other (Ibid.). The statement in November 1997 was thus the pre-phase to this political initiative and agreement. In that statement the three governments made it clear that they wanted to launch various measures to enhance transnational industrial collaboration, and in it they urged the national champions to present a plan and timetable for industrial restructuring and integration (Schmitt, 2000c).

Paradoxically, the political vision at the time was focused on the creation of *one* company, a European Defence and Aerospace Company.[8] There were several rounds of discussion regarding the make-up of this company, in politics as well as in the industry. There were many hurdles. One stumbling block was the general lack of a European company statute. The Commission stated in a Communication in 1992 that with the European company statute, 'the Community will provide the European aircraft industry with a legal framework for adapting its industrial and legal structures to the conditions of global competition' (COM, (92), 164, p. 24).

Rather soon the industrial development turned away from moving towards the creation of one company. In January 1999, British Aerospace confirmed that it would buy General Electric Company's Marconi Electronics, which created the third largest defence and aerospace group in the world. Germany's DASA warned that the creation of a pan-European aerospace and defence company might be postponed indefinitely (*Financial Times*, 25 January 1999). Prior to the take-over it was often mentioned in the specialised press that the best way to push forward plans for a consolidated European Aerospace and Defence Company (EADC) was through a link-up between BAE and DASA.

In October 1999, a merger between Aérospatiale Matra and DASA was announced. The new company, which would form a military aviation joint venture, was named EADS (European Aeronautic Defence and Space Company), not to be confused with EADC.

What is interesting with the new company (EADS) is the fact that 'for the first time, "national champions" are merging all their assets (with the exception of Dasa's aero-engine subsidiary MTU, which will be retained in the DaimlerChrysler group). With the recent inclusion of CASA, what began last October as a Franco-German rapprochement is turning into a truly European grouping' (Schmitt, 2000a, p. 4). The new European grouping will enjoy a dominant position in the European aerospace industry. In May 2000 the European Commission cleared the creation of the new company (*Financial Times*, 14 May 2000). Even though the companies involved have overlapping interests, the political pressure on the Commission is very high from the governments concerned (*European Voice*, 4-10 May 2000).

Thus, the political vision of one big European company, EADC, is dead. The idea has been questioned from an industrial competitiveness perspective and as a symbol for fortress Europe. 'We have the capability but in doing that it is essential that we do not establish fortress Europe by creating a single acquisition agency and only one international industry in each industrial area. That would merely lead to plan economy' (Senior executive Vice-President of Saab, Lars Josefsson, Statement at 5th Forum Defence Industries Conference, 23 May 2000, Brussels). One of my interviewees in the Commission said in September 1999 that very few believed in the creation of *one* company. The notion of EADC was instead an effective way to provoke and thus generate action to get rid of various trade and market barriers.

From a European political perspective it is of course a crucial question what kind of linkages the European companies will have with American companies. In August 1999 John Weston stated 'We never conceived EADC as something that represented Fortress Europe, with everything in it. We actually saw it as a mechanism for how to get some of these deals together across the national boundaries of Europe' (John Weston, *Defense Daily*, 10 August 1999). In fact the companies are mixed up with each other already (Interview with former Secretary-General of EDIG, Woodcock, September 1999). Interestingly, in February 2000 the French co president executif of EADS, Philippe Camus, stated that EADS would not constitute a fortress Europe (*Le Monde*, 25 February 2000).[9]

In December 1999 it was stated that BAE Systems of the UK and Boeing, the U.S. aircraft and defence manufacturer, were engaged in exploratory talks which could result in a merger of their defence businesses (*Financial Times*, 13 December 1999). BAE and Boeing are already involved in a number of collaborative defence-related projects and the two governments have stressed the potential benefits of defence cooperation between the UK and the U.S. (Ibid.). Indeed, one scenario in about a five years time is that BAE's linkages with Boeing will intensify and that Lockheed Martin 'could become the American fiend of EADS' (*The Economist*, 23 December 2000—5 January 2001, p. 112). BAE also has a long-standing partnership with Lockheed Martin. In November 2000 BAE bought parts of Lockheed Martin, which made it one of world's largest defence groups (Ibid.).

The logic that makes the Atlantic option attractive is of course compelling. The military hardware budgets have been decreasing on both sides of the Atlantic. The production of high technology that is so important for the military is dependent on global and commercial business. Hence, a market-driven consolidation tends to lead towards closer transatlantic relations. Politically, however, governments seem to be rather reluctant towards a more market-driven and transatlantic consolidation. One political problem is the uncertainty regarding the future role of the U.S. and NATO in European security affairs. From an industrial and business community perspective it could be argued that the political polarisation between the U.S. and Europe will be (or is perhaps already) less relevant among the defence companies. It could therefore be argued that in the long run there will be U.S. firms 'that become European and European firms that become American, within and across product lines, enhancing companies and efficiency in a broader transatlantic market' (Gordon Adams in *Financial Times*, 3 February 1999).

Euro-American Competition: The Case of the Eurofighter

From the European Commission's perspective it is, however, very important to create a strong Europe versus the U.S. Indeed, the European consolidation of the European defence industry must include measures to build in mechanisms that will prevent American companies from buying European companies (Interview with senior official, DG III, September 1999).

An illustration of the competition between Europe and the U.S. is the arming of the Eurofighter, which is a fighter project involving the United Kingdom, Germany, Spain and Italy. Whether the European countries chose the missile manufactured by Raytheon or one produced by the European Meteor consortium was seen as an indication of whether U.S. fears of a 'fortress Europe' may be realised or not. Indeed, the decision by the governments in the UK, Germany, Spain and Italy, is seen as crucial in the ongoing consolidation of the aerospace industry (*Financial Times*, 18 February 2000). From a European industrial as well as political perspective Meteor is primarily about breaking a U.S. monopoly in the missile sector. The European consortium consists of a joint venture by Aérospatiale Matra and BAE Systems and the American company Boeing. In February of 2000 the deputy chief director of Matra BAE, Alan Garwood, declared that this cooperation provided 'a very clear signal to the U.S. government that strong relationships with American industry are very important to us' (*Financial Times*, 18 February 2000). In May 2000 the British government decided it would buy Meteor air-to-air missiles and not the American Amraam missile (FT May 17 2000). 'For the first time Europe will equip its fighter aircraft with a European air-to-air missile, creating interoperability and independence to export' (Fabrice Bregier, CEO of Matra BAE Dynamics, *Aviation Week & Space Technology*, 22 May 2000, p. 25).

To sum up, the European defence industry is traversing a period of dramatic change. The earlier vision of one European aerospace company is dead. Instead Europe is doing what the U.S. did earlier, namely creating a small number of large companies able to compete with the U.S. giants.

Concluding Analysis

In the wake of the end of the Cold War and the creation of the internal market the Commission has revitalised the classic lagging-behind theme between Europe and the U.S. Like a Trojan horse the Commission has pursued a market frame in order to gain influence over an issue that has traditionally been framed as a defence and security issue. In other words, the defence industry has been 'desecuritised.' The Commission has, together with the industry, special journals and policy centres such as CEPS created a political crisis awareness pointing to various economic, industrial and technological threats from the U.S.

An image of a Europe in disarray is presented which legitimises a stricter interpretation of Article 296 and the protection of national security interests. Important values are at stake which make it necessary to think in European and global terms. In the 1980s it was the economic threat that SDI (the Strategic Defence Initiative) posed to the Europeans that was one of the driving forces behind the creation of the internal market (Sandholtz et al, 1992, p. 82).

The nation-state as the important territory for technological innovations was replaced by the notion of a European territory. In the 1990s the turn has come to the defence industry. Thus, the ongoing liberalisation of the national defence industries is part of the liberalisation trend in the European Union that started with the creation of the internal market. This market integration entails the gradual harmonisation of standards, or at least the creation of a framework within which a standardisation process could take place.

The U.S. is clearly perceived as the model for Europe and has become an important component in EU policymaking and European identity building. The technological and economic threat of the U.S. is not simply a matter of objective and exogenous changes. It is a social construction. Ideas must be conceptualised and put on the political agenda. By interpreting the issue of defence equipment into a market frame the Commission and industry have assigned a clear meaning to the issue and guided future political actions—to deregulate the national defence industry. Through the market framing activity—by contrasting Europe against the U.S.—a sense of European unity and identity is created. Thus, framing is not only about strategic interests, it also constitutes the identity of actors. A sense of European actorness is created.

Scholars who study the linkage between security and international political economy suggest that the end of the Cold War has led to a power struggle between states on economic and technological terms. States' struggle for economic growth, knowledge and competitiveness has partly replaced the more military and territorially oriented security policy (Crawford, 1995; cf. Strange, 1992). Nye argues that '[i]n assessing power in the information age, the importance of technology, education, and institutional flexibility has risen, whereas that of geography, population and raw materials has fallen' (1996, p. 22).

The popular notion of competitiveness 'has been widely used to create a sense that the U.S. and Europe are 'losing' to each other in some kind of knock-out competition' (Cable, 1995, p. 310; Hart, 1992). The increasing competitiveness is thus often described in realist terms—as economic warfare between leading countries in the world. There is a struggle between independent actors striving to maximise their own utility—the classic logic of anarchy in the international system. The U.S., the EU, Japan (and increasingly China):

> are essentially adversaries though the weapons in countering threats to national security are economic policy measures rather than Cruise missiles and Stealth bombers. By combining a 'realist', Machiavellian, approach to international relations with the language of security and the economic insights of 'strategic trade theory', advocates of a more mercantilist approach have achieved some intellectual respectability and made some impact, in the U.S. especially (Cable, 1995, p. 307).

The empirical analysis in this chapter shows that the European Commission has now transferred this reasoning on the importance of knowledge-based power and the view of the adversary to the European defence industry context. The emerging alliances between European and American defence companies are, however, driven by market frames. In markets there are no enemies, only competitors. In a world of economic globalism in which production becomes decoupled from individual states, 'it becomes more and more difficult to constitute an Other that might be transformed into a threatening enemy' (Lipschutz, 1995, p. 220).

Notes

1. These issues are further analysed in a forthcoming book (Mörth, 2001).
2. This means that 'actors both calculate consequences and follow rules' (Laegreid & Roness, 1999, p. 308; March and Olsen, 1998; Marcusson et al, 1999; Green Cowles et al, 2001).
3. The new number after the Treaty of Amsterdam is 308.
4. See for instance the Marchécal report in 1967. The Marchéal Committee was created in 1965 to 'review national scientific and technological policies, reported to the first-ever meeting of the EEC Council of Science Ministers in 1967' (Peterson and Sharp, 1998, p. 31). At the Hague summit in 1969 it was declared that the agreement to formulate a research programme lay near in the future (Nau, 1975).
5. See for instance Presidency Conclusions from Copenhagen in 1990, Dublin and Florence in 1996, Luxemburg in 1997, Cardiff and Vienna in 1998 and the so-called Vienna Strategy for Europe, Helsinki in 1999 and Lisbon in 2000. At the European Council's meeting in Lisbon March 2000 it was stated that 'The European Union is confronted with a quantum shift resulting from globalisation and the challenges of a new knowledge-driven economy. These changes are affecting every aspect of people's lives and require a radical transformation of the European economy' (Presidency Conclusions, para, p. 1). For that reason the Council outlined a 'new strategic goal for the next decade: *to become the most competitive and dynamic knowledge-based economy in the world capable of sustainable economic growth with more and better jobs and greater social cohesion*' (Ibid., p. 5).
6. EDIG stands for the European Defence Industrial Group and AECMA stands for the European Association of Aerospace Manufacturers.
7. For an overview of European Aerospace Consolidation see for instance *Aviation Week & Space Technology* (24 July 2000).
8. The company would include the Airbus partners (France-Aérospatiale, Germany-Dasa, United Kingdom-British Aerospace, Spain-Casa) and Italy's Finmeccania-Alenia and Sweden's Saab. Initially, however, the companies involved were Aerospatiale, BAE and DASA.
9. The transatlantic linkages already exist, for instance, in October 1999 it was announced that Marconi Electronic Systems (owned by BAE), Aérospatiale Matra and DaimlerChrysler Aérospace agreed to merge their space activities into a new company, Astrium (*Aviation Week & Space Technology*, 25 October 25 1999, and 5 June 2000). Furthermore, the same month it was also announced that Aérospatiale Matra, British Aerospace and Italy's Finmeccanica were about to merge their missile businesses (Ibid.). If Finmeccanica enters into Airbus a transatlantic problem is created. This is because Finmeccanica already has a close relationship with Boeing—the arch-rival of Airbus (*Financial Times*, 14 April 2000).

Conclusion: Towards a Theory of Threat Politics

JOHAN ERIKSSON

Threat politics is about competing images of threats, risks and scapegoats. In the perspective of late modernity, threat politics could be seen as characteristic of societies with highly developed technologies and infrastructures, including nuclear power and information technology—features that make them extremely vulnerable. In a contrasting perspective, threat politics could be associated with war-torn or deeply divided societies plagued by hatred, bloodshed and poverty. Both perspectives are flawed. Threat politics should not be associated with a particular type of society or historical period. Though the patterns of threat politics change over time and show great diversity across societies, it cannot be done away with. This concluding chapter attempts to synthesise the discrete analyses of previous chapters with the intent of teasing out some general propositions on what shapes the societal salience of threat images.

The various ways in which threat images can take on societal salience have been vividly exposed in the contributions to this book. This includes how threats and risks are framed among public opinion and political elites. It is also about how news reporting does not simply reflect episodes but rather contains recurrent narratives of how the world is to be understood. Furthermore, it is about how focusing events implying urgency, uncertainty and threatened core values—crises—impact on agenda setting and decision-making. It can also be about big business leaders who are lobbying political leaders to get their attention to particular threat images.

Posturing on major themes of fear is either legitimating or challenging master frames in politics and societal debate. Therefore the politics of framing is an important instrument of power. This entails responsibility as well as opportunity. Threat politics may facilitate or hinder the realisation of political goals. Threat politics may solve, underpin or even create policy controversies. Threat politics can challenge or reinforce conceptions of collective identity.

In the following, the diverse explanations of why threat images take on societal salience that have been unfolded in this volume are brought together in a coherent, albeit tentative, explanatory framework. I conclude by reflecting on the cross-fertilisation that arguably is needed for furthering the understanding of threat politics.

Explaining the Societal Salience of Threat Images

In the introductory chapter it was suggested the societal salience of threat images largely could be explained by threat politics, and that the primary feature of this is a struggle between advocates of competing problem frames. It was argued that the analysis should take into account the type of referent object of a threat image, the type of framing actor, frame characteristics, and patterns of reframing. The initial discussion presented a conceptual framework, but only hinted at possible explanations, primarily by focusing on the impact of framing.

This argument can now be qualified. The factors identified here, as influencing societal salience are either of a *general* or *circumstantial* nature. The contention is that the complexity of threat politics cannot be explained either by a parsimonious universal theory or a very detailed contextually limited theory. What are suggested here are therefore some contributions to a middle-range theory. The general factors are categorised as cognition, framing and culture. The circumstantial factors that are emphasised here are epistemic communities, bureaucratic politics, identity politics, and a final category labelled the referent objects of threat images (actors, events and structural conditions). The general factors are considered to be necessary but not sufficient, while those of a circumstantial nature are neither necessary nor sufficient, except under very specific circumstances. Hence, an explanation of why some threat images take on societal salience but not others takes into account the general factors, as well as one or more of the circumstantial factors.

It must be stressed that the contribution here is not so much the analysis of the specific factors as the synthesis. Cognition, framing, culture, epistemic communities and so forth have been studied elsewhere. What is presented here is rather a new way of combining factors seldom addressed in a comprehensive framework. Specifically, as our explanations emphasise ideational factors such as cognition, framing and culture, they go beyond neo-utilitarianism (Ruggie, 1998, Adler, 1997). Moreover, though explaining is an ambitious goal, it must be emphasised that the intent never was to be more than exploratory. The preliminary answers suggested here are neither comprehensive nor conclusive, in the analytical as well as empirical sense.

General Factors: Cognition, Framing and Culture

Cognition, culture and framing are three general factors of an ideational nature that generally appear to have an impact on the societal salience of threat images. The three are not of the same kind, however. Cognition is about common individual perceptions of threats and risks. Framing emphasises agency and choice. Culture calls attention to structural context. The reasons for focusing on these three as general explanations are the following. Explaining why some images but not others take on societal salience must begin with what happens in the minds of people. The basis of this are some general observations made in risk studies and psychological research. That framing is given a general explanatory status should come as no surprise. Frame analysis has provided the basic conceptual framework presented in the introductory chapter, and can now be given a more explicit position in our explanatory framework. Focusing on the impact of culture is the result of systematically applying cultural theory in the study of risk perceptions and threat politics. The general impact of cultural context is shown most forcefully by Bjereld, but is also addressed by Robertson in her study of the media, and briefly also in the contributions by Sjöberg, Stern and Hansén.

Cognition The main cognitive point is this: perceived risks have greater salience than perceived gains. When faced with a choice between risk aversion and an opportunity to gain something, people tend to opt for risk aversion. This is a basic argument in the psychological literature on prospect theory (Kahneman, Slovic and Tversky 1982; Farnham 1994; Levy 1997), and is corroborated by contributors to this volume (Sjöberg; Stern and Hansén). Thus there is a basic cognitive explanation for the salience of threat images. People are only likely to accept risk when the aversion of that risk would imply that they loose something they value. Of this an example is the willingness to take to arms (accept the risk of being killed in battle) when facing a threat to political freedom (avoid losing a core value).

Paying attention to cognitive factors follows a general trend in the social sciences, what Emanuel Adler (1997, p. 320-21) calls 'cognitive revolution.' This takes into account but goes beyond the contention that people do not act in response to reality as it is, but on the basis of how they interpret this reality. This is not only about perceiving but also about representing problems to others. This involves asking why some interpretations of reality are collectively taken for granted, while others are considered as biased or perverse. That there is room for political manoeuvring on such issues can be concluded from our studies showing differences between the risk perceptions of mass and elite (see Sjöberg; Bjereld, this volume).

Framing That framing influences the societal salience of issues has been argued and illustrated throughout this volume. The basic point is that the impact is not only explained by *what* is identified as a threat, but largely also by *how* it is represented to others. This latter aspect is what framing is about. Three specific observations can be made.

First, risks that are framed as *general* (risk to others) rather than *personal* (risk to oneself) have a much greater potential for taking on societal salience. One reason for this is that risks framed as general tend to be perceived as much bigger than risks framed as personal. In general people tend to see themselves as safe, but think that others face much greater risks. Another reason is that government responsibility for risk mitigation tends to be seen as much bigger if risks are framed as general rather than personal. There is one exception, however, i.e. if risks are framed as personal but also as something that people feel they have little or no control, such as radioactive fallout. In such cases there will be a demand for governmental action, despite the fact that the risk is perceived as personal. Sjöberg in his convincing survey of risk perceptions makes these observations.

Second, *elaborated* frames take on societal salience more easily than *restricted* frames. Of this an example is the elaborated frame of 'information operations,' which since the mid 1990s has been widely employed in the securitisation of IT, without any noticeable opposition either among experts or politicians (Eriksson). Likewise, Karlsson shows that the elaborated threat frames addressed by big business leaders have been almost the same as those identified by national governments. The reason for such consensus is that elaborated frames allow a wider range of interpretations and applications of the same issue. In effect, potential controversies between actors representing contrasting views can be downplayed or concealed. The issue can be securitised (addressed as a security problem), but at the same time depoliticitised (open political conflict over the issue is avoided). The distinction between 'elaborated' and 'restricted' frames is also emphasised in general framing theory (Snow and Benford, 1992).

Third, *thematic* frames have a greater societal salience than *episodic* frames. While short-lived news items are represented in episodic frames that constantly replace each other, thematic frames—also known as grand narratives or master frames—are underlying, long-running serials that structure public debate and political decision-making. Robertson shows this in her comparative study of news framing. Illustrative of this are the significant differences between the thematic frames employed by British *BBC World* and Swedish Television's *Rapport*, as shown by Robertson. The former stresses continuity with the Cold War era, the inevitability of threatening situations and tragedies, and seldom gives voice to actors involved. In contrast, Swedish *Rapport's* master frame emphasises change in world politics, blames actors as responsible for tragedies, and gives voice to actors concerned. As will be argued in the subsequent section, such differences are largely explained by cultural context.

Focusing on framing implies an emphasis on agency. Framing does not come out of the blue. There is always a framing actor, a concept that is equitable with 'policy entrepreneur' in agenda setting theory (Kingdon, 1995) and 'securitising actor' in securitisation theory (Buzan, Wæver and del Wilde, 1998). Cunning political actors may exploit knowledge about the impact of framing. If the goal is to get public attention to an issue, the actor is likely to me more successful if it is framed as a general rather than a personal problem. Reframing an issue from a controversial to a generally more acceptable frame is important. Mörth shows in her study that the European Commission has been more successful in solving political stalemates concerning defence industry by reframing the issue from a 'defence frame' to a 'market frame.'

That reframing can be used for solving intractable policy controversies is also argued more generally in framing theory (Schön and Rein, 1994). This is not to say that all actors are aware of these effects of framing, or that those who are, are actually using this knowledge. Understanding the nature of framing is not to be equated with assuming that rationality explains behaviour. On the contrary, our conception of framing is that it is more of a skill or art. Some employ it and others do not. Some use it consciously and others do not really reflect on their framing activities. Some are good at it while others fail.

Culture Arguing that culture has a general impact on the societal salience of threat images might seem paradoxical. It could easily be argued that an emphasis on culture reveals the circumstantial rather than the universal features of threat politics. But this is exactly the point: the societal salience is generally affected by the cultural context in which a threat image is identified. The success for competing problem frames largely depend on the dominant culture in a society. This subject has been addressed in recent contributions to security studies (McSweeney, 1999; Katzenstein, 1996; Wæver et al, 1993), and could be seen as reflecting a general trend in the social sciences (Lapid and Kratochwil, 1996). However, studying the impact of culture is hardly a novel idea emanating from security studies.

Drawing on general Cultural Theory à la Wildavsky, Bjereld shows that the typology of individualistic, egalitarian, hierarchical and fatalistic cultures is purposeful for addressing this issue. Therefore, the results of the case studies presented in this book cannot easily be generalised. There are good reasons to believe that case studies in other cultural contexts than those presented here might reveal quite different patterns. This is apparent with regard to what threat images take on societal salience (e.g. refugees are more likely to be framed as threats in countries with a more hierarchical culture than Sweden). In addition, the demand for governmental mitigation of threats and risks is likely to be higher in countries with a weaker tradition of welfare statism and a stronger culture of liberal individualism than Sweden. Moreover, Karlsson shows the impact of a culture in his study of how both big business leaders and national governments frame threats in accordance with a liberal perspective. Thus there is need for comparative studies, including cases representing different cultural contexts.

The impact of cultural context is also shown in Robertson's comparative media study. The differences between the master frames that were identified in British *BBC World* and Swedish *Rapport* can be traced back to cultural differences. The specific content of these differences have not been clarified, however. If this is to be attempted, it will be necessary to go beyond national culture in the broader sense, and also look more specifically at corporate and newsroom cultures. News framing is influenced both by media globalisation and local newsroom cultures. The general impression is that while globalisation influences *what* is addressed, culture affects *how* it is represented.

Circumstantial Factors

Epistemic communities, bureaucratic politics, identity politics, and referent objects are four concepts considered as circumstantial factors. In a given situation, one or more of them can be but do not necessarily have to be, necessary factors. However, they are never sufficient explanations for the societal salience of threat images, as they always have to be seen in combination with the three general factors. This point implies a critique of the separate discourses that have emerged on these themes, especially those on epistemic communities, bureaucratic politics, and identity politics. In each of these fields, which now have a substantial body of literature on their own, there is a tendency to consider the particular concept in focus as a universal explanation for change in policy. In our perspective, such single factor explanations cannot account for the complexity of threat politics. By contrast, the present model is more comprehensive, though simultaneously being more watery than a single factor approach.

Why, then, are these particular factors addressed and not others? The simple reason is that they are the factors that truly stand out after scanning the individual contributions to this book. In addition, they do seem to fit together, especially when adopting a pragmatic constructivist approach, as argued more thoroughly below.

Epistemic communities Mainly as a result of modernisation and the increasing complexity of societal issues, networks of knowledge-based experts—epistemic communities—have become increasingly influential in public debate, the media, and policy-making. Studies of 'epistemic communities' show that control over knowledge and information is an important dimension of power (Haas, 1992). These 'knowledge elites' play an important role in articulating causes and effects, framing issues for public debate, and shaping policy options. Epistemic communities are influential only under specific conditions, however. First, if there is a consensual worldview and problem framing among the experts. This is not always the case, as witnessed for instance in the professional debate on the BSE disease in Europe. Yet there is a strong drive toward consensual knowledge in professional communities. Second, if the issues at hand are technically complicated. Third, and of particular importance for our focus on threat images, their role is most noticeable 'in the face of uncertainty, and more so in the wake of a shock or crisis' (Haas, 1992, p. 14).

In this book, all three criteria—knowledge consensus, technical complexity, and uncertainty—are applicable to the decision-making crises characterising the submarine incidents (Bynander), and the Palme assassination (Stern and Hansén). In the submarine case, politicians have reported that they found their range of options, concerning framing as well as solutions, severely constrained by the navy experts and their analyses. In both cases, specific epistemic communities emerged, such as the navy and the police, which greatly influenced problem framing and decision-making. However, epistemic communities do not only play a role in crises characterised by urgency and drama. As observed in my own study of IT security and information warfare, the influence of experts may not only emerge through incidents, but also because of the uncertainty and technical complexity characterising the issue area.

The circumstantial significance of epistemic communities is also indicated in Karlsson's study of how big business leaders try to influence the threat frames of governments in the Baltic Sea area. It was observed that though a 'technocratic approach' was available, the big business leaders preferred the 'power approach' of talking directly to the governments.

Bureaucratic politics While epistemic communities are based on consensus, bureaucratic politics is about rivalry and contending frames. It is a well-known thesis that crises and perceptions of external threat make people put aside their internal quarrels and join forces (cf. Rosati, 1981). In their analysis of the Palme murder, however, Stern and Hansén corroborate the contrasting view that bureaucratic politics may appear and even get stronger during crises (cf. Rosenthal, 't Hart and Kouzmin, 1991; Stern and Verbeek, 1998; Ripley, 1995).

Thus, bureaucratic politics make contending threat frames salient, but also make it more difficult for a single threat frame to take on a *dominant* position in public debate, the media and political decision-making. Dominant threat frames seem to require an epistemic community, or maybe a broader consensus even beyond the 'knowledge elite.'

Bureaucratic politics are not limited to threat framing, however. If there is an epistemic community making the framing of threats uncontested, bureaucratic politics may revolve around the responsibility for and management of identified problems. This is shown in my study of IT security and information operations. Though there is consensus among politicians and the military-bureaucratic establishment about the framing of information operations as a serious security threat, there is an ongoing turf battle about responsibility and solutions.

Identity politics Identity has become a central topic in security studies, risk studies and crisis management research—primarily as a result of the constructivist turn in the social sciences. In response to rationalistic theories, identity theorists argue that security and risk policy, including the formation of threat images, are not expressions of national interests, but rather shaped by conceptions of identity (McSweeney, 1999; Katzenstein, 1996; Ruggie, 1998). The 'we-them' distinction helps to explain why some are considered potential enemies and others are defined as friends or allies. This is captured by the notion of societal security, which emphasises national identity as a core value (Wæver et al, 1993; Buzan, Wæver and de Wilde, 1998). While sovereignty is the core value of states—the traditional concern in security policy—identity is the core value of national communities.

However, in contrast to cognition, framing and culture, identity does not always shape the societal salience of threat images. Identity is not an overarching explanation of problem framing and decision-making. The impact of identity is most likely strongest in situations when collectivities (states, nations, ethnic groups etc.) are redefining their most fundamental relationships, including making and breaking alliances, integrating and seceding from polities. Noreen demonstrates this in his study of how Estonia is adapting its national identity to western conceptions. According to way of reasoning, the Baltic countries want to join NATO and the European Union because this would confirm their reorientation from Russia to the western 'family' of democratic European nations. Thus it cannot simply be explained by military precautions for providing security from a potential Russian attack. The Baltic states are seeking a new identity in post-Cold War Europe. Paying attention to identity politics makes the Baltic silence on 'the Russian threat' understandable. The Baltic countries have learned to speak the security language of NATO and the European Union, and this implies an emphasis on 'cooperative security,' 'soft security,' and identity. The Estonian reframing from hard-core realist conceptions of power and military threats to an emphasis on the European 'family' they wish to join is captured only if identity politics is part of the explanatory framework.

In her analysis of the EU Commission's policy on defence industry, Mörth emphasises the constitutive dimension of framing European competitiveness as a 'technology gap' to the United States. She argues that this contributes to a creating a European identity. With the U.S. being framed as the 'other,' the European 'self' can more easily take shape. In addition, in her study of mediated threats, Robertson argues that by paying attention to the sense-making narratives, and not only to the informational aspects of news reporting, an important political implication is revealed. That is, what Robertson calls the identity function, the juxtaposition of 'us' with threatening 'others.'

Referent objects: events, actors and structural conditions In the introductory chapter it was argued that explaining the societal salience of threat images also must account for the distinctive features of the phenomena that the images are about. Events, structural conditions and actors may or may not be the targets of threat images. It was suggested that dramatic events take on societal salience more easily than both structural conditions and actors. This was corroborated by our case studies of Swedish national crises—the submarine intrusions (Bynander) and the assassination of Prime Minister Olof Palme (Stern and Hansén). Indeed, it is a central claim argument in agenda setting theory (Kingdon, 1995, pp. 94-109), crisis studies (Stern, 1999) and classical theories of international politics (Jervis, 1976, ch. 6) that incidents of this calibre often provide the push for getting the attention of decision-makers, the media and the public opinion.

The grounding of the Soviet submarine U137 in 1981—the 'Whiskey on the rocks'—undoubtedly was a triggering event. Importantly, however, previous submarine incidents, especially the hunt at Utö in 1980, did not catch the same attention either of the politicians or the media. Unlike the U137 crisis, any commissions of inquiry or upgrading of submarine hunting capability did not follow the Utö incident. However, the much more visible U137 crisis—a Soviet submarine grounded deep into the Swedish archipelago—also set the scene for the agenda setting of subsequent incidents. Though the great many incidents that followed this crisis for the layman (including politicians and the media) appeared similar to the Utö incident, they took on much greater salience, including series of commissions of inquiry. This supports a main thesis of ours – that the nature of external events do not necessarily determine whether the end up on the agenda or not. Events have to be identified and framed, preferably by influential actors. Additional facilitating conditions are also required. In the case of submarine incidents, Bynander shows an interesting combination of on the one hand an epistemic community—the navy—providing 'compelling evidence' for the submarine threat and, on the other hand, separate branches and individual actors involved in bureaucratic rivalry about how to combat the perceived threat.

Several of the other contributions to this book provide examples of how focusing events have taken on societal salience. Of particular interest is the withdrawal of Russian forces from Estonian territory in August 1994, which definitely provided the push for an official 'desecuritisation' of Russia. The withdrawal was probably a necessary but hardly a sufficient explanation for the reframing of Estonian security rhetoric, changing from a hawkish to a much softer official policy, emphasising cooperation with rather the defense against Russia. My own chapter on information security observed the impact of the Y2K bug for the 'securitisation' of IT. The Y2K bug, however, was neither a sufficient nor necessary explanation. But it helped to explain why the dramatisation of IT was intensified at the turn of the millennium.

Though focusing events tend to take on societal salience more easily than both structural conditions and actors, they easily fade from the busy agendas of politicians and the media. In parallel to the distinction between episodic and thematic frames, structural conditions can be associated with the latter. If and when these have taken on societal salience their staying power tend to be much stronger. Of this a number of examples can be given from our case studies. Mörth shows the impact of the structural condition of European economic competitiveness, framed as a 'technology gap' in relation to the U.S. Likewise, Robertson shows the remarkable staying power of a traditional Cold War frame in *BBC World's* reporting on Russia. Interestingly, this stands in stark contrast to the Swedish *Rapport* perspective, in which the situation in Russia is depicted as dramatically different from the Cold War era. Thus the impact of culture and framing is emphasised once again.

Finally, what comes out most clearly is that it is the combination of all three types of referent objects—events, structural conditions and actors—when an incident like the murder of Olof Palme not only becomes a temporary murder mystery, but also calls attention to the structural vulnerability of state security, and provokes a blaming process targeting not only individuals but whole groups of actors. This is in accordance with the notion of 'coupling the streams,' which Kingdon (1995) calls the unique situations in which several facilitating conditions converge in a given time and place.

How Does it All Hang Together?

The factors and explanations discussed above are compatible in that they all fit together within a 'middle ground' constructivism (Adler, 1997). In our case, this implies that threat images are socially constructed through a framing process that is generally affected by cognition and culture, in combination with some contingency of epistemic communities, bureaucratic politics, identity politics, and/or some set of referent objects of the images at hand. These explanatory factors interact in many ways, and it goes beyond our purpose to sort out the complex pattern of thinkable interactions.

The relationship between culture and identity politics warrants particular attention. Identity should not be equated with culture, one of the general explanatory factors discussed above. Collective identity—a sense of belonging together—may exist with or without a shared culture in the form of common traditions, language, worldview, religion, and so forth. Collective identity is often strengthened if there is also a common culture, and people who share a common identity often produce a common culture. But they are not the same. Identity research, particularly that on nationalism, has shown that there are no given or obvious 'cultural traits' that will come to symbolise a common identity (Anderson, 1991; Hylland Eriksen, 1993). The groups involved in the Ulster conflict, for example, do not identify themselves according to language (as both speak English).

Indeed, even religion plays a subordinate role in this conflict, despite the fact that the groups refer to themselves as Catholics and Protestants. Religious arguments are very seldom used in political rhetoric or for mobilising support. The notions of Catholics and Protestants are not simply about contrasting versions of Christianity, but are rather about more fundamental perceptions of two separate 'peoples' (ethnic groups).

Moreover, culture affects the successfulness of different frames. Attempting to frame refugees as a threat to social order, for example, is more likely to be successful in a society dominated by a hierarchical culture than in societies dominated by egalitarian and individualistic cultures.

This kind of interactions should be studied in more depth, including the relationships between circumstantial factors, and between general and circumstantial factors. Of this an example is the suggestion that the existence of strong epistemic communities are likely to minimise bureaucratic politics, at least concerning problem framing (but not necessarily concerning the search for solutions).

However, since the question at hand is what explains the societal salience of threat images, less attention has been paid to the equally interesting question of what shapes cognition, framing, culture, epistemic communities, bureaucratic politics and so forth. Subsequent case studies and comparative analyses will have to demonstrate more specifically in what ways these factors interact, and how given situations define what combinations of general and circumstantial factors are significant.

Going Ahead: Cross-fertilisation

This book makes the case for academic bridge building. This has been an underlying theme in this volume. Let me conclude by making some explicit reflections on this subject.

If the study of how fears, threats and risks are framed and managed in modern society is to be furthered, there is much to gain by engaging in theoretical cross-fertilisation. The theoretical framework suggested above represents one such attempt. Indeed, cross-fertilisation is not only relevant for the study of threat politics, even if the conclusion stems from our preliminary analysis of this particular subject.

An important lesson from studying threat politics is that the analyst cannot solely rely on what has been discovered within the nearby fields of security, risk and crisis management. The theories underpinning the explanations suggested here are not merely drawn from studies of threats and risks, but from more general theories on framing, agenda setting and communication, including media studies. This is not always recognised in studies of security, risk and crisis management, and references to these more general theories are often absent.

Cross-fertilisation is also warranted between the academically disassociated but thematically overlapping disciplines and subfields in which the subject of threats and societal fears primarily are dealt with are, i.e. security studies, risk studies, and crisis management. The absence of cross-fertilisation between these subfields has resulted in a lack of coherence of the field as a whole, and in an inability to learn from each other's advancements and mistakes.

Security studies have been and still are generally focused on the state and threats to national sovereignty, even after the widely acknowledged broadening of the security concept. As a result, there is not much concern for fears and risks that do not necessarily take on national and existential dimensions. Risk studies have been focused on risks associated with modernity, such as nuclear power, modern infrastructure, and health risks, often and sometimes explicitly excluding 'security policy' issues. Crisis management studies have been more open to include studies of all kinds of problems, regardless of whether they concern traditional issues of security policy or risks of modern society. On the other hand, crisis management has been focused on the relatively short periods of dramatic events, and consequently has contributed less to the understanding of how particular actors or structural conditions take on societal salience.

These differences partly explain the lack of cross-fertilisation, but they are hardly acceptable as excuses. There is obviously a common ground—and here we must return to the study of the very basic functions of society and politics. Fears, threats, and risks—or whatever we call these ubiquitous problems of life—are ultimately legitimating our polities. They fuel collective identity—the separation of a familiar 'us' from a threatening 'them'—and they justify power—the separation of rulers from the ruled. It would definitely be an advancement if the specialised scholars in security studies, risk studies and crisis management at least on occasion would address these questions, not as something particular for their subfields, but as the general problems that they are. This requires a readiness to communicate across academic boundaries.

Bibliography

Adam, B., Beck, U. and Van Loon, J. (eds.) (2000) *The Risk Society and Beyond: Critical Issues for Social Theory*. London: Sage.

Adler, E. (1997) 'Seizing the Middle Ground: Constructivism in World Politics,' *European Journal of International Relations* 3 (3): 319-363.

AECMA (the European Association of Aerospace Industries) (1996) *Towards a European Aerospace Policy – Perspectives and Strategies for the Aerospace Industry*. AECMA: Brussels.

Aftonbladet. Stockholm, tabloid.

Agrell, W. (1985) *Bakom ubåtskrisen*. Stockholm: Liber.

—— (2000) *Morgondagens krig. Tekniken, politiken och människan*. Stockholm: Ordfront.

Älmeberg, R. (1999) 'Sverige rustar för IT-krig,' Interview with Swedish Defence Minister Björn von Sydow, *Riksdag & Departement*, (38): 4-7.

Andrén, N. (1996) *Maktbalans och alliansfrihet: Svensk utrikespolitik under 1900-talet*. Stockholm: Norstedts.

Anderson, B. (1991) *Imaged Communities. Reflections on the Origin and Spread of Nationalism*. 2nd edn. London: Verso.

Andersson, J.J. (ed.) (2000) *Internationalization, Economic Dependence and National Security*. Stockholm: The Swedish Institute of International Affairs.

Allan, S. (1998) 'News from NowHere: Televisual News Discourse and the Construction of Hegemony,' in Garret, A. and Garrett, P. (eds.) *Approaches to Media Discourse*. London: Blackwell.

Allison, G.T. (1971) *Essence of Decision: Explaining the Cuban Missile Crisis*. Boston: Little Brown & Co.

Allison, G.T. and Zelikow, P. (1999) *Essence of Decision: Explaining the Cuban Missile Crisis*. 2nd edn. Longman: New York.

Archer, C. and Jones, C. (1999) 'The Security Policies and the Concepts of the Baltic States—Learing from their Nordic Neighbours?,' in O.F. Knudsen (ed.) *Stability and Security in the Baltic Sea Region*. London: Frank Cass.

Åsheden, A-M. (1987) *Jakten på Olof Palmes mördare - de tre första månaderna*. Stockholm: Bonniers.

Aumont, J. (1997) *The Image*. London: British Film Institute.

Aviation Week & Space Technology.

Baldwin, D. (1996) 'Review Article: Security Studies and the End of the Cold War,' *World Politics* 48 (1): 117-141.
Baltic Sea Business Summit (1996) *The Stockholm Declaration on Growth and Development in the Baltic Sea Region*. Stockholm April 24-25, 1996.
— (1998) *Memorandum on Conditions for Growth and Development in the Baltic Sea Region*. Stockholm, 1 January 1998.
Bangemann, M. (1996) 'The Future of Europe's Defence Industry,' Opening Speech at 'The Future of Europe's Defence Industry Conference,' Brussels, 18 June 1996.
Barkin, S.M. (1984) 'The Journalist as Storyteller: An Interdisciplinary Perspective,' *American Journalism*, Winter, pp. 27-33.
Baumgartner, F.R. and Jones, B.D. (1993) *Agendas and Instability in American Politics*. Chicago: University of Chicago Press.
BBC World News.
Beck, U. (1992) *Risk Society: Towards a New Modernity*. London: Sage.
— (1999) *World Risk Society*. London: Polity.
Bell, A. (1994) 'Telling Stories,' in Graddol, D. and Boyd-Barrett, O. (eds.) *Media Texts: Authors and Readers*. Clevedon: The Open University.
Bennett, W.L. and Edelman, M. (1985) 'Toward a New Political Narrative,' *Journal of Communication* 35: 156-171.
Bergström, L. och Åmark, K. (1999) *Ubåtsfrågan: En kritisk granskning av den svenska nutidshistoriens viktigaste säkerhetspolitiska dilemma*. Uppsala: Verdandi Debatt.
Berkowitz, D. (1992) 'Who Sets the Media Agenda? The Ability of Policymakers to Determine News Decisions,' in Kennamer, D.J. (ed.) *Public Opinion, The Press, and Public Policy*. Westport, Ct.: Praeger.
Betts, R.K. (1997) 'Should Strategic Studies Survive?,' *World Politics* 50 (1): 7-33.
Bignell, J. (1997) *Media Semiotics*. Manchester: Manchester University Press.
Bjereld, U. (1992) *Kritiker eller medlare? Sveriges utrikespolitiska roller 1945-1990*. Stockholm: Nerenius & Santérus.
Blanchard, J-M.F., Mansfield, E.D. and Ripsman, N.M. (eds.) (2000) *Power and the Purse: Economic Statecraft, Interdependence, and National Security*. London: Frank Cass.
Bondebjerg, I. (1992) 'Intertextuality and metafiction. Genre and narration in the television fiction of Dennis Potter,' in Skovmand, M. and Schrøder, K.C. (eds.) *Media Cultures. Reappraising Transnational Media*. London: Routledge.
Boulding, K. (1959) 'National images and international systems,' *Conflict Resolution* 11 (2): 120-131.
Bourdieu, P. (1996) *The Rules of Art—Genesis and structure of the Literature Field*. Cambridge: Polity Press.

Bovens, M. A. P. and 't Hart, P. (1996) *Understanding Policy Fiascoes*. New Brunswick, N.J.: Transaction Publishers.
Brecher, M. (1993) *Crises in World Politics*. Oxford: Pergamon Press.
Buchanan, W. and Cantril, H. (1953) *How Nations See Each Other*. Urbana: University of Illinois Press.
Burns, W.J. et al (1993) 'Incorporating structural models into research on the social amplification of risk: Implications for theory construction and decision making,' *Risk Analysis* 13: 611-623.
Buzan, B. (1991) *People, States and Fear: An Agenda for International Security Studies in the Post-Cold War Era*. 2nd edition. New York: Harvester Wheatsheaf.
Buzan, B., Wæver, O. and de Wilde, J. (1998) *Security: A New Framework for Analysis*. London: Lynne Rienner.
Bynander, F. (1998) 'The 1982 Swedish Hårsfjärden Submarine Incident: A Decision-Making Analysis,' *Cooperation and Conflict* 33 (4): 367-407.
— (2000) 'Review Article: Management of Third World Crises in Adverse Partnership: Theory and Practice. Imtiaz Bokhari,' *Journal of Contingencies and Crisis Management* 8 (2): 125-127.
Cable, V. (1995) 'What Is International Economic Security,' *International Affairs* 71 (2): 305-324.
Cameron, D. (1994) 'Words, words, words: The power of language,' in Dunant, S. (ed.) *The War of the Words: The Political Correctness Debate*, pp. 15-34. London: Virago Press.
Caporaso, J.A. and Levine, D.P. (1992) *Theories of Political Economy*. Cambridge: Cambridge University Press.
Capella, J. N. and Hall Jamieson, K. (1996) 'News Frames, Political Cynicism, and Media Cynicism,' *Annals, AAPSS*, 546, pp. 71-84.
Carlsson, I. (1999) *Ur skuggan av Olof Palme*. Stockholm: Hjalmarsson och Högberg.
Castells, M. (1997) *The Power of Identity. The Information Age: Economy, Society and Culture*. Vol. 1. 2nd edn. Oxford: Blackwell.
— (2000) *Information Age: Rise of the Network Society*. Vol. 1. 2nd edn. Oxford: Blackwell.
Cate, F. (1997) *Privacy in the Information Age*. Washington, D.C.: The Brooking's Institution.
CBSS Secretariat (2000) *Survey on the Implementation of Recommendations adapted from the January 1998 'Memorandum on Conditions for Growth and Development in the Baltic Sea Region,'* Stockholm, January 2000.
CEPS (Centre for European Policy Studies) (1999) 'Future Cooperation among European Defence Industries in the light of European Multinational Forces.' *Report of a CEPS Working Party*.

Chaiken, S., Giner-Sorolla, R., and Chen, S. (1996) 'Beyond Accuracy: Defense and Impression Motives in Heuristic and Systematic Information Processing,' in Gollwitzer and Bargh (eds.) *The Psychology of Action.* London: The Guilford Press.
Charlick-Paley, T. and Sylvan, D. (2000) 'The Use and Evolution of Stories as a Mode of Problem Representation: Soviet and French Military Officers Face the Loss of Empire,' *Political Psychology* 21 (4): 697-728.
Chilton, P.A. (1996) *Security Metaphors: Cold War Discourse from Containment to the Common House.* New York: Lange.
Cini, M. and McGowan, L (1998) *Competition Policy in the European Union.* London: Macmillan.
Cobb, R.W. and Ross, M.H. (eds.) (1997) *Cultural Strategies of Agenda Denial: Avoidance, Attack, and Redefinition.* Lawrence, Ks.: University Press of Kansas.
Cohen, B. (1963) *The Press and Foreign Policy.* New Jersey: Princeton University Press.
Commission on Threats and Risks (1995) *SOU 1995:19. Ett säkrare samhälle.* Stockholm: Ministry of Defence.
Couldry, N. (1999) 'Disrupting the media frame at Greenham Common: a new chapter in the history of Mediations?,' *Media, Culture and Society* 21: 337-358.
Council of the Baltic Sea States (1992) *The Copenhagen Declaration.* Conference of Foreign Ministers of the Baltic Sea States, Copenhagen, March 5-6, 1992.
Cohen, B.L. (1985) 'Criteria for technology acceptability,' *Risk Analysis* 5: 1-2.
Combs, B. and Slovic, P. (1979) 'Newspaper coverage of causes of death,' *Journalism Quarterly* 56: 837-843, 849.
Crawford, B. (1995) 'Hawks, Doves, but no Owls: International Economic Interdependence and Construction of the New Security Dilemma,' in Lipschutz, R. (ed.) *On Security.* New York: Columbia University Press.
Czarniawska, B. and Sevón, G. (eds.) (1996) *Translating Organizational Change.* Berlin, New York: Walter de Gruyter.
Dagens Nyheter (DN). Stockholm, daily.
Dearing, J.W. (1996) *Agenda-Setting.* Thousand Oaks, CA.: Sage.
Defence Commission of Sweden (1996) *Ds 1996:51. Omvärldsförändringar och svensk säkerhetspolitik.* Stockholm: Ministry of Defence.
— (1998) *Ds 1998:9. Svensk säkerhetspolitik i ny omvärldsbelysning.* Stockholm: Ministry of Defence.
— (1999a) *Ds 1999:2. Förändrad omvärld – omdanat försvar.* Stockholm: Ministry of Defence.
— (1999b) *Ds 1999:55. Europas säkerhet – Sveriges försvar.* Stockholm: Ministry of Defence.

— (2000) 'Världsläget kräver vidgad säkerhetssyn'. Debate article signed by all members of the Defence Commission (excluding the Conservatives), published in the Swedish daily *Svenska Dagbladet* October 19, p. 12.
— (2001) *Gränsöverskridande säkerhet – gemensam säkerhet.* Ds 2001:14. Stockholm: Ministry of Defence.
Defence News.
Defense Daily.
Demchak, C.D. (2000) ' "New Security" in Cyberspace: Emerging Intersection between Military and Civilian Contingencies,' *Journal of Contingencies and Crisis Management* 7(4).
Denning, D.E. (1999) *Information Warfare and Security.* Reading, Mass., Harlow, England: Addison-Wesley.
Dewey, J. (1929) *The Quest for Certainty: A Study of the Relation of Knowledge and Action.* New York: G.P. Putnam Capricorn Books.
Dillman, D.A. (1991) 'The design and administration of mail surveys,' *Annual Review of Sociology* 17: 225-249.
Dillon, M. (1996) *Politics of Security: Towards a Political Philosophy of Continental Thought.* London and New York: Routledge.
DiMaggio, P.J. and Powell, W.W. (1991) 'The Iron Cage Revisited: Institutional Isomorphism and Collective Rationality in organizational Fields,' in DiMaggio, P.J. and Powell, W.W. (eds.) *The New Institutionalism in Organizational Analysis.* Chicago/London: The University of Chicago Press.
Douglas, M. (1970) *National Symbols. Explanations in Cosmology.* New York: Pantheon Books.
— (1992) *Risk and Blame. Essays in Cultural Theory.* London: Routledge.
Douglas, M. and Wildavsky, A. (1982) *Risk and Culture: An Essay on the Selection of Technical and Environmental Dangers.* Berkeley: University of California Press.
Dror, Y. (1986) *Policymaking Under Adversity.* New Brunswick: Transaction.
Drottz-Sjöberg, B-M. (1993) 'Risk perceptions related to varied frames of reference,' in Hubert, P. and Poumadère, M. (eds.) *SRA Europe Third Conference. Risk analysis: underlying rationales in Paris*, pp. 55-69. SRA-Europe.
— (1996) *Stämningar i Storuman efter folkomröstningen om ett djupförvar.* SKB, Projekt Rapport PR D-96-004.
— (1998) *Stämningar i Malå efter folkomröstningen 1997.* SKB, Projekt Rapport PR D-98-03.
— (1999) 'Divergent views on a possible nuclear waste repository in the community: Social aspects of decision making,' in Andersson, K. (ed.) *VALDOR: Values and Decisions in Risk.* Stockholm: European Commission: DG XI.

Dunn, D.H. (1997) *The Politics of Threat: Minuteman Vulnerability in American National Security Policy.* Houndmills, Basingstoke, Hampshire, London: MacMillan.

Durant R. and Diehl, P. (1989) 'Agendas, Alternatives and Public Policy: Lessons from the U.S. Foreign Policy Arena,' *Journal of Public Policy* 9: 170-205.

Economist, The.

EDIG (European Defence Industries Group) Position papers 1995-1999.

Commission of the European Communities
— 'Industrial Policy in an Open and Competitive Environment: Guide-lines for a Community Approach', COM (90) 556 final.
— 'The European aircraft Industry—first assessment and possible Community Actions,' COM (92) 164 final.
— 'Research After Maastricht: an assessment, a strategy,' SEC (92) 317 final.
— 'Growth, Competitiveness, Employment,' COM (93) 700 final.
— 'Green Paper on Innovation' (1995).
— 'The Challenges Facing the European Defence-related Industry, A Contribution for Action at European Level,' COM (96) 10 final.
— 'The European Union and Space,' COM (96) 617 final.
— 'Concerning the 5th framework of the European Community for research, technological development and demonstration activities,' COM) (97) 142 final.
— 'The European aerospace industry is in urgent need of restructuring—Meeting the Global Challenge,' COM) (97) 466 final.
— 'Implementing European Union Strategy on Defence-Related Industries,' COM (97) 583 final.
— 'Draft Action Plan for the Defence Related Industry,' Directorate General for Enterprise and Information Society (1997) (former DG III).

Eesti Päevaleht.

Efinger, M.P., Mayer and Schwarzer, G. (1993) 'Integrating and Contextualizing Hypotheses. Alternative Paths to Better Explanations of Regime Formation?,' in Rittberger, V. (ed.) *Regime Theory and International Relations.* Oxford: Clarendon Press.

Eilders, C. (2000a) 'Media Acting in Political Editorials: Issue Focusing and Selective Emphases in Germany's Prestige Press,' paper presented at the ECPR Joint Sessions in Copenhagen, April 2000.

Eilders, C. and Albrecht L. (2000) 'Germany at war: competing framing strategies in German public discourse,' *European Journal of Communication Research.*

Elliott, P., Murdock, G. and Schlesinger, P. (1986) 'Terrorism' and the state: a case study of the discourses of television,' in Collins, R. *et al, Media, Culture and Society. A Critical Reader.* London: Sage.

Entman, R.M. (1993) 'Framing: Toward Clarification of a Fractured Paradigm,' *Journal of Communication* 43 (4): 51-58.

Esaiasson, P., Holmberg, S. and Brothén, M. (1995) *Riksdagsenkät 1994. Dokumentation.* Stencil. Statsvetenskapliga institutionen. Göteborgs universitet.
— (1996) *Representation From Above. Members of Parliament and Representative Democracy in Sweden.* Aldershot: Dartmouth.
Eriksson, J. (1999a) 'Observers or Advocates? On the Political Role of Security Analysts,' *Cooperation and Conflict* 34 (3): 311-30.
— (1999b) 'Debating the Politics of Security Studies,' *Cooperation and Conflict* 34 (3): 345-52.
— (2000a) 'Agendas, Threats and Politics: Securitization in Sweden,' *Aberdeen Studies in Politics* Spring 2000, No. 7. University of Aberdeen.
— (2000b) 'Explaining Security Agenda Setting: Beyond the Domestic Realm,' in O. Knudsen (ed.) *Security and Cooperation in the Baltic Sea Region.* Stockholm: Södertörn University College.
— (2001) Book review: Buzan, B., Wæver, O. and de Wilde, J. (1998) Security: A New Framework for Analysis. London Lynne Rienner, *Journal of Contingencies and Crisis Management* 9 (1): 61-3.
Estonian Review.
European Commission Senior Officials (personal interviews by Ulrika Mörth), especially concerning external relations, industrial affairs and RTD), Swedish MEPs, Swedish and French officials at the Ministry of Defence dealing with the Letter of Intent Initiative, the former chairman of EDIG and other representatives from the European defence industry.
European Council Presidency Conclusions 1990-2000.
Euronews.
European Parliament, (1997) 'Defence-related industry Resolution on the Commission communication on the challenges facing the European defence, a contribution for action at European level,' (A4-0076/97) (Committee on Foreign Affairs, Security and Defence Policy, Rapporteur: Mr Gary Titley).
European Voice.
Expressen. Stockholm, tabloid.
Fairclough, N. (1995) *Media Discourse.* London: Edward Arnold.
Farnham, B. (Ed.) (1994) *Avoiding Losses/Taking Risks: Prospect Theory and International Conflict.* Ann Arbor: University of Michigan Press.
Featherstone, M. (1995) *Undoing Culture. Globalization, Postmodernism and Identity.* London: Sage.
Financial Times.
Findahl, O. (1998)'Media som folkbildare. Malå och kärnavfallet,' in Lidskog, R. (ed.) *Kommunen och kärnavfallet. Svensk kärnavfallspolitik på 1990-talet,* pp. 211-242. Stockholm: Carlsson Bokförlag.
Fischer, F. and Forester, J. (1993) *The Argumentative Turn in Policy Analysis and Planning.* London : UCL.

Fisher, A. and Sjöberg, L. (1990) 'Radon risks: People's perceptions and reactions,' in Majumdar, S.K., Schmalz, R.F. and Miller, E.W. (eds.) *Environmental Radon: Occurrence, Control and Health Hazards*, pp. 398-411. Pittsburgh: Pennsylvania Academy of Science.

Fiske, S. and Taylor, S. (1991) *Social Cognition*. 2nd ed. New York: McGraw-Hill.

Flaherty, D.H. (1989) *Protecting Privacy in Surveillance Society*. Chapel Hill, London: The University of North Carolina Press.

Flynn, J., Slovic, P. and Mertz, C.K. (1994) 'Gender, race, and perception of environmental health risks,' *Risk Analysis* 14: 1101-1108.

Fordham, B. (1998) 'The Politics of Threat Perception and the use of Force: A Political Economy Model of U.S. Uses of Force, 1949-1994,' *International Studies Quarterly* 42: 567-590.

Foucault, M. (1972) *The Archeology of Knowledge*. London: Routledge.

Foucault, M. (1984) 'The Order of Discourse,' in Shapiro, M.J. (eds.) *Language and Politics*. Oxford: Blackwell.

Franklin, J. (ed.) (1998) *The Politics of Risk Society*. London: Polity.

Frieden, J. and Lake, D. (2000) *International Political Economy. Perspectives on Global Power and Wealth*. 4th ed. Bedford: St.Martins.

Friman, H., Sjöstedt G. and Wik, M.W. (eds.) (1996) *Informationskrigföring: några perspektiv*. Stockholm: The Swedish Institute of International Affairs.

Giddens, A. (1991) *Modernity and self-identity. Self and society in late modern age*. Cambridge: Polity Press.

Gilljam, M. och Holmberg, S. (1995) *Väljarnas val*. Stockholm: Norstedts Juridik.

Gilpin, R. (1987) *The Political Economy of International Relations*. Princeton: Princeton University Press.

Gitlin, T. (1980) *The Whole World is Watching*. Berkley: University of California Press.

Goffman, E. (1974) *Frame Analysis: An Essay on the Organization of Experience*. Boston: Northeastern University Press.

Goldmann, K. (1999) 'Politikens internationalisering – en introduktion,' in Goldmann, K. et al, *Politikens internationalisering*. Lund: Studentlitteratur.

Government of Sweden (1987a) SOU 1987:14. *Juristkommissionens rapport om händelserna efter mordet på statsminister Olof Palme*, del 1. Stockholm: Ministry of Justice.

— (1987b) SOU 1987:72. *Juristkommissionens rapport om händelserna efter mordet på statsminister Olof Palme*, del 2. Stockholm: Ministry of Justice.

— (1988) SOU 1988:18. *Rapport av parlamentariska kommissionen med anledning av mordet på Olof Palme*. Stockholm: Ministry of Justice.

— (1989) SOU 1989:1. *Rapport av den särskilde utredaren för granskning av hotbilden mot och säkerhetsskyddet kring statsminister Olof Palme*. Stockholm: Ministry for Civil Service Affairs.

— (1996a) Proposition 1996/1997;11. *Beredskapen mot svåra påfrestningar i samhället i fred.* Stockholm: Government of Sweden.
— (1996b) Proposition 1995/96:125. *Åtgärder för att bredda och utveckla användningen av informationsteknik.* Stockholm: Government of Sweden.
— (1998) Regeringens skrivelse 1998/1999:33. *Beredskapen mot svåra påfrestningar på samhället I fred.* Stockholm: Government of Sweden.
— (1999a) Proposition 1999/2000:30. *Det nya försvaret.* Stockholm: Government of Sweden.
— (1999b) Proposition 1998/1999:74. *Förändrad omvärld – omdanat försvar.* Stockholm: Government of Sweden.
— (1999c) SOU 1999:88. *Granskningskommissionens betänkande i anledning av brottsutredningen efter mordet på statsminister Olof Palme.* Stockholm: Ministry of Justice.
— (2001) SOU 2001:41. *Säkerhet i en ny tid.* Stockholm: Ministry of Defence.
Graber, D.A. (1984) *Mass Media and American Politics.* Washington D.C.: CQ Press.
Gray, M. (1992) *A Dictionary of Literary Terms.* Beirut: Longman, York Press.
Green-Cowles, M., Caporaso, J. and Risse, T. (eds.) (2001) *Transforming Europe: Europeanization and Domestic Change.* Ithaca, N. Y.: Cornell University Press.
Green-Cowles, M. (1995) 'Setting the Agenda for a New Europe: The ERT and EC 1992,' *Journal of Common Market Studies*, 33: 501-506.
Greenwood, J. (1997) *Representing Interests in the European Union*, London: Macmillan.
Grendstad, G. och Selle P. (eds.) (1996) *Kultur som levemåte.* Oslo: Det Norske Samlaget.
Grendstad, G. och Rommetvedt, H. (1996) 'Fem tyver på samme marked,' in Grendstad, G. och Selle, P. (eds.) *Kultur som levemåte.* Oslo: Det Norske Samlaget.
Gurevitch, M. (1996) 'The Globalization of Electronic Journalism,' in Curran, J. and Gurevitch, M. (eds.) *Mass Media and Society.* London: Arnold.
Gustafsson, L. (1988) *Problemformuleringsprivilegiet.* Stockholm: Norstedts.
Haab, M. (1998) 'Estonia,' in Mouritzen, H. (ed.) *Bordering Russia. Theory and Prospects for Europes's Baltic Rim.* Ashgate.
Haas, P.M. (1992) 'Epistemic Communities and International Policy Coordination,' *International Organization* 46 (1). Washington: The MIT Press.
Hall, S. (1994) 'Encoding/Decoding,' in Graddol, D. and Boyd-Barrett, O. (eds.) *Media Texts: Authors and Readers.* Clevedon: The Open University, pp. 200-211. (The original article is from 1980.)
Halperin, M. (1974) *Bureaucratic Politics and Foreign Policy.* Washington: Brookings inst.

Hansen, L. (1999) 'The absence of gender in the Copenhagen school: lessons for feminist/security studies,' paper presented at the Threat Images conference at the Swedish Institute of International Affairs, Stockholm, October 15-16.

Hansén, D. and Stern, E. (2001) 'The Palme Assassination as a National Trauma,' in Rosenthal, U., Comfort, L. and Boin, A. (eds.) *Coping with Crises*.

— (in press) 'From Crisis to Trauma: The Palme Assassination Case,' in Rosenthal, U., Boin, R.A. and Comfort, L.K. (eds.) *Managing Crises: Threats, Dilemmas, Opportunities*, Springfield: Charles C. Thomas.

Hansén, D. (1998) 'The Occupation of the West-German Embassy in Stockholm, 1975,' Stockholm: Crismart, mimeo.

Harshberger, E. and Ochmanek, D. (eds.) (1999) 'Information and Warfare: New Opportunities for U.S. Military,' pp. 157-178 in Khalilzad, Z.M. and White, J.P. (eds.) *Strategic Appraisal: The Changing Role of Information in Warfare*. Santa Monica: RAND.

't Hart, P. (1990/1994) *Groupthink in Government: A Study of Small Groups and Policy Failure*. Amsterdam: Swets and Zeitlinger; Baltimore: Johns Hopkins University Press.

Hart, J. (1992) *Rival Capitalist—International Competitivieness in the United States, Japan and Western Europe*. Ithaca: Cornell University Press.

Hart, T. (1976) *The Cognitive World of Swedish Security Elites*. Stockholm: The Swedish Institute of International Affairs.

Hartley, J. (1995) *Understanding News*. London: Routledge.

Heberlein, T.A. and Baumgartner, R. (1978) 'Factors affecting response rates to mailed questionnaires: a quantitative analysis of the published literature,' *American Sociological Review* 43: 447-462.

Heider, F. (1958) *The Psychology of Interpersonal Behavior*. New York: Wiley.

Heisbourg, F. (2000) *European Defence: Making It Work*, Institute for Security Studies, WEU, Chaillot Papers 42.

Hellberg, A. and Jörle, A. (1984) *Ubåt U137. Tio dagar som skakade Sverige*. Stockholm: Atlantis.

Hellman, M. and Alexa R. (1997) *A Day in the Aktuellt Newsroom*. Stockholm: Stockholm University, Department of Political Science.

Hermann, C.F. (1963) 'Some Consequences of Crises which Limit the Viability of Organizations,' *Administrative Sciences Quarterly* 8:61-82.

— (1990) 'Changing Course: When Governments Choose to Redirect Foreign Policy,' *International Studies Quarterly* 34: 3-21.

Hinnfors, J. (1995) *På dagordningen? Svensk politisk stil i förändring*. Stockholm: Nerenius & Santérus.

Hodges, M. (1983) 'Industrial Policy: Hard Times or Great Expectations?,' in Wallace, H., Wallace, W. and Webb, C. (eds.) *Policymaking in the European Community*. London: John Wiley & Sons.

Holmér, H. (1988) *Olof Palme är skjuten!* Wahlstrand & Widstrand.
Holsti, K. et al (1982) *Why Nations Realign: Foreign Policy Restructuring in the Postwar World.* London: George Allen and Unwin.
Horowitz, I.L. (1963) *The War Game: Studies on the New Civilian Militarists.* New York: Paine-Whitman.
Houghton, D.P. (1996) 'The Role of Analogical Reasoning in Novel Foreign-Policy Situations,' in *British Journal of Political Science* 26 (4).
Hox, J.J. and De Leeuw, E.D.D. (1994) 'A comparison of nonresponse in mail, telephone, and face-to-face surveys,' *Quality and Quantity* 28: 329-344.
Huysmanns, J. (1995) 'Migrants as a security problem: dangers of "securitizing" societal issues,' in Miles, R. and Thänhardt, D. (eds.) *Migration and European Integration: The Dynamics of Inclusion and Exclusion,* 53-72. London: Pinter.
Hyland, Eriksen, T. (1993) *Ethnicity an Nationalism: Anthropological Perspectives.* London: Pluto Press.
Ilves, T.H. (1996) to the Riigikogu on 5 December 1996. http://www.vm.ee/eng/pressreleases/speeches
— (1997a) Estonian Minister for Foreign Affairs, at the Institute of International Affairs, Stockholm, January 9, 1997. http://www.vm.ee/eng/pressreleases/speeches
— (1997b) at the International Conference on the Security Environment in the Baltic Sea Region after the Madrid Summit. September 5, 1997. Tallinn. http://www.vm.ee/eng/pressreleases/speeches
— (1997c) 'Estonia's European Security and Defence Policy and the Western European Union,' date released (WWW version): September 08, 1997. http://www.vm.ee/eng/pressreleases/speeches
— (1997d) 'A Strategy for the Baltic Rim,' date released (WWW version): September 10, 1997. http://www.vm.ee/eng/pressreleases/speeches
— (1997e) 'Implications of EU and NATO Enlargement Policies for the Baltic state,' date released (WWW version): November 9, 1997. http://www. vm.ee/eng/ pressreleases/speeches
— (1997f) 'The Road to European Integration: EU and NATO,' date released (WWW version): November 9, 1997. http://www.vm.ee/eng/pressreleases/speeches
— (1998a) 'Estonia's Return to Europe,' lecture by, Minister of Foreign Affairs of Estonia in Cyprus, January 14, 1998. http://www.vm.ee/eng/pressreleases/speeches
— (1998b) at the opening of the Estonia's accession negotiations with European Union Brussels, 31 March 1998. http://www.vm.ee/eng/pressreleases/ speeches
— (1998c) at the Carnegie Endowment for International Peace, 18 September 1998, Washington D.C. http://www.vm.ee/eng/pressreleases/speeches

— (1999a) Opening Remarks by, Minister of Foreign Affairs, at the 'North Atlantic Treaty at 50 and NATO Enlargement' symposium, 7 April 1999, Tallinn. http://www.vm.ee/eng/pressreleases/speeches
— (1999b) 'Estonia's main foreign policy priorities,' address by T. H. Ilves, Minister of Foreign Affairs, on behalf of the Government of the Republic of Estonia to the Riigikogu, June 1999. http://www.vm.ee/eng/pressreleases/speeches
— (1999c) Statement at the 54th Session of the UN General Assembly, 1 October 1999. http://www.vm.ee/eng/pressreleases/speeches
— (1999d) 'Estonia's main foreign policy priorities,' address by T. H. Ilves, Minister of Foreign Affairs, on behalf of the Government of the Republic of Estonia to the Riigikogu, 25 November 1999. http://www.vm.ee/eng/pressreleases/speeches
— (1999e) Speech to the Swedish Institute for International Affairs, 14 December 1999, Stockholm. http://www.vm.ee/eng/pressreleases/speeches
Innovation & Technology Transfer.
Iyengar, S. (1996) 'Framing Responsibility for Political Issues,' *Annals, AAPPSS*, 546: 59-70.
Jachtenfuchs, M. (1996) *International Policy-Making as a Learning Process?* Aldershot: Ashgate.
James, A. (1998) *Post-Merger Strategies of the Leading US Defence Aerospace Companies.* Research Report, Stockholm: Swedish Defence Research Establishment.
Jane's Defence Weekly.
Jensen, K.B. (1995) *The Social Semiotics of Mass Communication.* London: Sage.
Jensen, T. (1999) 'Risk Perceptions among Members of Parliament: Economy, Ecology, and Social Order,' in Esaiasson, P. and Heidar, K. (eds.) *Beyond Westminster and Congress: The Nordic Experience.* Columbus: Ohio State University Press.
Jervis, R. (1976) *Perception and Misperception in International Politics.* Princeton: Princeton University Press.
Johnson, R.H. (1997) *Improbable Dangers: U.S. Conceptions of Threat in the Cold War and After.* Houndmills, Basingstoke, London: Macmillan.
Jönsson, C. *et al* (1995) 'International Organizations and Agenda Setting,' unpublished paper. Lund: Lund University, Department of Political Science.
Kahler, M. (1998) 'Rationality in International Relations,' *International Organization* 52 (4).
Kahneman, D. Slovic, P. and Tversky A. (eds.) (1982) *Judgements under Uncertainty: Heuristics and Biases.* Cambridge: Cambridge University Press.

Kallas, S. (1995) Meeting of Foreign and Defence Ministers of the Western European Union, 14 November 1995, Madrid. Internet: http://www.vm.ee/eng/pressreleases/speeches
— (1996a) Deutsche Gesellschaft für auswürtige Politik, 15 April 1996, Bonn. Internet: http://www.vm.ee/eng/pressreleases/speeches
— (1996b) Address to the Riigikogu, 30 May 1996, Tallinn. Internet: http://www.vm.ee/eng/pressreleases/speeches
Kapferer, J.N. (1989) 'A mass poisoning rumor in Europe,' *Public Opinion Quarterly* 53: 467-481.
Karlsson, P. (2000) 'Bulltoftadramat, 1972,' Stockholm: National Defence College, Crismart, mimeo.
Karlsson, M. (1996) *Hi-Tech Visions as Global Fashion: The International Diffusion of Information Technology Policy*. PhD. Diss., Linköping: Linköping University, Tema T.
Karlsson, M. (1995) *Partistrategi och utrikespolitik: Interna motiveringar och dagspressens agerande i Catalina-affären 1952 och EEC-frågan 1961/62*. PhD Diss. Stockholm: Stockholm University, Department of Political Science.
— (1998) 'The Catalina DC3 Crisis,' Stockholm: National Defence College, Crismart, mimeo.
— (1999) 'Transnationale Beziehungen in der Ostsee-Region. Das Beispiel Des Baltic Sea Business Summit,' *WeltTrends*, 7: 9-29.
Karlsson, M., and L. Sturesson (1995) *Världens största maskin*. Stockholm: Carlssons.
Karvonen, L. (1981) *Med vårt västra grannland som förebild – En undersökning av policydiffusion från Sverige till Finland*. PhD. Diss., Åbo: Åbo Akademi.
Kasperson, R.E. (1992) 'The social amplification of risk: progress in developing an integrative framework,' in Krimsky, S. and Golding, D. (eds.) *Social theories of risk*, pp. 153-178. Westport: Praeger.
Kasperson, R.E. et al (1988) 'The social amplification of risk,' *Risk Analysis* 8: 177-187.
Katzenstein, P.J. (ed.) (1996) *The Culture of National Security: Norms and Identity in World Politics*. New York: Columbia University Press.
Kellner, D. (1995) 'Reading the Gulf War,' in Kellner, D. (ed.) *Media Culture. Cultural Studies, Identity and Politics between the Modern and the Postmodern*. London: Routledge, pp. 198-228.
Keohane, R.O., Nye, J.S. and Hoffmann, S. (1993) *After the Cold War. International Institutions and State Strategies in Europe, 1989-1991*. Cambridge, Mass.: Harvard University Press.
Keohane, R.O. (1993) 'The Analysis of International Regimes. Towards a European-American Research Programme,' in Rittberger, V. (ed.) *Regime Theory and International Relations*. Oxford: Clarendon Press.

Khong, Y.F. (1992) *Analogies at War: Korea, Munich, Dien Bien Phu, and the Vietnam Decisions of 1965*. Princeton: Princeton University Press.
Kingdon, J.W. (1995) *Agendas, Alternatives and Public Policy*. 2nd edn. New York: HarperCollins College Publishers.
Knight, G. and Dean, T. (1982) 'Myth and the Structure of News,' *Journal of Communication* 32:144-161.
Kone, D. and Mullet, E, (1994) 'Societal risk perception and media coverage,' *Risk Analysis* 14: 21-24.
Krusell, I. (1998) *Palmemordets nakna fakta*. Stockholm: Fischer & Co.
KU 1986/87: 33. *Regeringens åtgärder med anledning av mordet på statsminister Olof Palme*, with appendices: A6, A7, A9, A16 and A21.
Kuhn, T.S. (1996) *The Structure of Scientific Revolutions*. 3rd edn. Chicago, Ill.: University of Chicago Press.
Laegreid, P. and Roness, P. (1999) 'Administrative Reform as Organized Attention,' in Egeberg, M. and Laegreid, P. (eds.) *Organizing Political Institutions*. Bergen: Scandinavian University Press.
Larsen, H. (1999) 'British and Danish European Policies in the 1990s: A Discourse Approach,' *European Journal of International Relations*, Vol. 5 (4).
Larson D.W. (1985) *Origins of Containment: A Psychological Explanation*. Princeton.
Layder, D. (1994) *Understanding Social Theory*. London: Sage.
Lebow, R.N. and Stein, J.G. (1993) 'Afghanistan, Carter, and Foreign Policy Change: The Limits of Cognitive Models,' in Caldwell, D. and McKeown, T.J. (eds.) *Diplomacy, Force, and Leadership: Essays in Honor of Alexander L. George*. Westview Press, pp. 95-127.
— (1994) *We all lost the Cold War*. Princeton, N.J.: Princeton University Press.
Le Monde.
Levy, D. (1997) *Tools of Critical Thinking: Meta Thoughts for Psychology*. London: Allyn and Bacon.
Lidskog, R. (1994) *Radioactive and Hazardous Waste Management in Sweden: Movements, Politics and Science*. Uppsala: Acta Universitatis Upsaliensis.
— (eds.) (1998) *Kommunen och kärnavfallet*. Stockholm: Carlsson Bokförlag.
Lindén, M., Posacki, R. and Wallström, P. (1999) *Nationella strukturer för skydd mot informationsoperationer*. Fö 19993025. Stockholm: Mandator and the Ministry of Defence.
Lippmann, W. (1941) *Public Opinion*. New York: Macmillan (first published 1922).
Lipschutz, R. (1995) 'Negotiating the Boundaries of Difference and Security at Millennium's End,' in Lipschutz, R. (ed.) *On Security*. New York: Columbia University Press.

Lipsky, M. (1980) *Street-Level Bureaucracy: Dilemmas of the Individual in Public Service.* New York: Russel Sage.
Ljung, L. (1980-1986) *Diary.* Stockholm: Royal War Archive.
Lones, P. (1998) *Millennieskiftet: klarar du dig förbi år 2000?* Stockholm: Bonnier Icon.
Loshitzky, Y. (1996) 'Travelling culture/travelling television,' *Screen* 37 (4): 323-335.
Luciani, G. (1989) 'The Economic Content of Security,' *Journal of Public Policy* 8 (2): 151-173.
Luik, J. (1994a) Swedish Institute of International Affairs, 2 March 1994, Stockholm. http://www.vm.ee/eng/pressreleases/speeches
— (1994b) 49th General Assembly of the United Nations, 28 September 1994, United Nations, New York City. http://www.vm.ee/eng/pressreleases/ speeches
Lübcke, P. (ed.) (1997) *Filosofilexikonet.* Stockholm: Forum.
Löfstedt, R. and Frewer, L. (eds.) (1998) *Risk and Modern Society.* London: Earthscan Publications.
Marcussen, M. *et al* (1999) 'Constructing Europe? The evolution of French, British and German nation state identities,' *Journal of European Public Policy* 6: 614-633.
March, J. and Olsen, J. (1998) 'The Institutional Dynamics of International Political Orders,' *International Organization* 52: 943-969.
Marinnytt, 1977-1983.
McDermott, R. (2001) *Risk-Taking in International Politics: Prospect Theory in American Foreign Policy.* Ann Arbor: The University of Michigan Press.
McSweeney, B. (1996) 'Identity and security: Buzan and the Copenhagen school,' *Review of International Studies* 22 (1): 81-93.
McQuail, D. (1994) *Masscommunication Theory.* London: Sage.
Merton, R.K (1965) *On the Shoulders of Giants.* New York: The Free Press.
Meyer, J. and Rowan B. (1991) 'Institutionalized Organizations: Formal Structure as Myth and Ceremony,' in Powell, W. and DiMaggio, P. (eds). *The New Institutionalism in Organizational Analysis.* Chicago: Chicago University Press.
Milbrath, L. (1981) 'Citizen surveys as citizen participation,' *Applied Behavioral Science* 17: 478-496.
Milburn, T.W. and Watman, K.H. (1981) *On the Nature of Threat: A Social Psychological Analysis.* New York: Praeger Special Studies.
Mingst, K. (1995) 'Uncovering the Missing Links: Linkage Actors and Their Strategies In Foreign Policy Analysis,' in Neack, L., Hey, J.A.K. and. Haney, P.J. (eds.) *Foreign Policy Analysis. Continuity and Change in Its Second Generation.* Englewood Cliffs: Prentice-Hall.

Molander, R., Riddile, A.S. and Wilson, P.A. (1996) *Strategic Information Warfare: A New Face of War*. Santa Monica: RAND.
Molin, K. (1991) *Omstridd Neutralitet: Experternas kritik av svensk utrikespolitik 1948-1950*. Stockholm: Tiden.
Morrison, S. (2000) 'Y2K bug prophet is unrepentant,' *Financial Times* 3 January.
Mortensen, P. (1999) 'Framtidens anfall kommer på nätet,' *Dagens Nyheter* 18 October, p. A6.
Mälk, R. (1998) 'Estonia's Main Foreign Policy Priorities,' address by Mälk, R., Minister of Foreign Affairs, for the Government of the Republic at Riigikogu, 26 November 1998. http://www.vm.ee/eng/pressreleases/speeches
Mörth, U. (1996) *Vardagsintegration – La vie quotidienne – i Europa*. PhD Diss. Department of Political Science, Stockholm University.
— (1998) 'Policy Diffusion in Research and Technological Development: No Government is an Island,' *Cooperation and Conflict* 33 (1): 35-58.
— (1999) 'Framing the defence industry/equipment issue—the case of the European Commission,' *SCORE Rapportserie*, 1999:1. Stockholm: Stockholm University.
— (2000) 'Competing frames in the European Commission—the case of the defence industry and equipment issue,' *Journal of European Public Policy* 7: 173-189.
— (2001) *Organising Europe: Constructing an Organisational Field on Defence Equipment*. Unpublished manuscript.
Mörth, U. and Sundelius, B. (1998) *Interdependens, konflikt och säkerhetspolitik : Sverige och den amerikanska teknikexportkontrollen*. Stockholm: Nerenius & Santérus.
National Defence College of Sweden (1999) *Informationskrigföring – hotuppfattning och skyddsåtgärder i USA, Norge och Finland*. FHS Report 21105:61456. Stockholm: National Defence College of Sweden.
'Nationelle samordnaren på kärnavfallsområdet,' (1998) in *Kampanj med kunskaper och känslor. Om kärnavfallsomröstningen i Malå kommun 1997*, ed. O. Söderberg. SOU 1998:62. Stockholm: Miljödepartementet.
Nau, H. (1975) 'Global Responses to R&D problems in Western Europe: 1955-58 and 1968-1973,' *International Organization* 29: 616-654.
Neuman, I.B. (1998) 'Identity and the outbreak of war: Or why the Copenhagen school of security studies should include the idea of "violisation" in its framework of analysis,' *International Journal of Peace Stuidies*, 3 (1).
Neumann, W.R., Just, M.R. and Crigler, A.N. (1992) *Common Knowledge. News and the Construction of Political Meaning*. London: Chicago University Press.
Neustadt, R. and May, E. (1986) *Thinking in Time: The Uses of History for Decision-Makers*. New York: Free Press.

Neveu, E. (1999) 'Politics on French Television. Towards a Renewal of Political Journalism and Debate Frames?,' *European Journal of Communication* 14 (3): 379-409.

Nilsson, Å., Sjöberg, L. and af Wåhlberg, A. (1997) *Ten years after Chernobyl: The reporting of nuclear and other hazards in six Swedish newspapers*. Center for Risk Research, Rhizikon: Risk Research Report 28.

Nisbett, R.E. and Ross, L. (1980) *Human Inference: Strategies and Shortcomings of Human Judgement*. Englewood Cliffs, NJ: Prentice Hall.

Nisbett, R.E. and Wilson, T.D. (1977) 'Telling more than we can know: Verbal reports on mental processes,' *Psychological Review* 84: 231-259.

Noreen, E. (1994) *Brobygge eller blockbildning. De norska och svenska utrikesledningarnas säkerhetspolitiska föreställningar 1945-1948* Stockholm.

— (1997) 'The Security Policy Beliefs of the Norwegian and Swedish Foreign Ministers 1945-1948,' in Runblom, H. et al (eds.) *Fifty Years after World War II. International Politics in the Baltic Sea Region 1945-1995*. The Baltic University Programme. Uppsala-Gdansk.

North, D.W. (1998) 'Nuclear waste management: shifting the paradigm,' *Reliability Engineering and System Safety* 59: 123-128.

Nye, J.S. (1990) *Bound to Lead—The Changing Nature of American Power*. New York: Basic Books.

Nye, J.S. and Owens, W. (1996) 'America's Information Edge,' *Foreign Affairs* 75: 20-36.

Okrent, D. (1998) 'Risk perception and risk management: on knowledge, resource allocation and equity,' *Reliability Engineering and System Safety* 59: 17-25.

Oskarson, M. (1994) *Klassröstningen i Sverige. Rationalitet, lojalitet eller bara slentrian?* Stockholm: Nerenius & Santérus Förlag.

Peffley, M. and Hurwitz, J. (1992) 'International Events and Foreign Policy Beliefs: Public Response to Changing Soviet-U.S. Relations,' *American Journal of Political Science* 36 (2): 431-61.

Peters, G. (1999) *Institutional Theory in Political Science*. London, New York: Pinter.

Peterson, J. (1992) *The Politics of European Technological Collaboration An Analysis of the Eureka initiative*, PhD Dissertation, London School of Economics and York University.

Peterson, J. and Sharp, M. (1998) *Technology Policy In the European Union*. London: Macmillan.

Petersson, B. (1998) 'Russian Self-Images,' in Karlsson, K-G., Petersson, B. and Törnquist-Plewa, B. (eds.) *Collective Identities in an Era of Transformations*. Lund: Lund University Press, pp. 37-73.

Pettman, J.J. (1996) *Worlding Women. A Feminist International Politics*. London: Routledge.

Postimees.
Preston, P. (1997) *Political/Cultural Identity. Citizens and Nations in a Global Era.* London: Sage.
Price, C., Morrison, S. and Chaffin, J. (2000) 'Worldwide relief as millenium bug fails to bite,' *Financial Times* 3 January, p. 1.
Price, M. (1995) *Television, the Public Sphere and National Identity.* Oxford: Clarendon Press.
Ramsberg, J. and Sjöberg, L. (1997) 'The cost-effectiveness of life saving interventions in Sweden,' *Risk Analysis* 17: 467-478.
— (1998) 'The importance of cost and risk characteristics for attitudes towards lifesaving interventions,' *Risk—Health, Safety & Environment* 9: 271-290.
Reinart, V. (1994) Head of the Division for International Organisations and Security Policy of the Ministry of Foreign Affairs of Estonia, Council of Europe, 20 January 1994, Strasbourg. http://www.vm.ee/eng/pressreleases/speeches
Reiter, D. (1994) 'Learning, Realism, and Alliances: The Weight of the Shadow of the Past,' *World Politics* 46.
Reiter, D. (1996) *Crucible of Beliefs: Learning, Alliances and World Wars.* Cornell University Press.
Renard, L. (2000) 'Framing and Intertextuality in the late nineties: political broadcasting on French TV,' paper presented at the ECPR session on Political Journalism, Copenhagen.
Renn, O. *et al* (1992) 'The social amplification of risk: Theoretical foundations and empirical application,' *Journal of Social Issues* 48: 137-160.
— (1998) 'The role of risk perception for risk management,' *Reliability Engineering and System Safety* 59: 49-62.
Ripley, B. (1995) 'Cognition, Culture, and Bureaucratic Politics,' in Neack, L., Hey, J. and Haney, P. (eds.) *Foreign Policy Analysis: Continuity and Change in its Second Generation,* pp. 85-97. Englewood Cliffs, NJ: Prentice Hall.
Risse-Kappen, T. (1994) 'Ideas Do Not Float Freely: Transnational Coalitions, Domestic Structures, and the End of the Cold War,' *International Organization* 40 (2): 185-214.
Risse-Kappen, T. (1995) *Cooperation Among Democracies: Norms, Transnational Relations, and the European Impact on U.S. Foreign Policy.* Princeton University Press.
— (ed.) (1995) *Bringing Transnational Relations Back In. Non-State Actors, Domestic Structures, and International Institutions.* Cambridge: Cambridge University Press.
— (1996) 'Collective Identity in a Democratic Community: The Case of NATO,' in Katzenstein, P.J. (eds.) *The Culture of National Security. Norms and Identity in World Politics.* Columbia University Press.

Roberts, D.F. and Maccoby, N. (1985) 'Effects of mass communication,' in Lindzey, G. and Aronson, E. (eds.) *Handbook of Social Psychology*, pp. 539-598. II. New York: Random House.

Robertson, A. (1999b) 'Kommunikation i den globala byn,' in Goldman, K. et al, *Politikens internationalisering*. Lund: Studentlitteratur.

Rochefort, D.A. and Cobb, R.W. (1994) 'Problem Definition: An Emerging Perspective,' in Rochefort, D.A. and Cobb, R.W. (eds.) *The Politics of Problem Definition: Shaping the Policy Agenda*. Lawrence, Ks.: University Press of Kansas.

Rorty, R. (1991) *Objectivity, Relativism and Truth*. Cambridge: Cambridge University Press.

Rosamond, B. (1999) 'Discourses of globalisation and the social construction of European identities,' *Journal of European Public Policy* 6: 652-668.

Rosati, J.A. (1981) 'Developing a Systematic Decision-making Framework: Bureaucratic Politics in Perspective,' *World Politics* 33 (2): 234-252.

— (1995) 'A Cognitive Approach to the Study of Foreign Policy,' in Neack, L. et al (eds.) *Foreign Policy Analysis. Continuity and Change in Its Second Generation*. Englewood Cliffs: Prentice-Hall.

Rose, R. (2000) 'New Baltic Barometer IV: A Survey Study,' *Studies in Public Policy*. 338, University of Strathclyde, Glasgow.

Rosenthal, U., Charles, M.T., 't Hart, P. (eds.) (1989) *Coping With Crises: The Management of Disasters, Riots and Terrorism*, Springfield, Illinois: Charles C. Thomas.

Rosenthal, U., 't Hart, P., Kouzmin, A. (1991) 'The Bureau-Politics of Crisis Management,' *Public Administration* 69: 211-233.

Rothstein, B. (1994) *Vad bör staten göra? Om välfärdsstatens moraliska och politiska logik*. Stockholm: SNS Förlag.

Royal Society Study Group. (1992) *Risk: Analysis, perception and management*. London: The Royal Society.

Ruggie, J.G. (1998) *Constructing the World Polity. Essays on International Institutionalization*. Routledge: New York.

Sande, G.N. et al (1989) 'Value-Guided Attributions: Maintaining a Moral Self-Image and Diabolical Enemy-Image,' *Journal of Social Issues* 45 (2): 91-118.

Sandholtz, W. (1992) *High-Tech Europe—The Politics of International Cooperation*. Berkeley/Los Angeles/Oxford: University of California Press.

— et al (1992) *The Highest Stakes—The Economic Foundations of the Next Security System*. London/New York: Oxford University Press.

SCB (2001) *IT i hem och företag. En statistisk beskrivning*. Stockholm: Statistics Sweden.

Schafer, M. (1999) 'Cooperative and Conflictual Policypreferences: The Effect of Identity, Security, and Image of the Other,' *Political Psychology*, 20 (4).

Schimmelfennig, F. (1999) 'NATO Enlargement: A Constructivist Explanation,' in Chafetz, G., Spirtas, M. and Frankel, B. (eds.) *The Origins of National Interests*. London: Frank Cass.
— (2000) 'International Socialization in the New Europe: Rational Action in an Institiononal Environment,' *European Journal of International Relations* 6 (1).
Schlesinger, P. (1997) 'From cultural defence to political culture: media, politics and collective identity in the European Union,' *Media, Culture and Society*, 19: 369-391.
Schmitt, B. (2000a) 'EADC is dead—long live EADS!' *Newsletter*, No 28, Western European Union Institute for Security Studies, Paris.
— (2000b) 'Task Force: "European Armaments Sector." Fourth Session, "Towards a Common European Demand for Defence Goods," ' *Western European Union Institute for Security Studies*, January 2000, Paris.
— (2000c) *From Cooperation to Integration: Defence and Aerospace Industries in Europe*, Chaillot Papers 40, Institute for Security Studies, WEU, Paris.
Schreiber, J-J. (1969) *The American Challenge*. Harmondsworth: Penguin.
Schudson, M. (1995) *The Power of News*. London and Cambridge, Massachusetts: Harvard University Press.
Schwartau, W. (1996) *Information Warfare*. 2nd edn. Thunder's Mouth Press.
Schön, D.A. and Rein, M. (1994) *Frame Reflection: Toward the Resolution of Intractable Policy Controversies*. New York: Basic Books.
Sharp, M. and Shearman, C. (1987) 'European Technological Collaboration,' Chatham House Paper No 36.
Shimko, K (1995) 'Foreign Policy Metaphors: Falling Dominoes and Drug Wars,' in Neack, Hey and Haney (eds.) *Foreign Policy Analysis: Continuity and Change in its Second Generation* pp. 71-85. Englewood Cliffs: Prentice Hall.
Silverstein, B. and Holt, R.R. (1989) 'Research on Enemy Images: Present Status and Future Prospects,' *Journal of Social Issues* 45 (2): 159-175.
Simon, A. and Xenos, M. (2000) 'Media Framing and Effective Public Deliberation,' paper presented at the Communicating Civic Engagement conference in Seattle, May 2000.
Sinijärv, R. (1995) Minister of Foreign Affairs of Estonia, Meeting of Foreign and Defence Ministers of the Western European Union, 15 May 1995, Lisbon. http://www.vm.ee/eng/pressreleases/speeches
Sjöberg, L. (1989a) 'Mood and expectation,' in Bennett, A.F. and McConkey, K.M. (eds.) *Cognition in Individual and Social Contexts*, pp. 337-348. Amsterdam: Elsevier.
— (1989b) *Radon risks: Attitudes, perceptions and actions*. U.S. Environmental Protection Agency, Office of Policy Analysis, EPA-230-04-89-049.
— (1994) 'Attityder till svenskt medlemskap i EU och riskperception,' Stockholm. EU-medlemskap: Styrelsen för psykologiskt försvar.

— (1998a) 'Avfallet är kärnfrågan i platsvalsprocessen' *Nucleus* 3 (17): 28-35.
— (1998b) 'Why do people demand risk reduction?,' in Lydersen, S., Hansen, G.K. and Sandtorv, H.A. (eds.) *ESREL-98: Safety and reliability,* pp. 751-758. Trondheim: A. A. Balkema.
— (1999a) 'Consequences of perceived risk: Demand for mitigation,' *Journal of Risk Research* 2: 129-149.
— (1999b) 'Neglecting the risks: The irrationality of health behavior and the quest for La Dolce Vita,' Lund University. The 19th Arne Ryde Symposium 'Individual decisions and health': Center for Health Economics.
— (1999c) 'Perceived competence and motivation in industry and government as factors in risk perception,' in Cvetkovich, G. and Löfstedt, R.E. (eds.) *Social Trust and the Management of Risk,* pp. 89-99. London: Earthscan.
— (1999d) 'Policy implications of risk perception research: A case of the emperor's new clothes?,' in Hubert, P. and Mays, C. (eds.) *Proceedings of the 1998 Annual Conference. 'Risk analysis: opening the process'*, pp. 77-86. Paris: IPSN.
— (1999e) 'The psychometric paradigm revisited,' University of Warwick. Annual conference: Royal Statistical Society.
— (1999f) 'Risk perception in Western Europe,' *Ambio* 28: 543-549.
— (2000a) 'The different dynamics of personal and general risk,' in Cottam, M.P. et al (eds.) *Foresight and Precaution. Volume 1*, pp. 1149-1155. Rotterdam: A.A. Balkema.
— (2000c) 'Specifying factors in radiation risk perception,' *Scandinavian Journal of Psychology* 41: 169-174.
—'Consequences matter, "risk" is marginal,' *Journal of Risk Research* (in pressc.)
Sjöberg, L., af Wåhlberg, A. and Kvist (1998) 'The risk of risk: Risk related bills submitted to the Swedish parliament in 1964-65 and 1993-95,' *Journal of Risk Research,* 1: 191-195.
Sjöberg, L., af Wåhlberg, A. (1996) *Sandsjöolyckan.* Centrum för Riskforskning, RHIZIKON: Rapport från Centrum för Riskforskning 6.
Sjöberg, L. and Drottz-Sjöberg, B-M. (1993) *Attitudes to Nuclear Waste.* Center for Risk Research, RHIZIKON: Risk Research Report 12.
— (1994) 'Risk perception,' in Lindell, B. et al (eds.) *Comprehending radiation risks. A report to the IAEA,* pp. 29-59. Vienna: International Atomic Energy Agency.
Sjöberg, L., Frewer, L., Prades, P. and Truedsson, J. (2000a) 'Through a glass darkly: Experts and the public's mutual risk perception,' mimeo.
Sjöberg, L., Jansson, B., Brenot, Frewer, L., Prades, A. and Tönnesen, A. (2000b) *Radiation Risk Perception in Commemoration of Chernobyl: A Cross-National Study in Three Waves.* Center for Risk Research, Rhizikon: Risk Research Report 33.

Sjöberg, L., Jansson, B. and Viklund, M., 'Risk perception by the Swedish public 10 years after Chernobyl' (in preparation).
Sjöberg, L., Kolarova, D., Rucai, A-A. and Bernström, M-L. 'Risk perception and media risk reports in Bulgaria and Romania,' in Renn, O. and Rohrmann, B. (eds.) *Cross-Cultural Risk Perception*. In press.
Sjöberg, L. and Truedsson, J. 'Perceived risks of information technology,' *Risk Analysis* (in press).
Sjöberg, L., Viklund, M. and Truedsson, J., 'Attitudes and opposition in siting a high level nuclear waste repository,' in Lesbirel, H. and Shaw, D. (eds.) (forthcoming). New York: Columbia University Press.
Sjöstedt, G. (1987) *The Structure of Non-Military Power*. Gower: Aldershot.
Slovic, P. (1993) 'Perceived risk, trust, and democracy,' *Risk Analysis* 13: 675-682.
— (1998) 'The risk game,' *Reliability Engineering and System Safety* 59: 73-77.
Slovic, P. Flynn, J.H. and Layman, P.M. (1991) 'Perceived risk, trust, and the politics of nuclear waste,' *Science* 254: 1603-1607.
— (1993) 'Perceived risk, trust, and nuclear waste: Lessons from Yucca Mountain,' in Dunlap, R.E., Kraft, M.E. and Rosa, E.A. (eds.) *Public reactions to nuclear waste*, pp. 64-86. Durham: Duke University Press.
Smith, R. and Rutherford (1979) 'Mythic Elements in Television News,' *Journal of Communication*, Winter, pp. 75-82.
Snow, D.A. and Benford, R.D. (1992) 'Master frames and cycles of protest,' in Morris, A.D. and McClurg Mueller, C. (eds.) *Frontiers in Social Movement Theory*. New Haven and London: Yale University Press, pp. 133-155.
Snyder, R., Bruck, H.W., and Sapin, B. (1963) *Foreign Policy Decision Making*. Glencoe: The Free Press.
Snyder, C.A. (1999) 'Regional Security Structures,' in Snyder, C.A. (ed.) *Contemporary Security and Strategy*. Houndmills, Basingstoke, Hampshire, London: Macmillan.
Starr, H. (1999) *Anarchy, Order, and Integration. How to Manage Interdependence*. Ann Arbor: The University of Michigan Press.
Starr, C. (1969) 'Social benefit versus technological risk,' *Science* 165: 1232-1238.
Staw, B.M. and Ross, J. (1987) 'Behavior in Escalation Situations: Antecedents, Prototypes and Solutions,' in *Research in Organizational Behavior*, 9: 39-78.
Staw, B.M., Sandelands, L. and Dutton, J. (1981) 'Threat-Rigidity Effects in Organizational Behavior: A Multi-Level Analysis,' *Administrative Science Quarterly* 26: 501-524.
Stefenson, B., Interview, 20 May 1996.
Stefenson, B. (1992) *Krishantering: U 137-krisen*. Stockholm: Royal Academy of War Sciences.

Stern, E. (1999a) 'The case for comprehensive security,' in Deudney, D.H. and Matthew, R.A. (eds.) *Contested Grounds: Security and Conflict in the New Environmental Politics*, pp. 127-54. New York: State University of New York Press.

— (1999b) *Crisis Decisionmaking: A Cognitive Institutional Approach*. PhD Dissertation. Stockholm: Department of Political Science, Stockholm University.

Stern E. and Kuipers, S. (forthcoming) 'Credibility and Crisis Management,' draft working paper.

Stern, E. and Sundelius, B. (1998) 'In Defense of the Swedish Crown: From Triumph to Tragedy, and Back?,' in Gray and 't Hart, P. (eds.) *Public Policy Disasters in Western Europe*, pp. 135-151. London: Routledge.

— (1992) 'Managing Assymetrical Crisis: Sweden, the USSR and U-137,' in *International Studies Quarterly* 36, 213-239.

Stern, E. and Verbeek, B. (eds.) (1998) 'Whither the Study of Governmental Politics in Foreign Policymaking: A Symposium,' *Mershon International Studies Review* 42: 205-255.

Stevenson, N. (1995) *Understanding Media Cultures. Social Theory and Mass Communication*. London: Sage.

Stone, D. (1997) *Policy Paradox: The Art of Political Decision Making*. New York: Norton.

Strange, S. (1995) 'States, Firms and Diplomacy,' in Frieden, J.A. and Lake, D.A. (eds.) *International Political Economy. Perspectives on Global Power and Wealth*. 3rd ed. London: Routledge.

Strange, S. (1992) 'States, Firms and Diplomacy,' *International Affairs* 68:1-16.

Stütz, G. (1999) *Opinion 99. Svenskarnas syn på samhället, säkerhetspolitiken och försvaret hösten 1999*. Styrelsen för Psykologiskt försvar. Meddelande 152.

Sundelius, B. (1983) 'Coping with Structural Security Threats,' in Höll, O. (ed.) *Small States in Europe and Dependence*. Vienna: Braumüller.

Sundelius, B., Stern, E. and Bynander, F. (1997) *Krishantering på svenska: teori och praktik*. Stockholm: Nerenius & Santérus.

Sun Tzu (1963) *The Art of War*. Trans. S.B. Griffith. Oxford: Oxford University Press.

Svenska Dagbladet (SvD). Stockholm, daily.

Svensson, K-G. (1986) 'Erfarenhetsberättelse avseende utredningen av mordet på Olof Palme' 1 September 1986. Åklagarmyndigheten Stockholm: 7:e åklagarkammaren.

SVT, Swedish Television's *Rapport*.

Swedish Agency of Civil Emergency Planning (2000) *Översikt: verksamhet med anknytning till IW (IO)*. ÖCB dnr 5-18/2000 incl. appendixes. Stockholm: The Swedish Agency of Civil Emergency Planning.

Swedish Submarine Commission, The (1995) SOU 1995:135. Stockholm: Ministry of Defence.
Sylvan, D. and Voss, J. (eds.) (1998) *Problem Representation in Foreign Policy Decision Making*. Cambridge: Cambridge University Press.
Tarand, I. (1994) Permanent Under-secretary of the Ministry of Foreign Affairs of Estonia, Parliament of Finland, 4 May 1994, Helsinki. http://www.vm.ee/eng/pressreleases/speeches
— (1996) Permanent Under-secretary of the Ministry of Foreign Affairs of Estonia, Institute for East West Studies Conference on Baltic Security, 24 August 1996, Riga. http://www.vm.ee/eng/pressreleases/speeches
Tarrow, S. (1998) *Power in Movement. Social Movements and Contentious Politics*. 2nd ed. Cambridge: Cambridge University Press.
Thompson, J.B. (1995) *The Media and Modernity. A Social Theory of the Media*. Cambridge: Polity Press.
Truedsson, J. and Sjöberg, L. (2000) 'Information technology and risk perception in Swedish society,' in Cottam, M.P. *et al* (eds.) *Foresight and precaution. Volume 1*, ed.. 49-56. Rotterdam: A. A. Balkema.
Tuchman, G. (1976) 'Telling Stories,' *Journal of Communication*, Autumn.
Tuchman, G. (1978) *Making News: A Study in the Construction of Reality*. London: The Free Press.
Tversky, A. and Kahneman, D. (1981) 'The framing of decision and the psychology of choice,' *Science* 211: 453-58.
Uhlin, A. (1995) *Democracy and Diffusion: Transnational Lesson-Drawing among Indonesian Pro-Democracy Actors*. Lund: Lund Political Studies.
Van Ginneken, J. (1998) *Understanding Global News*. London: Sage.
Velliste, T. (1993a) NUPI-Csis Conference on Baltic and Nordic Security, 21 September 1993, Oslo. http://www.vm.ee/eng/pressreleases/speeches
— (1993b) Committee of Ministers of the Council of Europe, 4 November 1993, Strasbourg. http://www.vm.ee/eng/pressreleases/speeches
— (1993c) Ministerial Meeting of the Conference for Security and Cooperation in Europe November 1993, Rome. http://www.vm.ee/eng/pressreleases/ speeches
— (1993d) Meeting of Foreign Ministers of the North Atlantic Cooperation Council 3 December 1993, Brussels. http://www.vm.ee/eng/pressreleases/speeches
Vertzberger, Y.Y.I. (1990) *The World in Their Minds: Information Processing, Cognition, and Perception in Foreign Policy Decisionmaking*. Stanford, CA: Stanford University Press.
— (1997) 'The Antinomies of Collective Political Trauma: A Pre-Theory,' *Political Psychology* 18 (4): 863-876.
Viscusi, K. (1990) 'Do smokers underestimate risks?,' *Journal of Political Economy* 98: 1252-1269.

Väyrynen, R. (1984) 'Regional Conflict Formations: An Intractable Problem of International Relations,' *Journal of Peace Research* 21 (4): 337-359.
Wæver, O. (1989) 'Security the speech act: Analysing the politics of a word,' Working Paper No. 19. Copenhagen: Center for Peace and Conflict Research.
— et al (eds.) (1993) *Identity, Migration and the New Security Agenda in Europe.*
— (1995) 'Securitization and Desecuritization,' in Lipshutz, R.D. (ed.) *On Security*, 46-86. New York: Columbia University Press.
— (1997) *Concepts of Security.* PhD Diss. Copenhagen: Institute of Political Science, Copenhagen University.
— (1999) 'Securitizing Sectors? Reply to Eriksson, *Cooperation and Conflict*,' 34 (3): 334-340.
Wagnsson, C. (1999) *Russian Language and Public Opinion on the West, and Checnya. Securitisation Theory Reconsidered.* PhD Diss. Department of Political Science, Stockholm University.
Wåhlberg af, A. and Sjöberg, L. (2000) 'Risk perception and the media,' *Journal of Risk Research* 3: 31-50.
Wallenberg, P. (1996) *Opening address by Dr Peter Wallenberg at the Baltic Sea Business Summit in Stockholm*, April 25, 1996. Stockholm.
Wayman, F.W. and Diehl, P.F. (1994) *Reconstructing Realpolitik.* University of Michigan Press.
Weber, M. (1962) *Basic Concepts in Sociology.* London: Peter Owen.
Weinstein, N.D. (1984) 'Why it won't happen to me: Perceptions of risk factors and illness susceptibility,' *Health Psychology* 3: 434-457.
— (1987) 'Unrealistic optimism about illness susceptibility: Conclusions from a community wide sample,' *Journal of Behavioral Medicine* 10: 481-500.
— (1989) 'Optimistic biases about personal risks,' *Science* 185: 1232-1233.
Weinstein, N.D., Klotz, M.L. and Sandman, P.M. (1988) 'Optimistic biases in public perceptions of the risk from radon,' *American Journal of Public Health* 78: 796-800.
Weinstein, N.D. and Nicholich, M. (1993) 'Correct and incorrect interpretations of correlations between risk perceptions and behaviors,' *Health Psychology* 12: 235-245.
Weldes, J. (1996) 'Constructing National Interests,' *European Journal of International Relations* 2 (3): 275-318.
Wendt, A. (1999) *Social Theory of International Politics.* New York: Cambridge University Press.
Wennersten, P. (1999) 'The Politics of Inclusion. The Case of the Baltic States,' *Cooperation and Conflict* 34 (3).
Wentland, E.J. and Smith, K.W. (1993) *Survey responses. An evaluation of their validity.* San Diego: Academic Press: Academic Press.

Wildavsky, A. (1987) 'A Cultural Theory of Responsibility,' in Lane, J-E. (ed.). *Bureaucracy and Public Choice*. London: Sage Publications.

Wildavsky, A. and Dake, K. (1991) 'Theories of Risk Perception: Who Fears What and Why?,' *Daedalus: Journal of the American Academy of Arts and Sciences* 119: 41-59.

Wilson, J.Q. (1989) *Bureaucracy*. New York: Free Press.

Winnerstig, M. (1996) *Shared Values or Power Politics. Transatlatic Security Relations 1981-94*. Research Report 26. The Swedish Institute of International Affairs.

Winter, H. (pseudonym) (1988) *Operation Garbo: En thriller om en möjlig verklighet*. Stockholm: Timbro.

Wood, B.D. and Peake, J.S. (1998) 'The Dynamics of Foreign Policy Agenda Setting,' *American Political Science Review* 92 (1): 173-184.

Working Group on Information Warfare [AgIW] (1997) *Åtgärder och skydd mot informationskrigföring. Rapport nr 1 från arbetsgruppen för informationskrigföring*. Stockholm: Ministry of Defence.

— (1998) *Åtgärder och skydd mot informationskrigföring: förslag till ansvarsfördelning m.m. Rapport nr 2 från arbetsgruppen för informationskrigföring*. Stockholm: Ministry of Defence.

Wyatt-Walter, A. (1995) 'Globalization, corporate identity and European technology policy,' *Journal of European Public Policy* 2: 427-446.

Wyn Jones, R. (1999) *Security, Strategy, and Critical Theory*. London: Lynne Rienner.

Year 2000 Delegation, The (2000) *SOU 2000:24. 2000-säkringen i Sverige: Myt och verklighet*. Stockholm: Ministry of Industry, Employment and Communications.

Index

Adler, Emanuel, 213
Agenda setting, 4, 10-12, 14-16, 127-29, 142, 151-54, 215, 220
Allison, Graham, 128
Aumont, Jaques, 64-65

Bangemann, Martin, 194-95, 198-99
Baresic, Milo, 174-75, 180, 187 (fn 10, 13, 16)
Bildt, Carl, 130-137
Boulding, Kenneth, 66
Bureaucracy, 108, 118, 123, 146, 148, 155
Bureaucratic politics, 126-29, 139, 146, 178, 218
Business leaders, ch. 5 (100-118)
Buzan, Barry, 18 (fn 1)

Cameron, Deborah, 5
Carlsson, Ingvar, 142, 167-68, 175, 187 (fn 9, 10)
Carlsson, Roine, 177
Coalition-building approach, 104
Cognition, 135, 179, 212
Cognitive-institutional approach, 165, 174, 176, 183
Competitiveness, 189, 191, 193-94, 196, 200, 204, 208
Constructivism, 90-91, 99 (fn 7)

'Copenhagen school' of security studies, 9, 14, 18 (fn 1), 146
Corruption, 109-10, 113-18
Crisis management, 129, 134, 136, 160-61, 163, 167-69, 172, 176-79, 211, 216
Culture, ch. 2 (38-56), 64-65, 72, 204-05, 215
 egalitarian, hierarchical and individualistic cultures, 42-43, 51, 112, 115, 208, 215
Cultural Theory, 41, 42, 45, 51-52, 56 (fn 2), 212, 215

Dake, Karl, 42
Defence industry, 197-206
Denning, Dorothy, 154
Desecuritization (see Securitization)
Dewey, John, 3

Eilders, Christiane, 62, 67-68
Entman, Robert M., 67
Environmental pollution, 28, 43-53, 109, 112-14, 116-18
Epistemic communities, 150, 217-18, 221-23
Esaiason, Peter, 45
Experts, 22-24, 29, 31, 33, 43, 150-58, 214, 217-18

European Commission, 114, 189, 195, 200-01, 204-05
European Union, 67, 77-81, 85, 89, 92-94, 98 (fn 5), 110-11, 115, 118, ch. 9 (189-209)

Featherstone, Mike, 64
Frame analysis, 7-16, 62-66, 211-15
   Cold War frame, 76, 221
   defence frame, 199
   elaborated frame, 16, 111, 159-60, 214
   episodic frames, 69
   framing, 5-16, 24-25, 62, 66-69, 82, 160-61, 168, 176-77, 189, 193, 199, 202, 207
   market frame, 189, 197, 199, 207
   master frame, 12-16, 210-11, 214
   restricted frame, 16, 155, 214
   thematic frame, 69
   threat frame, 11-13, 16, 101-05, 113, 116, 172-81, 214-15

Globalisation, 64, 73, 80, 190, 194, 196-97, 200, 208, 209 (fn 5)
Goffman, Erving, 7, 67
Greenwood, Justine, 106

Halperin, Morton, 128
't Hart, Paul, 129
HIV/AIDS, 2, 10, 13, 28
Holmberg, Sören, 45
Holmér, Hans, 168-72, 175, 180-81, 184-85
Identity, 68, 84, 90-96, 189-90, 207, 219-20
Ilves, Toomas Hendrik, 87-94

Information operations (IO), 148-49, 151, 154, 158-60, 162
Information technology (IT), 1, 12, 34, ch. 7 (145-63), 194, 197
Information warfare (IW), 145, 147-49, 152, 154, 156-57, 160-62
Institutional setting, 109-10, 117-18, 190-91
Internet, 30, 35, 92, 145, 157, 163
Iyengar, Shanto, 69

Jager, Peter de, 157
Jensen, Torben, 46, 51-53

Kennedy, John F., 27, 164, 182
Kingdon, John W., 10, 150-51, 222
Kosovo, 1, 68
Kuhn, Thomas S., 12, 16

Liberalism, 102-04, 114, 118
Lippman, Walter, 66-68
Luik, Jüri, 89

Marxism, 102-03
Media, 28-30, 34-36, ch. 3 (59-83), 119, 128-30, 133-34, 136-38, 140-41, 166, 174, 184-85
Mitterand, François, 186

Narrative, 63-65, 66-69, 83, 210, 214, 220
Nation-building, 84-86, 90-91
NATO, 84-85, 89-96, 149-50
Neutrality, 126, 136
Nuclear power, 23-26, 28-37
Nye, Joseph S., 208

Organised crime, 11, 101, 109-10, 112-14, 114-16, 117-18

Palme, Lisbet, 164, 173-75, 187 (fn 13)
Palme, Olof, 79, 136-38, 142-43, ch. 8 (164-87)
Policy diffusion, 153-56
Price, Monroe, 65, 72, 82-83
Prospect theory, 180, 184, 188 (fn 22)
Protectionism, 101-03, 109, 111, 113, 117-18
Psychometric Model, 31-32
Public opinion, 22-27, 45-51

Realism, 89-90, 98 (fn 3), 99 (fn 7), 201
Refugees, 41-53, 73, 75, 79-83
Rein, Martin, 7
Research and (technological) development (R&D and RTD), 191-93, 195, 198, 200, 202
Risk, 3, 6, 8-9, 21-22
    general vs. personal risk, 25-29, 206
    risk mitigation, 27-28, 32
    risk perceptions, 3, 22, 30, 35 (fn 2), ch. 2 (38-56), 205-07
    risk society, 1, 34-35
Rosati, Jereld, 113
Ruggie, John, 13-14
Russia, 73-79, 84-96, 111, 115

Schimmelfennig, Frank, 95, 97 (fn 3), 99 (fn 9)
Schuback, Bengt, 124, 137
Schön, Donald, 8
Security, 2, 5-10, 15, 17, 18 (fn 1), 84, 87-90, 94-95, 127, 133

Securitisation and desecuritisation, 9-10, 13, 18 (fn 1), 86-87, 89, 98 (fn 10), 124, 126-28, 136, 139-43, 145-46, 150-54, 157-63, 214-15, 221
Societal salience, 4-5, 127-29, 133-34, 136, 141-42, 149-50, 161-62, 180, 210-211
Speech act, 96
Stakeholders, 33
Statism, 102-03, 118
Sun Tzu, 156
Sundelius, Bengt, 11
Sydow, Björn von, 162

Technocratic approach, 105-06, 118, 218
Technology gap, 192, 199
Terrorism, 2, 28, 69, 75-76, 87, 147, 159, 173, 175-76, 178
Threat image, 3-6, 11-14, 63, 104, 108-18, 146, 152-53, 162, 177
Threat politics, 5-6, 13-16, 61, 101, 104, 114-18
Transnational relations, 101-105, 110-14, 116, 118, 153, 156
Trust, 30-31

Unemployment, 43-54, 193

Wallenberg, Peter, 107-08, 114-15
Wæver, Ole, 18 (fn 1)

Velliste, Trimivi, 88, 98 (fn 4)
Verbal politics, 85, 97 (fn 2)
Wildavsky, Aaron, 42, 56 (fn 2), 215

Y2K bug, 1-2, 153-54, 157-59, 162, 221